Italian Wines

FABER BOOKS ON WINE
General Editor: Julian Jeffs

ITALIAN WINES

PHILIP DALLAS

new edition

faber and faber

LONDON · BOSTON

FOR MY WIFE, NINNIXEDDA
AND MY SISTER, GERALDINE

First published in 1974
by Faber and Faber Limited
3 Queen Square London WC1N 3AU
Revised edition first published in paperback in 1983
This third edition first published in 1989

Phototypeset by Input Typesetting Ltd, London
Printed in Great Britain by
Richard Clay Ltd, Bungay, Suffolk

A CIP record for this book is available from the British Library

ISBN 0-571-15390-9
0-571-15179-5 (Pbk)

Contents

CONTENTS

CONTENTS

Acknowledgements

For this new and revised edition the author would like to express his appreciation for the kind assistance of the following:

Ezio Rivella, Chief Executive, Villa Banfi, Rome; Marco Trimani, Vintner and Editor, Rome; Giancarlo Panarella, Wine-writer and Publisher, Rome; Lucia Pintore, Chief Sommelier, and Ernesto Collu, Director, Sardinian Sommelier Association, Cagliari; Toni Santarelli, Grower and Estate Bottler, Rome; Giorgio Lungarotti, Estate Bottler, Perugia.

PART ONE

I

The Age of Abundance

The Age of Abundance is with us; only human folly succeeds in turning abundance into redundance. We have the resources and the know-how for the first time in history to clothe the poor, feed the hungry, house the homeless, and cure the sick; and we have the electronics to teach and entertain them all. We can even supply most of them with well-made wine, a product that was a luxury a generation ago.

For all that, there is too much wine. The drop in consumption throughout most of Europe and the United States means that there will be ever more unsold and undrunk wine which seems a pity, especially as wine has never been as good as it is today. Italy makes a fifth of the wine produced in the world, and everywhere in Italy you can find wine that costs much the same price as milk, Coca-Cola or beer. I have always maintained that wine-making was a sign of civilization and depended on a state of peace so that the humblest worker could enjoy his litre. We are, it seems, over-civilized today, as we produce more wine than we can consume. But perhaps our civilization has changed while most of the wine-makers are hanging on to the past rather than changing with the times.

So many things have happened in the wine world since 1948 when I came to live in Italy and even more since 1974 when the first edition of *Italian Wines* was published. The next edition was a half-way book published in 1983 in paperback which surprisingly, though tentatively, predicted much of the new state-of-the-art of 1989. This edition, I hope, will nail down fairly definitely the new, ebullient nature of Italian wine and its makers and give more than a clue to the future.

There has been no rush of books on the subject, in either English or Italian, that can be considered definitive opinion-formers. After Cyril Ray's early book of 1966, in which he expressed little enthusiasm for the subject and discovered and disliked a number of Italian wines that scarcely existed, there was Burton Anderson's *Vino* (1980), in which he personally visited hundreds of wineries and stressed the virtues of the small low-tech producers. Then there was Victor Hazan's book, *Italian Wine* (1984), which pointed to a lot of non-DOC wines of fine quality, and Nicolas Belfrage's *Life Beyond Lambrusco* (1985), which does much to explain the current innovative philosophy of Italian wine-makers. There was also my Italian section of Serena Sutcliffe's *André Simon's Wines of the World*. These latter books were labours of love unlikely to alter the destiny of most Italian wines (or their destination), which seems rigidly anchored to the past; but they may have done a lot towards giving selected wineries greater prestige. They all offer a consensus of what is good and what is great. They start pessimistically and finish in praise of Italian wines and their makers; and, it must be said that, in later years, Cyril Ray became a noted expert and admirer of Italian wines. All these books, however, were written and published before the current wave of future-looking Technology got underway, led by Ezio Rivella, the President of the International Enologists' Union, which, though it has not increased overall sales overnight, has impressed the world's experts with its great dynamic potential. At long last, I hear the countdown and foresee a sparkling and urbane future.

In brief, I propose to describe the technological breakthroughs and the creative talent that have revolutionized almost every basic idea about wine-making. The huge pages devoted to wine-making in the *Larousse Memento Encyclopedia* of 1937 read not much better than a medieval parchment. Following its counsel, one would not make very good wine.

If you want to know the latest news about wine today, I suggest a visit to your local data-bank and that you hook up, via Chicago, with the enological faculty of Davis University in California and with the Italian network at Frascati and see what happens. My experience is that of being flooded with polyglot technology . . . what I call the New Enology.

The paragraph that follows was the first to come out of the Frascati data-bank (and in English) and I think it is a fair demonstration that considerable strides have been taken since *Larousse*'s recommendation to crush grapes by foot to avoid squashing the pips:

Experimental Enology Institute, Asti. Category Code: H. (alcoholic and non-alcoholic beverages): from magazine *Enotecnico*, Vol 22 No. 3., pp. 287–304, 1986, in Italian. The possibility of producing light wines with low alcoholic degree (5–7 deg) to suit modern consumer requirements is explored and experiments, carried out at the Villa Banfi (Montalcino) laboratories, are reported. Musts of 1984 white Muscat, Sangiovese and Tuscan Trebbiano grapes were fermented with a strain of Saccharomyces cerevisae to produce base wines (characteristics tabulated) of 10–10.5 deg. Equipment used subsequently for cold (–5 deg C) vacuum de-alcoholization (with vol. reduction of .02) is fully described. Gas chromato-filtration, bottling and pasteurization. Tests covered volatile and terpene components, higher alcohols, ethyl acetate and methyl alcohol (results tabulated in detail). The fresh, sharp wines produced, of approximately pH 3 and 5–7 deg. alcohol, had low volatile activity, small contents of higher alcohols, ethyl acetate, SO_2 and acetaldehyde and negligible amounts of methyl alcohol. Volatile evaluation was favorable. The acqueous alcoholic distillate obtained during the process (approx. 10% of base wine) had an alcoholic degree of 5 deg and, as brandy, could largely recover processing costs. Considerable detail is given of the assessment of consumer reaction to light wines in different parts of Italy.

The enologist today does have rather more analytical information available than, say, twenty years ago, but I doubt that the reader will want to know much more. But let us press the Control C button just to see what comes out next. The reader is welcome to skip it, though it does have its relevance to what follows much later in this book.

Institute of Agrarian Technology, Tuscia. In view of Italian wine surpluses, alternative uses for must are being sought. A new beverage called Kiwine has been produced using juice from undersized, twin or damaged Kiwi fruit, an Orvieto must and a stabilized grape juice from Sicily (Canigatti). Selected yeasts (saccharomyces, ellipsoideus 1090), bentonite, SO_2 and pecti-nase are added to a 70–30 mixture of must and Kiwi juice and fermented for 6 to 7 days at 12 deg C. until 5% alcohol content is reached when fermentation is stopped on pasteurization. Then follows addition of grape juice (25%) and bottling. The resultant Kiwine is pale yellow, clear and slightly acid but pleasant to taste. Its analytical data (tabulated) shows a residual sugar content of 80.0 g/l: total acidity (as tartaric acid) is 11.8 g/l. Detailed chemical composition is given.

Thus, we have the birth of a new, low-alcohol, fruit beverage wine and the complexities of its manufacture. Fruit wines and 'coolers' were invented in South Africa and California, while Italy was, and is still, in the rearguard due to legislation contrary to anything except what grandfather did. As for de-alcoholizing wine, who has ever heard of it? After all, in much of Europe, wine's natural alcoholic content is low. De-alcoholizing could only be needed for Californian and Italian wines whose alcoholic content can run up from 10 to 17 per cent without chaptalization.

Here again, this is more than you may wish to know about wine-making. Unfortunately, in this technological age, you need to understand at least a few of the novelties employed in wine-making and some of the often mistaken and often sound legislation.

Another print-out has arrived on my desk to tell me that RIUN-ITE, the major producer of Lambrusco (but the very special non-DOC Lambrusco tailor-made for the US market), has followed up with a white wine, a rosé, a traditional wine called D'Oro (gold), two sparkling 6 atm charmat wines – a red and a rosé – and three fruit-flavoured ones (for export only) – peach, raspberry and apple – with the promise of two more new wines before long: perhaps Kiwine? or a new non-DOC neo-classic wine to be called Blush. All this for the USA, but perhaps for England, too: Villa Banfi, I see, has swallowed Alvini Trestini importers and several Villa Banfi wines are on Harrods' wine-list. This, along with the acquisition of the sole importing rights of fine wines from five non-European countries, is a major entrepreneurial breakthrough that has no paragon and, for that matter, no rival.

Mr Belfrage would not have had far to look for *Life Beyond Lambrusco*. It is in the same winery and the same importer's office.

This now broad choice of charmat (tank-method, as I note this being called nowadays) sparkling wines at economy prices from the RIUNITE co-operative has, over the last twenty years, risen from 1,200 bottles of Lambrusco in 1967 to the astonishing grand total of one billion, two hundred million (1,200,000,000) bottles sold over the whole twenty-year period. And yet the rest of Italian wines continue their traditional destiny and destination despite great technical and agronomic innovations.

There seems to be a conflict of trends and even logic which has been only exacerbated by the utter folly of a handful of Italians who put methyl alcohol into wine to make a quick lira; men who would have destroyed Italy's reputation as a wine-producer for ever and a day had not the Lambrusco-makers and the many respected vintners with an international renown for their fine wines (and good sense) saved the name of Italy by the absolute trust that everyone – in particular, the wine-writers of the rest of the world – had in their integrity. Only ten years ago, the international and national press would have run the Italian wine industry through its own endless screw crushers.

The small-time tricksters (none exporters and none even slightly known on the home market) had been enticed and inveigled by loopholes in the seemingly thoughtless legislation of the Common Market (the distillation of surplus wine) and then by the inexplicable defiscalization of wood-alcohol which could hike the alcoholic content and cash value of such surplus wine – all at negligible cost. The final stroke of sinister genius was to switch the destination of this souped-up surplus wine from the Common Market-controlled distilleries to the open market of négociants who wanted some cheap and strong cutting wine. The die was cast. Those responsible for this chain of greed, folly and cretinous cunning will perhaps only be discovered by the judge when they come to trial. The matter was swiftly circumvented, however, and at no time were exports involved.

A curiosity on this subject is that even if quality-control by professionals and analysts had been carried out, the sophistication of the wine would not have been discovered. Normal analysis does not include looking for methyl alcohol, since no enologist in his right mind would use it as an additive (even though it exists in minute quantities in any wine by nature) and, since the wine-

5

tasters spit out the wine after tasting it, they would not have been harmed.

There was also a brief crisis when minimal and quite harmless quantities of anti-freeze were found in some Lambrusco by the US authorities. The RIUNITE plant was halted and US experts and their equipment were invited to Italy to check on the spot: a minute leak was found in one of the innumerable refrigeration vats. Here, again, the Italians did not have the fine-tuned analytical equipment for registering 'minute' quantities: they do now. After causing heavy losses ($33 million) in Lambrusco alone withdrawn from the market, the US government concluded that its embargo had been quite unnecessary.

In its way, the Austrians' recent intentional and generous lacing of their wines with anti-freeze (which, oddly enough, gives a wine a warm, rich flavour) was ethically more reprehensible because it was deliberate, even if not harmful. These shocks and the three or more million bottles of Bordeaux removed from the market in 1987 are surely enough to make the wine trade watch its step in the future, while the 'news' that 50 per cent of Beaujolais is adulterated (they don't say how), announced by the University of Nantes research department in the French consumers' magazine *Que Choisir*, on the basis of a 'new and infallible' magnetic nuclear resonance method of analysis, true or false, is damaging to confidence.

To my mind, these crises have changed the situation. In one of my previous books I recommended that, among other data available to the public, the name of the qualified enologist (called an enotechnician in Italy) responsible for processing and quality-control should be printed on, say, a back label. The days of amateurism must end and not only in Italy. For example, if someone says today that a wine is made by enologist Ezio Rivella or Giacomo Tachis, you buy it with confidence as a properly made wine since it is reckoned nowadays that 60 per cent of the kudos for a white wine and 40 per cent for a red is due to the enologist, leaving the balance to the agronomist. Not only would enologists (and, for that matter, agronomists, if listed) become famous, like great chefs, but we would all be the better for it. Another change is that, unlike in the past, when the products of only a few co-operatives were recommended, many more should be taken into serious consideration, for the good reason that it is difficult to get two vintners to agree to do something new, and impossible to get 3,000 co-op members to connive for baser motives.*

Sophistication has always been around. If you turn to Julian Jeffs's delightful and informative book, *Sherry*, you will read about Hamburg sherry, made of potato alcohol, molasses, water and cheap white wine in the last century and, no doubt, with a beautiful printed label, the only genuine part of the fraud. Jeffs points out the inability of experts to analyse wine then. Even today, it is not easy: fraud, in every field of commerce, is rife and the most one can do to protect oneself is to buy from reputable merchants who in turn buy from reputable producers.

The Italian Wine Law of 1963 regulates the growing of vines, the production of wine and the labelling of bottles of those wines that are considered of 'particular reputation and worth'. It aims to protect such wines when produced in specifically defined areas and under clearly prescribed conditions. This legislation is called Denominazione di Origine Controllata (DOC).

DOC-Garantita (DOC-Guaranteed) means that 'select wines of particular excellence' are subject to more rigorous controls. 'Guaranteed' refers to direct government control and the sealing of each bottle with a government stamp, as is also the case with spirits. The first wines included in this new category are Barolo, Barbaresco, Brunello di Montalcino, Chianti Classico and Chianti, Vin Nobile di Montepulciano and Albana di Romagna.

The descriptions given under each DOC zone mentioned in Part Two of this book are the bare-bones requirements of the law and do not take into account the myriad subtleties and nuances of the various wines produced by the infinite number of factors involved in their production. Alcohol is expressed in percentage of volume and refers to the minimum total alcoholic content required by DOC regulations. Ageing requirements are also mentioned.

What is called plonk in England is what you get when the importer

---

* Cantine Sociali Cooperatives. CAVIT (Trento), Produttori di Barbaresco (Piedmont), Terre del Barolo (Piedmont), Santa Maria della Versa (Lombardy), RIUNITE (Emilia), Castelgreve (Tuscany), Cupramontana (Abruzzi), Casal Thaulero (Abruzzi), Torre Melissa (Calabria), Settesoli (Sicily), Dolianova (Sardinia) are amongst the best producers.

buys by price alone, forcing the producer not to be too fussy about the quality of his grapes and to skip various processes in the vinification. Verona wines are often written off glibly as plonk (the Germans buy them and complain, too) but if you buy Classico or Superiore, and even more so when you choose Recioto Amarone, you will find the story changes appreciably. Valpolicella, Bardolino and Soave are not the greatest of Italian wines, but they are not plonk in the pejorative sense: equally, a gentleman from Verona might well dub a lot of English beer plonk.

At this point, I would like to go out on a limb and make a rash statement. It is that wine-making only became serious and professional in the last twenty-five to thirty years. Previously, it was solemn and amateur. The exceptions to this are fortified wines such as port, sherry, marsala, madeira, Vin Santo and various dessert wines from the south and, of course, champagne. These are exceptions, not because broad enological problems had been solved by their makers but because they dodged them with great finesse. The reader will wonder how I can wriggle out of such a rash statement.

2

The Age of Eno-technology

All wine books tell the ancient history of wine-making – that of the Greeks, the Etruscans, the Phoenicians and the Romans (and some even start with Noah). This arcane wine, though alcoholic, must have been pretty rudimentary *vis-à-vis* today's wine. The Romans often boiled it down and added aromatic substances. They also hit on the good idea of ageing wine in terracotta vases kept in attics rather than cellars so that it stabilized itself with a slow fermentation during the summer, as a Tuscan Vin Santo does today.

The bishop St Martin of Tours (a former Roman Legion officer and the same St Martin of London's Trafalgar Square church) became famous both as a holy man throughout rural Europe and as a promulgator of the vine through his homilies.

In the Dark Ages, the Benedictines kept alive a flickering light of enology and white-wine production for sacramental uses, while a lot of barbarians also acquired a taste for it or at least for the alcoholic content thereof. Despite these heroic efforts, the wine itself was rarely, surely, fit for serving at a Wine and Food Society dinner today. In the late Middle Ages and the Renaissance, things got better in Tuscany with Florence Red, which was not very stable, and Spanish Sack, fortified with alcohol (like sherry), which was. The idea of adding alcohol was surely an Arab one, since they were the first to learn how to distil wine and foolish enough not to drink it and enjoy the results of their ingenuity.

For centuries the barrel was the normal receptacle for wine. It was the French who first made bottles with necks sturdy enough to take a cork, leaving the Italians (who had cork forests and Empoli green bottle-glass) a century behind when it came to logistics. Most importantly, this technological breakthrough in bottle-making, more than an advance in enology, made champagne production a practical reality. However, it was the French Revolution that changed everything, even the colour of the wine. It was the expropriation of ecclesiastical lands and their being sold to private citizens that brought about a huge new market for wine, but increasingly for red wine, rather than the white that the prelates, monks and friars had always produced. 'White wine is the wine of the rich,' wrote Bertall in 1848. 'Red wines are French wines par excellence . . . blue wines are for the poor. . .'*

This was the first important period, the early nineteenth century, when wine became not only big business but the passion of every Frenchman. In Italy, too, French enologists such as Louis Oudard were employed and Italian growers went to study in France to bring back, in particular, the know-how for making 'big' red wines and champagne. The making of simple sparkling wine with lots of sediment had been known in Italy for centuries: it was the *rémuage* and the *dégorgement* that were new, as well as the bottles.

The second important period was that of the vine rootstock plague of *phylloxera* bugs towards the end of the century that came from the United States: it wrought havoc in the vineyards. This disaster, which spread through most of Europe, made everybody stop to think. The consensus was that there was a fortune in wine but not the way everyone was treating it at that time: even Pasteur got it wrong, being convinced that wine needed abundant oxygen to ferment and mature; when, in fact, only that amount that can seep through the seams of a well-bunged barrel can possibly, but not necessarily, be useful.

It was also realized that to make a big fortune in wine, you needed to invest a small fortune and put such technology, hygiene and marketing experience as existed to work. The French managed to overcome the *phylloxera* period without going bankrupt chiefly by buying wine from the Veneto and Friuli for both wine and cognac production and, in no time, reputations went into orbit: the same *phylloxera* hit Italy later, when the French had already got their wineries in full production, using American roots and with the aid of Algerian cutting wine. One of the curious trivia about *phylloxera* is that Chile sent healthy, pedigree Chardonnay

---

* Bertall was a Parisian painter of no notable fame who wrote an entertaining book, *L'Arte di Bere Bene* (Canesi, Rome, 1971, Italian edition).

and Cabernet ungrafted vines to France where they were grafted on to American roots; and it is still today a proud claim of the Chilean wine-makers that their vines never suffered from *phylloxera* and were never grafted on to American roots.

Italy was struck down worst in the 1920s and 1930s, but profited from the French experience and quickly took preventive measures and replanted the country's vineyards with American rootstock grafted with native Italian vines. This was the time of autarky and Mussolini. The grafted vines were Trebbiano, Sangiovese, Montepulciano, Barbera and Nebbiolo, for the most part – good, reliable varietals that have served Italy well – and they were supplied free by the government. It is said that a lot of Italy's pre-*phylloxera* vines were of French origin but, for economic and nationalist reasons, autarky won out and perhaps put Italy back fifty years because nobody was investing a 'small fortune' in Italian wine. The Germans were producing well, with the aid of considerable additives. In the mid-1930s they invented 'hot-bottling' but never got round to using it, probably because they were too much occupied with hot-bottling Austria, the Sudetenland and, in general, preparing for the Second World War. Ezio Rivella, in the resuscitation of Europe after that war, was the first to understand the importance of the invention and equipped several of Italy's largest and best wineries (Corvo, Fazi Battaglia, Regaleali, Marino) with this new plant, after which it became a general usage, especially for stabilizing white and rosé wines (see p. 17).

In the 1920s and 1930s, Italy was fighting back and I remember in 1935 tasting my first Italian wine, a rosso Cònero, in London. I can still taste the delight of my palate and recall the expansion of my fifteen-year-old vision of life. I come from a long line of Scotch drinkers and have concluded, over the last few decades, that wine, in its various forms, is more user-friendly, though Scotch, taken with wisdom, is still a great comfort.

By this time, the 1930s, all sorts of other wine-producing countries were progressing – including Australia and South Africa and, after Prohibition, California, which shook the European wine industry.

The mammoth Gallo winery quickly became big enough to slake the American thirst and employed more Ph.D.s, as used to be said, than any other wine company: for Ph.D.s read enologists, physicists, chemists, engineers, etc. It was an operation that dwarfed Europe, and still does.

There was no wine-producer in Europe that had enough exports to the USA to use publicity and, at the same time, could double its output of branded products if successful – as Villa Banfi has done today. The nearest in approach was Portugal's Mateus and Germany's Liebfraumilch: that is the problem with wine. Its production is too atomized into thousands or tens of thousands of labels, making heavy publicity impossible. Only the port and sherry shippers, like those of Scotch, Cognac and various liqueurs, can keep their names in front of the public on a worldwide basis. I am told that, in this field, publicity reflects sales precisely: cut your publicity budget, cut your sales.

Chianti was Italy's flag-carrier throughout the world. Although some wine-writers ungenerously say it was so bad you couldn't give it away, the raffia-covered flasks are fond memories for several generations and millions of people who willingly paid good money for them. Certainly, these flasks of Chianti were not filled with Chianti Classico Riserva from one of the many aristocratic wineries of Tuscany – wines that were always there in their enormous black barrels and cobwebby bottles in old castle cellars, wines that needed ten years to reach perfection. But aged Italian wine, outside Italy, had not enough prestige, image or reputation for the foreigner to risk his own reputation in front of his guests by offering Italian wines that nobody knew about. Only those wine-lovers who trusted their own taste bought it and, in fact, paid very little.

Aged red wines can still be made with improved traditional methods in Europe, but the vintages will be variable. It is the young whites and young reds that needed a whole new programme to stop them oxidizing. Fermentation was the tricky moment and it was not till the 1970s that this was controlled by slow fermentation at a low temperature and the wine was protected from oxidation by a 'blanket' of inert CO_2 or nitrogen. Today, also, the enologist knows how to induce malo-lactic fermentation in both reds and whites, a required process that his father had never even heard of. He is also much better at handling the acidity and colour of his wines. There are still, however, no hard and fast rules for making wine even today; and Ezio Rivella lays down the disquieting edict to the effect that 'quality without technology can only be accidental'.

It was in the post-war period that wine-making made its great leap in technology. Italy no longer looked to France for its standards; it looked to California and to Davis University in particular. At Palermo airport last year I asked two enormous Californians what they were doing in Sicily: one replied: 'Monitoring the fermentation at a few co-operatives.' There has been and still is a lot of cross-pollination of thought and practice between Italy and California.

First, Italy had to manufacture a whole gamut of wine-making machinery to update the wineries after years of neglect during wartime. In this sector, the Italians excelled to the extent that for some years now they have exported most of their production even as far as the Soviet Union.

This machinery included endless-screws for de-stalking and crushing the grapes (and, recently, mobile ones for vineyard-crushing), machinery for refrigeration of the must and the wine, for filtering, centrifuging, temperature-controlling fermentation and 'charmating' (also with temperature control) along with hot-bottling, and the enormous hot showers-cum-conveyor-belts for pasteurization of bottled sparkling wines – and most of them automated and computerized. It is a formidable array and a far cry from 1937 and my *Larousse Memento Encyclopedia*. There was a pre-war and a post-war period in which most of the tanks (which to a great extent replaced the use of barrels for storage) were made of bricks and cement and, later, painted inside with epoxy resin, but these are getting rare to find on a high-tech level where stainless-steel reigns, while the whole is manipulated through an electronic console. It is also a far cry from the time that Italy was still licking its wounds after an ill-conceived war and beginning to feel the curative effects of the Marshall Plan.

In 1952, wine-making technology was a great improvement on that of 1852, but nothing in comparison with 1988. The great dessert and fortified wines are, perhaps, now made to modern criteria but it is not really necessary: the solera system and the addition of alcohol are enough to stabilize such wines. The Italian Vin Santos equally require no special modern treatment: in fact, they require benign neglect for five or six years to produce their liquid gold. These have all finessed their success, leaving us with sparkling wine which also has not changed its processing – at least in theory – over the centuries. To wind up, then, the art of grafting

European vines on to American roots has been acquired for over a hundred years: but today, these grafts are bombarded with gamma rays to accelerate mutations and to facilitate an automated production of clones made from selected vines. I think that, with this dissertation, I have demonstrated that everything started twenty-five to thirty years ago. For good measure, we could include the invention not only of relatively inexpensive sparkling wines which require a lot of technology but also Vino Novello of Beaujolais-style using carbonic maceration (see p. 257). We should mention the wide variety of innovative uses of *barriques*, both old and new, to reach new styles of wine. We could even add fruit-wines now, since they cannot be rejected with contumely as were the banana-and strawberry-flavoured marsalas of half a century ago.

3

The Age of Research and Development

Without new generations of enologists, agronomists, engineers of all disciplines and electronic and computer experts, none of what has happened could have occurred. At the same time, nothing earth-shaking has occurred in Italy's export figures with the astonishing exception of Villa Banfi and the RIUNITE co-operative.

Way back, it seemed as though the Winefood Company, with its acquisition (and subsequent modernization) of thirteen of Italy's foremost wineries – Bigi (Orvieto), Vini Vaja (South Tyrol), Val Panaro (Emilia), Umano Ronchi (Marches), Santi and Nino Negri (Valtellina), Lamberti (Veneto), Fontana Candida (Rome), d'Ambra (Ischia), Melini (Tuscany), Calissano (Piedmont), Vini Vulture (Basilicata) and Folonari (Tuscany and elsewhere) – would set standards and dominate public opinion. After its passing, by default, into the hands of the Crédit Suisse Bank, it has lost its one-time burgeoning leadership though it has maintained its quality and its exports. Seagrams also acquired an interest in Tuscan Ricasoli's Brolio and Piedmontese Bersano, but even these seemingly far-reaching mergers did nothing more than consolidate a distinguished status quo. Meanwhile, the growers and wineries of Italy were all cleaning up their act, even following DOC regulations by planting out specific varietals in specific areas though, as it turns out some twenty years later, the best way to make money and a reputation is to ignore these regulations. For all that, it was a discipline which, perhaps, the Italians needed and which served to get them all thinking in terms of research and development and innovative wine-making. Perhaps, more importantly, it gave them a discipline to mutiny against.

The 1960s were also the time of market-surveys which were to pressure Italian vintners towards lighter and more acidic wines (by nature, Italian wines are alcoholically strong and with a full body) by pruning their vines longer, training them along pergolas and harvesting early, rather than letting the grapes mature on five-foot high bushes as was much favoured in the past.

The cloning of selected varietals that had been bombarded with rays and mutated came much later, but at least vintners no longer racked their wine by the light of the full moon. It needed a new generation of enologists and they did not fail us. For the record, in 1964 my interest was further aroused in the novelties afoot and I prepared the English edition of a booklet on the Siena Enoteca which is still sited in the Medicea Fortress. This exhibition (with wine-tasting rooms) was the first timid and tentative presentation of the then state-of-the-art of Italian wines. They were not to be rejected. May I quote from my *Italian Wines*, 1974 edition:

> Back in the sixties, I suggested to the editor of an American magazine (*House and Garden*) that I write an article on Italian wines. The reaction of this lady was, to me, somewhat of a shock. She expressed surprise that anyone should wish to write about anything so second-rate. However, she offered to publish my article if I were able to prove to her readers that Italian wine was not poison and that it even had some merits. My article must have been among the first ever to have been written in praise of Italian wine to appear in a major magazine. Her attitude was harsh but I found her opinion widely held and to be widely held even today.

In 1989, her view is still by no means past history; only now it can be said to be pure prejudice with no objective basis.

The story of enologist Ezio Rivella, one of prudence and audacity, covers this period of technological flourishing until the present day and would seem to be more than valid for the future. Since 1981, he has been elected President of the International Enologists' Union, with headquarters in Paris, three times. He is the first Italian ever to preside over this distinguished association. He is also director of all Villa Banfi operations in Italy, with over 12,000 container-loads of wine exported annually to the States, including the construction and management of the largest wine-producing estate in Italy, near Montalcino in Tuscany, and three specialized small ones in Piedmont with a total of 3,000 acres of vineyards.

Ezio Rivella was the son of a small (circa 40,000 litres of Barbera a year) wine-producer in Piedmont and he soon saw that this was not enough to slake his ambitions. He took his degree in Eno-technology at Alba and went to do his military service in an Alpine regiment where he quickly became a commissioned officer. This, he says, taught him a lot about precision in large-scale organizations. He returned to civil life as a teacher at his Alma Mater, waiting to see what would happen next. Meanwhile he wrote two treatises on how wine should be made, using the then latest equipment: books that would probably make him smile indulgently if he read them today. He then went to Rome and set up shop as an enological consultant, and it might be said that he made Rome plonk drinkable by stabilizing it with hot-bottling, a basically simple system of heating the wine to circa 60°C for a minute or so as it passes down the tube from vat to bottle. This is something of an art in as much as if it is badly done (usually by overheating) the wine is cooked and spoiled; if it is done well, the wine is improved notably, gaining a smoothness and phoney-ageing (especially young reds) over and above the original intention of stabilizing it by overcoming the bacteria and oxygen, thus making it a wine fit to travel. It is, in fact, still a valid process (even if often derided by wine-writers), especially for low-alcohol and sparkling wines when, in the latter case, hot water is sprayed on to the already bottled wines for over an hour.

It was in the 1970s that I extended my experience of Italian wines and, after various articles published in England and the USA, was asked to write a book by both Faber and Doubleday. I quickly sent off some 400 letters to wineries asking for information and got quite a few replies, often touching ones from owners who had dreams that they were fulfilling, telling me of all their problems – letters typewritten with two fingers after office hours. I learned more from these than can be culled from the polished prose of the glossy wine magazines. At the same time, the Italian wine-makers were frightened of a writer, and a foreign one to boot – who knows what he will say? He might extort money from us to be flattering. I quickly understood this, and never (or almost never) met any of them.

I bought their wine on the open market and tasted it at home (like Victor Hazan), at wine trade fairs and at the Rome branch of the Wine and Food Society which I founded and which, owing to the migratory nature of foreigners, collapsed after a few years. It makes me smile now, decades later, to see the wine-makers skinned alive by the slick promotion and ad-men of Milan, when once upon a time they were terrified of the expense and risks of inviting me to lunch. In all events, glasnost arrived many years ago and the doors were happily opened to Burton Anderson and Nicolas Belfrage; I feel sure they were invited to luncheon.

Meantime, Ezio Rivella's little enological consultancy agency on the edge of Rome towards the Castelli Romani gathered skilled technical partners and started its career in restructuring wineries. Amongst these were several well-known companies, beginning with the Marino Co-operative at Frascati in 1958 and followed by the Palermo Corvo Co-operative and some twenty more. Rivella, during this period, acquired a small Chianti Classico estate, Il Caggio, but has never found time to manage it, leaving this task to his brother, also a skilled enologist. Rivella still had to wait for Lady Fortune to wave her wand even if, technologically speaking, he had done his part and had an enormous practical experience. She came transmogrified as a cultivated young New Yorker (Cornell University, I think), who had recently finished his stint with the US Occupation Forces in Germany and had rejoined his family firm of wine-importers; not a very large firm (though not a small one either), but one he and his younger brother, Harry, were soon to inherit. John Mariani met Rivella in Rome in 1966; the former was, amongst other things, looking for a new wine to market in the States and was convinced that he would find it in Italy. Despite patient searching, he had not succeeded. Already, his family firm handled a few dozen traditional wines from Germany, France and Italy. Sales were not impressive. He had noted (as others, too, have noted with northern Europeans) that most Americans talk 'dry' and drink 'sweet' and that they like bubbles. Rivella introduced him to Lambrusco which he found close to his ideal but still not quite right. These must have been the sweetest words that Rivella had ever heard because they encapsuled the secret that was to make him famous as a creator of wines.

I once knew this secret: one of his enologists told me but, perhaps fortunately, I have completely forgotten it. It has never been patented and Rivella has, presumably, told nobody outside his close circle of collaborators. He plays off acidity and sweetness on a low-alcohol regime to give a fruity and essentially non-cloying sweetish wine with bubbles at circa 2 atmospheres, just under the US Customs level for sparkling wine. This was what he had prepared for John Mariani by the RIUNITE for a meeting a year later. Mariani gave a modest order for a hundred cases. After that, the sales parameter went right up the wall and the rest is history ... backed by a $10 million yearly advertising budget. This was just the beginning of something more intellectually interesting and challenging for Rivella, though I hope he had a percentage on those Lambrusco sales! RIUNITE grew like Topsy and was counselled by the best brains of the enological faculty of Bologna University, led by young Antonio Maccieri as the in-house enological specialist. Rivella was to return to RIUNITE years later when Banfi and RIUNITE made a separate merger to produce wines other than Lambrusco.

It was in 1975 that the Mariani brothers decided to take a large part of the Lambrusco profits back to Italy with the sole purpose of making superb wines that could rival, and perhaps beat, the world's best. They said ironically that, moneywise, they would have done better to buy US Government Bonds. Fourteen years later, it must be admitted that they have done very nicely anyway. It was, however, to a mature Rivella, at the age of forty, that they gave *carte blanche* and $100 million to kick off with.

Within a couple of years, Rivella had searched Italy for land to buy and had acquired nearly 5,000 acres of vineyards, olive groves and cornfields in a lonely spot in Tuscany, some ten miles from the equally lonely little medieval township of Montalcino. It was a windswept plateau, mostly at 750 feet above sea-level, reached by tortuous country lanes that seem unending. (Nowadays, Rivella resolves his commuting problem by going there by helicopter.)

The task of taming this enormous area must have been daunting. I saw it on several occasions and in its various stages. In origin, the shape was rather messy, the way God made it, but, with a few heavy-duty bulldozers, gentle contouring was given to the land. First, however, enormous boulders, some weighing a ton and more, had to be unearthed and bulldozed into landfills: during this operation, the future vineyards took on the aspect of a lunar landscape. Finally, the topsoil was replaced and the lunar landscape was pushed aside in favour of the gentle contours. Rivella did this huge earth-moving job a few hundred acres at a time and, as soon as they were ploughed (over five feet deep), he set about planting vines. The only major building on this huge estate at that time contained three little offices, a tasting-cum-conference room, a canteen where everybody could get a hot lunch and a patio where the farm machinery was kept.

Then came the problem of planting out: why a problem? When you have to plant out two million vines and a million cement stakes to which to tie the vines (yes, they had a little open-air factory for making cement stakes), you don't just take a spade and tuck stakes and roots under your arm and go off to work singing, 'Hi ho, Hi ho!' The semi-automated planting of the stakes – one every forty seconds or so – was a sight to see: the stakes were on a truck, placed one after another into the grip of an adapted bulldozer that drove each stake into the ground and moved on immediately to the next one.

Artificial lakes were created, with drainage and irrigation networks (the use of the latter is permitted only in July when the vines risk death from thirst), because Montalcino, like Sardinia, is one of the most drought-prone areas of Italy. A few cottages were built for the permanent workers and, of course, roads sprang up everywhere. Communication was maintained by radio. In 1984, the estate's surface area was increased to 7,000 acres by the acquisition of the adjoining Poggio vineyards and castle. Here the vines were a trifle old but the medieval castle, by the grace of God, was in shipshape condition as it had been lived in by its previous owner. It had been damaged in the Second World War but admirably restored: its ancient halls, courtyard and loggias, though not enormous, were most attractive and the cellars (of what is now called Castello Banfi), were full of well-aged Brunello in casks and bottles. What more could you ask for? Maid Marion? In all events, though the infrastructure, contouring and fertilization of the land cost three times as much as the purchase price, Ezio Rivella had demonstrated that he knew the value of both money and land, all DOC-Guaranteed land. The inauguration dinner, celebrations and entertainment were held there in Renaissance style with dancers, singers, trumpet fanfares and flag-wavers. The guests were VIPs and wine-writers of the world, well over a hundred at table.

The computerized cost-accounting of every detail of this operation was something of a shock to the Tuscans. The little township of Montalcino is Communist-run: here were Yankee dollars exploiting both virgin land and innocent unarmed Marxists, and the rape of their Renaissance heritage. Rivella played a new role of politician and placator of ideological fervour. He seems to have succeeded since many of the local farmers bought themselves tractors and bulldozers and rented themselves and their farm machinery to Villa Banfi at a good market price. Since the vineyards will be being planted out for several more years to come, they have a bargain: the write-off of their investment is secure as well as the transferring of the know-how they have gathered at Banfi to their own farmland. And the solitary little township of Montalcino will finally be on the map . . . perhaps even the tourist map.

The entry of Villa Banfi on to the Italian landscape caused much envy and much sincere and insincere worry that uncomprehending Americans would smash up the market first of Brunello, Italy's prime wine, and then those of Chianti Classico, Barolo and heaven knows what else. But this was far from the intentions of either the Marianis or Rivella. They were aiming to produce a small quantity of Brunello, not enough to drive the price down but, rather, to increase it a bit, due to the new public exposure that they would give the Brunello DOCG zone throughout the media. In fact, many Brunello producers have done very well of recent years, hanging on to Banfi coat-tails.

A curiosity of the Mariani policy was that, though experts in promotion and publicity, they left their newly created wines, premium or otherwise, to make their own reputations . . . that is to say, without straight publicity or with only a minimum announcing of their existence and availability. The New York office would give wine-tastings and present the new wines to the professionals, confident that the editorials would be enough to sell their wines as, in fact, occurred, especially as they were and are still only available in relatively small quantities. So successful has this theory been that, if it were possible to put a cash valuation on wine-writers' recommendations, Villa Banfi might find that quite a lot of its land, plant and equipment had cost them next to nothing.

The first wine to meet the press was the Moscadello di Montalcino, the last style of wine that the Italians expected to be offered from a robust red wine area (Chianti Classico, Vin Nobile di Montepulciano and Brunello). It was a wine of no inconsiderable delicacy, resembling most the finest of Asti Spumante. It is said to have been a Tuscan wine of long ago which had fallen out of use for various reasons, chiefly the difficulty of making it and the unequal competition from Asti. Even now, Villa Banfi is finding unexpected difficulties in handling the grapes in the vineyard. That was one of the risks in Rivella's sweeping changes and technological dream-world: but Murphy's Law is unyielding! The Banfi Muscadello was planned to be the winery's major estate-bottled product but it is turning out to be more expensive than calculated.

Rivella told me one day he was planning to start planting out a Chardonnay to be called Fontanelle, a Pinot Grigio to be called San Angelo and a Cabernet Sauvignon to be named Tavernelle. He went on to describe each of them, tasting them in his imagination. They were, he said, to be a sporting challenge to his Californian friends, especially the Chardonnay with its strong oak finish. The Chardonnay would not appeal to the Italian palate, whereas the Cabernet would be full and rich and would suit all tastes, increasingly so as the vines themselves aged, as would also the Pinot Grigio, which is producing well particularly in the Friuli area of Venice's hinterland.

Villa Banfi, therefore, has a variety of vines that have reached maturity and some that are still on the way. The Brunello vines, not being old enough to produce grapes to rival Biondi Santi, mostly find their destiny in a younger-style wine which, of recent years, has become famous among serious wine-drinkers. Let me explain. Banfi's Centine is the same Brunello (but chiefly from young vines) which is run off the lees after a much briefer period than the DOCG, full-bodied Brunello, thus requiring less ageing in the *barrique*; therefore, a lighter (but not all that much) wine is presented that costs much less. The various Brunello estates of Montalcino are using this process and selling well after only a year in the wood, thus saving on the heavy cost of tied-up capital of the full ageing process. The serious drinker likes it, as to drink DOCG Brunello regularly is an expensive habit and a luxury few can afford, especially if they like to invite good drinking friends to their table. In all, Centine (or Vigneti di Brunello, 'from Brunello Vineyards') is an excellent compromise and some producers are coming round to the idea that this might be their major product rather than the traditional Brunello. They are not entirely mistaken. It is also a non-DOC table wine which leaves them complete freedom to make all the processing decisions themselves. A young Chardonnay – also called Centine – is beginning to be made: this also cuts costs and brings great pleasure.

On this subject of what are now sometimes called 'food wines', in contrast to 'boutique', *'barrique'* or 'premium' wines, the fact is that serious drinkers drink wine with lunch and with dinner: a fair percentage of Frenchmen and Italians find it difficult to eat without a bottle of wine within arm's reach. For them and others like them in other countries, Rivella has produced three 'house wines' which are traditional Italian table wines and of the sort you can drink day in, day out without *ennui*. Of course, a change can be a pleasure, especially if well chosen, but that does not mean one is necessarily weary of the house wine. Rivella is not permitted by law to declare the geographical or varietal origins of his table wines on the labels or elsewhere, but my feeling is that Umbria may be the major source of the bouquet and taste and that Puglia may play a part in the body and aftertaste. I would not risk an opinion as to what final processing and blending takes place.

The building of the Montalcino Winery (all five acres of it) was, clearly, a top priority and it was done while the first vines were still growing. For Rivella, the planning of processing machinery from the arrival of the grape to the final bottling and despatch was a return to his first profession.

The electricity supply alone, brought by pylons across the hills from some twenty miles away, cost many hundreds of thousand pounds. The plant in itself, however, was strictly utilitarian with little thought for aesthetics, though a satisfactory resolution of any mechanical problem tends to have its own personality and I suppose that this monster plant must reflect something of its author's character.

It has a capacity for storing wine in great refrigerator vats for 3.5 million bottles and an enormous underground, air-conditioned crypt where some million or more 'bottles' are maturing placidly in *barriques*, each of 350 litres. It is an impressive sight but with no romance, cobwebs or fancy-dress confraternities. It is probably the biggest set-up in Italy but only because some of the big co-operatives have, say, five or more fermentation and stockage wineries and only their bottling plant is centralized. There are bigger plants in California and there are more luxurious ones there, too. But Rivella's is almost certainly the most technologically up to date and I was told that, when it needs to, this plant can double its production economically and quickly.

Rivella has the equipment required for making Beaujolais-style

Vino Novello which, for Banfi, is a young Brunello wine labelled 'Santa Costanza Novello dei Colli della Toscana, Vino Rosso da Tavola'. The Banfi process is new. It does not repeat the French one and gives the wine a rather longer life. Basically, the grapes are put in a vat under vacuum conditions and then carbon-dioxide is injected. What follows is a curious biological process invented by the French enologist Flanzy. The bacteria, isolated from the oxygen, react against the sugar and the acids in such a way that the acidity stays high and the aroma of the grapes remains intact. The grapes are then pressed and, after a quick fermentation, the wine is ready to drink, fresh and full of life by early November.

When I wrote the 1983 edition of *Italian Wines*, there was a small import of Beaujolais *nouveau* into Italy and half a dozen noted Italian estates were producing very limited quantities – a matter of thousands or, at the most, a few tens of thousands of bottles of Novello. At that time, I looked most dubiously at this innovation and reckoned it was a fashion that would last a couple of years and not spread far south of rich Milan, blocked by Italian conservatism. Instead, this carbonic maceration process, as it is called, has extended its fascination throughout Italy and even to the wineries of Sardinia; and the style has effortlessly – and with no publicity – become a part of the Italian tradition. Today, over two million bottles are made and sold by eight major producers.

Needless to say, with only a few exceptions, the Novellos are non-DOC, since this deviation from the norm was not foreseen by the Founding Fathers of the DOC regulations. This goes, too, for the technological leap in the production of sparkling wines, both 2 atmosphere and 6 atmosphere ones, of which most are non-DOC with the major exceptions of Asti Spumante and Prosecco of Conegliano, near Venice.

The success of Asti Spumante is long founded. For years now, it has been selling around 50 million bottles annually, 30 million of which are sold abroad, mostly to the States and to France. However, it has reached the maximum permitted by DOC regulations; that is to say, the total of vineyard land is already being used to produce the special muscat grape used for its vinification. Since there was room for market growth in this field, this must have been one of the reasons that Rivella decided to make a plunge on Moscadello, which is a cousin to Asti, and also the style of wine that Rivella is a recognized master at creating. Equally, the Prosecco from Venice is a slightly sweet sparkling wine and enjoys a wide market and, since the perfecting of the charmat (tank-method) system of a natural second fermentation in vats, there has been a boom in Pinot Bruts, Chardonnay Bruts, Riesling Bruts and many other surrogate champagnes from all over Italy – even from Sicily and Sardinia in the south. When Pinot Bruts have been second-fermented over a long period at a low temperature, you get a wine that has a perlage and froth as delicate as a fine champagne. Though this slow process is the essence of high-quality sparkling wines, the law does not permit the producer even to note this on a back label. Despite this, the Italians are very proud of their charmats and justly so: the Pinots are champagne-like and the blanc de blanc Chardonnays are something on their own. The Italian champenois-system bubbly has been leaping ahead over the last decade, though it is still tonnes behind France in quantity of production.

All this intellectual and vinous fermentation obviously could not be left alone by either Rivella or the Mariani brothers, so they bought a small, old-established winery, Bruzzone, that was under-capitalized and needed a complete overhaul; even the façade had a face-lift of about ten feet.

Bruzzone winery was sited in the hilly countryside in south-east Piedmont (Rivella's homeland). Its major reputation was for its 'champagne' – some 60,000 bottles a year, of which, most surprisingly, a good part has been exported regularly to Belgium since the last century, something of a guarantee of its quality. Rivella went to work on both the quality and the quantity and, with a new label, 'Villa Banfi Brut – Metodo Champenois', this sparkler can often be found nowadays in New York and Jumby Bay (but that is another story). Rivella had demonstrated that he could blend a *cuvée* to perfection; 40 per cent Chardonnay for perfume and lightness, 50 per cent Pinot Noir for body and depth of taste and 10 per cent Pinot Blanco for roundness.

The Villa Banfi Cellars (ex-Bruzzone) were stripped down and, as I mentioned, grew ten feet taller to make room for offices and reception rooms, leaving, of course, the ancient cellars for making champenois-system sparkling wine. It was then equipped with the most up-to-date machinery for making charmat wines – to call them 'tank' wines is a coarse expression for the delicate operations involved. Unlike the Montalcino winery, which is formidable and has a huge potential, the Villa Banfi Cellars at Acqui are in comparison a jewel of technology, and move with the precision of a fine watch. In fact, while I was there, a technician had worked for twenty-four hours to get a bug out of the bottling line; finally, he announced triumphantly that a washer, worth two pence, was the cause of the trouble. He had replaced it. Incidentally, these Banfi Cellars show another side of Rivella's character – a technician's passion for detail.

While this winery was being reconstructed, Rivella put together an assault force (this sort of action, perhaps, he picked up when an Alpine regiment officer) to vineyardize a nice little hill he had acquired a few miles away in the Gavi (also called Cortese di Gavi) DOC zone. His Tuscan boys (many were in their early twenties) set to work with their tractors and bulldozers to contour the 250-acre hill, lay a good fertilized topsoil, plant the vines, ram home the concrete stakes and call it a day. They did it all in under a month. The local farmers watched, not believing their eyes. Here was to be produced some of Piedmont's best-known dry white wine, Gavi. This is a highly respected, traditionally rather hard masculine wine. Rivella changed its nature, giving it a transsexual fix so that his Principessa Gavia, as it is called, is soft, enticing and pétillant: almost too good to drink at table with food that can detract from its charms. Better as an apéritif before a gourmet supper.

The major production of Villa Banfi Cellars is yet another of Rivella's secrets: a light, slightly sweet – and, as always with Rivella's work, not cloyingly so – frizzante wine called Bell'Agio. It comes into the Moscadello category along with Asti Spumante (of which Rivella makes a little at the Cellars' Winery) but is a non-DOC that cannot announce its origins which, though they are plainly from the muscat grape, could come from anywhere in Italy, even the south.

'Even from the south', one adds still, only because the existence of the slow-fermentation method is not widely known yet. Wine, nowadays, in a broiling September in southern Italy, Sicily and Sardinia, is fermented in refrigerated vats at ambient temperatures lower than Germany; thus there is no longer the heaviness that was, throughout history, the mark of Mediterranean wines that had boiled furiously during fermentation. These wines, then, in the hands of Rivella, are re-fermented (the charmat process) even more slowly over a period of weeks and sometimes months so that they acquire a delicacy of nose and a fresh tiny-bubble perlage that is normally considered the prerogative of a fine champagne. The oxidation found, in the past, in still wines, is kept at bay nowadays by inert nitrogen (rather than inert CO_2) at the cellars at Strevi, according to the excellent Italian law that does not permit the presence of liquid CO_2 on the premises of a winery that makes sparkling wine, for fear that the owner may fall into temptation and use carbon-dioxide straight instead of fermentation to make his bubbles. Inert nitrogen can be recognized by its bigger bubbles.

Ezio Rivella has a sense of history but he likes to rewrite it himself. In Tuscany, at Montalcino he resuscitated the Moscadello of Montalcino and, I am confident, improved on the original appreciably. In Piedmont, he planted out a vineyard of Bracchetto d'Acqui DOC vines, a varietal that had almost died out. It recalls the Freisa, which is also a threatened species, both customarily, but not necessarily, processed as 2 atmosphere frizzante red wines. The Bracchetto is a most subtle dry wine with a trace of sweetness: it is a prime example of Rivella's tight rope-walking talent for balancing sweetness and acidity to make a truly three-dimensional wine. The Bracchetto grape is a 'serious' Piedmont product, whilst the bubbles give it a self-indulgent frivolity.

More traditional is Rivella's DOC Dolcetto d'Acqui, called Argusto, of which very little is made, thus following Villa Banfi's policy of not rivalling or embarrassing the old establishment of local producers, though it may give them something to think about. Argusto is aged briefly (four to six months) in small Yugoslav barrels and a year in the bottle. It is a most dignified wine for an experienced connoisseur.

'Prima Vera': the European tends to look at the bottle and judge it unfavourably before even tasting it. In all, it is a non-DOC, light-weight, low-calorie, low-alcohol, pétillant five-blend white wine. One fears that, like some whites that seem to have travelled a mile down pipes in some great co-operative so that there is little taste left – but no. It is a new style, not to be knocked. I may have started out my adventure with Italian wines with fewer prejudices than many wine-lovers, but I still have my little baggage of them which I try to ignore when facing up to reality and, for that matter, to Ezio Rivella, who, along with a handful of big names and a few hundred skilled eno-technicians and agronomists, has made it all possible. The wine panorama is just not what it was only a few years ago.

4

The Age of Non-DOC

Some years ago, there was an earthquake in the wine world – or rather there might have been. One fine day, the newspapers gave headlines to the news that Villa Banfi was buying Antinori, a most respected and old-established producer of Chianti Classico. Some editorialists screamed that, after the entry of Seagrams into Ricasoli-Brolio, this would be capitulation to the almighty dollar. Others acknowledged that Antinori needed new capital and, maybe, it was not a fate worse than death; it would give Antinori access to the best-qualified sales-force existing in the wine world today. Every consideration was debated in the press while the protagonists no-commented, till the story lost its impetus and died for lack of new fuel. If there was any truth in it, my guess is that, for political reasons (Tuscany is traditionally Communist), the government told one of its several nationalized banks to lend Antinori what it wanted on favourable terms to keep Antinori within the fold, conditions that previously, perhaps, had been refused by the banks. In all events, the great event was a non-event. In any case, what possible attraction could Antinori have had for Villa Banfi? It has fine offices in the centre of Florence, in a Renaissance palace, and a large production of estate-bottled Chianti Classico supervised by the distinguished enologist Giacomo Tachis, who had finally buried Baron Ricasoli's famous four-wine blend used to make Chianti. (Was the Baron mistaken – it would seem so – when he retired to Brolio Castle, near Siena with his beautiful wife, allegedly because of her too-many admirers in Florence, and dedicated himself to her and to enology?)

The famous four wines were red Tuscan Sangiovese, red Canaiolo, white Trebbiano and white Malvasia: they were used for Chianti and Chianti Classico and both for young wines and for those for long ageing. The fact is that the whites soften the harsh Sangiovese quickly and effectively and, therefore, for a wine to be bottled six months after its fermentation, can still be considered valid, but it also could be improved on. With wines for ageing, the whites served no useful purpose. What Tachis did was to remove the whites and the red Canaiolo and replace them with red Cabernet Sauvignon: a revolutionary heresy. The Iron Baron (as Ricasoli was rather ironically known) must have turned in his grave: let us hope that the Baroness was still by his side to comfort him.

Giacomo Tachis has been an Antinori consultant for over twenty-five years and he has upset all the precious ideas of Tuscan wine-making: this he did first while working for an Antinori uncle, Marchese Mario Incisa della Rocca. The Marchese, for reasons of his own, rather than any specific commercial purpose, planted some Cabernet Sauvignon in the hills south of Leghorn on the Tuscan Seaboard, an area previously not considered to have any particular vocation for wine production. This was back in 1942: the resulting wine was not impressive and he left it in barrels in his cellars and forgot it. Since Italy at that time was suffering the effects of the Second World War and its aftermath, he probably had more important matters on his mind. He broached the barrels in the 1950s to find excellent wine. Encouraged, he chose a more favoured vineyard, Sassicaia, near the sea at Bolgheri, and went ahead again, agreeing with Piero Antinori (also a Marchese) that Antinori would handle the marketing if the wine were successful. The first worthwhile parcel of wine, after four years' ageing (two in the wood and two in the bottle) was that of 1968 – 7,300 bottles. Fame, however, needed another ten years to arrive. It was in London in 1978 that Sassicaia 1974 won the laurels in competition with thirty-three of the world's best Cabernet Sauvignons. Tachis merits a lot of the kudos for this; Piero Antinori, too.

The remarkable success of the Cabernet led to experiments and marketing of Tignanello, a wine that was 80 per cent Tuscan Sangioveto (as Tuscan Sangiovese is called nowadays to distinguish it from the Sangiovese of the Abruzzi and Emilia-Romagna) and 20 per cent Cabernet Sauvignon. Tachis, far from insulting Italy's old standby, the Sangioveto, has enhanced its robust structure with the caresses of France's greatest gift to civilized living to make what he considers, after due *barrique*-ageing, should be the new Riserva Chianti Classico. 'Where Tachis goes, Tuscany mostly follows' is becoming a proverb. This is a non-DOC wine, as is Sassicaia, and both are labelled plebeanly 'red table wine' as the law requires, whereas they are crus of crus.

Tachis and Antinori have pushed the 'Villa Antinori Riserva DOCG' to the limits of the discipline in line with their new formula: that is to say, 15 per cent is Tignanello, the rest is Sangioveto with as little as legally possible of white wine and Canaiolo. All this until the day that the DOC regulations permit the Tignanello formula (which, for the record, is allowed to a certain extent in Carmignano, i.e. 10 per cent Cabernet).

Another non-DOC experiment has been that of Solaia, a 100 per cent Antinori estate-grown and -bottled wine, 75 per cent Cabernet Sauvignon and 25 per cent Cabernet Franc, aged two years in new *barriques*. These wines have given the wine world much to think and talk about. May I quote my own 1983 text on the subject:

... a lot of fine maverick wines can live outside the DOC legislation quite happily, though this seemed unlikely ten years ago. In fact, many producers are intentionally going beyond the limits and are planting non-DOC vineyards, confident that the good taste of the public, at home and abroad, will assure that their wines will be sold at sustained prices. Among these are Cabernets, Merlot, Chardonnay and Riesling which are currently enjoying considerable success in Italy.

The prestige of Antinori's Cabernet-based wines on a world level must have been Banfi's interest (if there was any), because prestige on a world level *is* Banfi's interest. Perversely, Brunello, Barolo, Barbaresco and Chianti Classico for that matter, which are considered Italy's best native red wines, cannot be compared with any precision to French, Californian and German wines. Only in the field of white wines is this possible and here we have quite a display of Chardonnays, Rieslings and white Pinots.

Starting with Villa Banfi, the Chardonnay is the woody varietal that Ezio Rivella wanted to produce as a sporting challenge to the Californians and which was and is well received in the States. The Italian-style Chardonnays (including the previously mentioned Centine) are remarkable for their highly distinguished and highly distinguishable personalities in a field in which many experts are saying that the quality of whites is of the highest, yet there is a general levelling – also at a high level – of the taste. This is due, they say, to the new methods of free-run musts, centrifuging, refrigeration, slow fermentation and, perhaps, early harvesting before the grape is mature. These are all New Enology processes that produce a clean, ultra perfect wine; but now many experts and wine-lovers are rethinking and saying they like some of the old Italian defects, though perhaps a little fermenting on the lees would be enough to give a stronger character.

In the second edition of this book, I recorded the increasing difficulty of identifying the origin of a wine from the organoleptic style due to the high-technology of processing which could make a Sardinian wine pass for one from more northerly latitudes. Giacomo Tachis is suggesting that fermentation temperatures might be raised to 25°C, from, say, 15°C, that part of the grape-skins be left in during fermentation and that a little old-style ageing in the wood be indulged in. My addition to this is that I find the high acidity produced by early harvesting to be excessive: particularly for those of us (and we are legion) who suffer from gastritis or worse.

Italy has been bombarded with advice over the last twenty years from well-wishers, ill-wishers, professional consultants, marketing experts, government bureaucrats and wine-writers. The general consensus has been that Italy must make quality wines, lighter wines, more acidic wines and less alcoholic wines – in fact, ultra-perfect wines – and this Italy has done. Now the pundits have asked for one step backwards, please.

Most of this is against nature and aimed only to produce wines to 'rival' French wines, not to make Italian wine as God wanted it. By nature, Italian wines come up with a full body, a generous alcoholic strength and a rich vinous bouquet. All this is put into a strait-jacket to produce French-style wines that have completely different growing conditions and a natural low-alcohol content and high acidity due to their wet and chilly summers. California's climate is closer to Italy's.

In fact, the wine-writers all fall in love with Fiano di Avellino, an aged-in-the-wood white from the mountains of the south behind Naples, which represents everything that market-survey wine isn't. Surprisingly, it is a DOC wine, despite its off-beat nature, made only by Mastroberardino of Atripaldi. Perhaps this might be the spirit of the new trend. And, incidentally, how wise Mastroberardino was not to have rushed to Madison Avenue, there to be told brusquely, and in the local dialect, to change his act or cop out of the wine business. He also produces a giant of a red wine called Taurasi; what is curiously perverse is that when a Cabernet, say, in the Napa Valley, comes up with a powerful 13 per cent alcohol content everybody is happy rather than talking of copping out.

5

The Age of Bubbles

⸺

The most impressive non-DOC category today is that of sparkling wines, both champenois-system and charmat. I am astonished to note that both retailers and wine-writers have a tendency nowadays to put them in the same category, without differentiation, despite their difference in processing and price.

France produces an astonishing 200 million bottles of champagne every year of which 125 million are drunk at home: England and Italy tie for second place with getting on for ten million bottles each, though the league table changes from year to year. Italy, however, has a ten-million-bottle production of local champenois-system sparkling wine (clearly marked Metodo Champenois and/or Spumante Classico, though this description may now have to be dropped under EEC regulations) and a vastly greater production of charmat: nearly fifty million bottles of sweet muscat Asti Spumante alone. There are now dozens of bubbly-makers. The raw materials – the various Pinots, Chardonnays and Rieslings (and there are many others) – were first grown in south-eastern Piedmont; later, in the hills above Trento, the hills south of Pavia and now, even more extensively, in the valleys around Brescia and in the South Tyrol. These wines may or may not be DOC, but since they are mostly second-processed and bottled far from their native habitat, they lose this medal. However, they often win a very special one: that of *pas dosé*. That is to say, they have not been sugared at all, in contrast to the finest champagnes which are often sugared three times during their journey from the first fermentation vat to the final *liqueur d'expédition* additive.

The whole field is brand new: one to which nobody can really bring any persuasive prejudices based on experience. There are only about half a dozen charmats imported into England and even

less Italian Spumante Classicos. The champenois-system production, though part of Italian tradition for over a hundred years,
was scarcely indulged in by Italian vintners. Only in the last twenty
years and less has production increased in the face of increasing
demand and appreciably rising prices.

Thirty years ago, I recall that I used to buy Cinzano Brut charmat
which I enjoyed immensely: a great party wine. This was at the
time that André Simon praised the champenois produced by Ferrari
of Trento. Sweet and brut charmat wines are now made all over
Italy. The technique for making them and the expensive autoclaves
needed (hermetically sealable stainless-steel vats) are widely available, as are the young enologists who supervise this new process.

I recall one day Prince Antonello Ruffo di Calabria inviting me
urgently to come and taste his latest wine. He had a 200-acre
vineyard and a new half-a-million pound sterling winery, from
which he produced a fine rich red Cesanese DOC and his own
improved-Cesanese non-DOC which he called La Selva. In the best
style of Italian eccentrics, he had landscaped a 200-acre garden
with artificial lakes and filled it with thousands of exotic birds,
from black Australian swans to flamingos and ostriches, a pro-
digality that cost him well over a million pounds, in those days
when a million was worth two million. His new wine, it turned
out, was a charmat sparkler of such brilliance and subtle flavour
that it was hard to believe it came from thirty miles south of Rome.
Antonello, himself, was as delighted as though he had fathered
triplets – all boys.

This charmat system has its negative side, too. Vast quantities
of sweet bubbly are made for the Christmas and New Year festive
season which sells for less than £1 a bottle: it is for family consumption; neither grandma nor the kids fuss too much about the
bouquet, the size of the bubbles or the persistence of the foam, but
they do like a good pop. These wines are made mostly from sweet
and surplus table-grapes – but, for all that, they keep Italy happy
and off the streets. They are not meant for foreign connoisseurs
or ambassadorial receptions, any more than is cheap Soave. Good
brut charmat, however, starts at around £3 a bottle, which is well
within the bounds of reason.

There lies *Beyond Lambrusco*, to recall Mr Belfrage's admirable
book, a panorama of pétillant-frizzante and sparkling wines which
the English palate should not reject. They have none of the historic

vices of Italian wines, except one: they are relatively inexpensive. Sparkling wine is a very delicate subject. In this field, I have always found experts very careful in choosing their words. Obviously, in most cases, it is easy to distinguish quality and the difference between charmat and champagne, but when they have been made with the same grape and the charmat has been fermented slowly for over three months, the perlage and bouquet can seem identical. Somehow, I succeed in tasting minimally the steel of the vat with the charmat, and the Italian product also tends to be a little softer, despite a French one often having a trace more sugar. The problem is that the second bottle is harder to adjudicate; the third more so. By which time, everybody has changed the subject. I speak from the unhappy experience of having organized several, hopefully educative, comparative tastings which all failed lamentably.

In this world of mergers and take-overs of fashion houses, perfume-makers, jewellers and even makers of claret by obscure multi-national cattle-feed and fertilizer corporations, I should not be surprised to see some of Italy's top wine houses gobbled up. Many wineries have had their new image, logo and label (designed by famous graphic artists in, say, San Francisco) readied for launching on an unsuspecting public: on their own, I don't think they will make it. RIUNITE would never have made it without Villa Banfi. One of the few who has made it, relatively speaking, on his own is a traditionalist–warrior, Giorgio Lungarotti. With a shrewd eye for the future, he put together the land of the various members of his family to make an estate of some 650 acres right after the Second World War. He produced fine traditional Umbrian wine of a quality never seen before – Sangiovese, Trebbiano and Vin Santo – just outside Perugia. When DOC came along, he even got his own zoning discipline. Of more recent years, he has been the host to annual blind tastings that brought to light many of the best wines that Italy has to offer, including his own new ones: Chardonnay di Miralduolo, Cabernet Sauvignon di Miralduolo and San Giorgio. Many producers of fine wines are unwilling to risk their reputations at blind tastings for a variety of fairly obvious reasons. In fact, winning competitions can cut both ways: nowadays, it is often considered, and rightly so, that the wine that wins the prize has all the 'right' characteristics but may not be a good wine at table. Presumably, the latter is the purpose of wine, rather than that of winning prizes, though this is arguable.

In fact, winning prizes is a sport of the rich in all sorts of luxury fields from prize bulls to speed-boats. The expenses are written off against profits elsewhere, while the prize bull may not be the most gifted at impregnating cows nor is the speed-boat necessarily the best way of going from A to B on water. This perversity does make a lot of wine-talk invalid and, as I have written on other occasions, the tasting of wine without consuming it is also invalid as the better part of a wine demonstrates itself not only in its after-taste but its subsequent effects – expectoration is like coitus interruptus and does not allow for any deepening of affection. You are not likely to fall in love with a wine by tasting it and spitting it down the drain. I also think that wine experts who lunch happily on a hamburger and Coke (and I have observed several with horror) should be disqualified, though this might be difficult to enforce.

Where then are the right criteria for judging wine? Perhaps in the market-place? The views and recommendations of wine-writers and prize juries? The reputation of the enologist? The reputation of the winery? Or, finally, your own choice, after a wide experience of tastings and a bit of knowledge of the origins and processing of the wine? The problem remains that it is not always clear whether one is comparing a cuddly spaniel with a mongrel truffle-hound: both have their merits but the rules, the criteria, are completely different; so, in the end, after adjudicating the authorities, the choice is purely subjective and, unfortunately, dominated by availability and the amount of money you have to spend.

6

The Age of Graceful Ageing

There have been two major changes in the ageing of wines in the last two decades. First, there has been the battle of wood (in the form of huge barrels) against stainless-steel vats, and now new *barriques* (mostly of 325 litres but some of 350) against all comers. It is a double battle that is still in progress and everyone is enjoying it thoroughly.

To explain: the purists first said that big-barrel ageing was out: it oxidized the wine, picked up a lot of tartrates and other junk from the ancient wood and, despite the fact that there wasn't much taste left in the wood (the barrels could be a hundred years old), the wine did somehow take on a very specific aged-in-the-wood style: all this mostly for old Barolos, Barbarescos, Chianti Classicos and many more in the traditional Italian spirit; big, strong wines with a rich winey bouquet.

The first to break the rules were big producers who, for economy's sake, said that half the time spent in the wood could just as well be spent in tanks or steel vats and that the wine lost nothing. They proved their point, too. Then came the purists who said the wine should ideally be aged in small glass barrels but that epoxy-resin-lined tanks or steel vats would do just as well. The basis for their argument was that you don't need that taste of wood, you don't want any extraneous tastes: you want the pure taste of the wine.

This line of thinking looked as though it was going to win the battle, chiefly because it has logic on its side. The purists quite reasonably posited that if Hannibal had beaten the Romans in 202 BC, we would probably be insisting that the élite barrels were made of Lebanese sandalwood or cedarwood (remember the poem: '. . . sandalwood, cedarwood and sweet white wine') rather than French or Yugoslav oak. As Scipio Africanus might well have said: 'It was a dam' near thing.' The Phoenicians lost out and the Romans and the Purists have all lost out, too, and the Californians have won, or so it would seem.

The novelties that the Californians have tossed into the ring are red grapes, quickly run off the lees, that are given a three- to eighteen-month rest in new *barriques*; the result is an altogether livelier wine, more exotic and more complex. The Italians are highly in favour. They are not, however, so convinced by *barrique* whites, particularly Chardonnay aged in fresh barrels, that seem to go too far from tradition for their taste; but that is not stopping their being made. This is a wonderful era of experimentation in breeding finesse. While the Europeans tend to maintain their traditions, the Californians are kicking over the traces and searching for (and finding) a lot of new delights. Plainly, wine does not 'need' *barrique*-ageing. It is just – I would not say a fad, that would be detracting from the talent involved – an extra titillation. It is breeding the loveliest of prize bulls that can, perhaps, even talk back and give their opinion on the local cows.

In all events, the 225-litre *barrique* (Ezio Rivella, for his own good reasons, uses 350-litre ones) has conquered Italy and taught wine-producers to go ahead with their experiments even if they lead out of the DOC fold. At the same time, there is a new conservative movement to put fine white wines in old barrels for a brief spell to soften their acidity. It is because of the changes in the style of so many wines that I nag about having more information from the producer about what he is doing and why.

Another of the innovations has been the planting out of vineyards. Having acquired the ideal cloned roots, the question arises of how to plant them out. Villa Banfi has plugged for generous space for every vine, to the extent that you can run a battle-tank between the rows. The principal reason for this theory is that each vine has plenty to eat without encroaching on its neighbour's territory. They are also trained high and long to reduce the sugar-alcohol and to shade the grapes from the fierce summer sun. If there is still a tendency to too great a yield, summer-pruning may be used. A Banfi-Rivella vineyard can be recognized from a mile away. At some later date in history, machine-harvesting of grapes and field-crushing will be possible: these will resolve oxidation problems and an eventual lack of grape-pickers.

The other major school doubles the number of vines planted and prunes them back to keep the yield down, the theory here being that each vine has to produce much less and, therefore, what it does produce will be much better. There are also new methods of deep ploughing in compacted soil. Twenty-five years ago, you could not plough five or six feet deep: the Caterpillar Corp. resolved that problem. Much more recently, there is a method of 'golf-hole' planting and a variety of new practices for de-weeding and fertilization of the soil around the vines. This latter is part of a long-term study and experimentation project that is just showing its results in the vineyards of the Giglio Estate on what were the Pontine Marshes just south of Rome: it is an area that produces abundantly and at high gradation.

All this mental ferment is changing Italian wines: some have gained notable reputations, many are on the way and all the rest are better for the experience. Perhaps the most interesting demonstration of technology and the fact that it is only twenty-five years old is in the centuries-old champagne industry. This was just ready for launching its export markets in England and America when the French Revolution came along: there was enough wine, there were even enough bottles, and French and English laws against trading wine in new-fangled bottles, instead of barrels, were repealed. Then came the Napoleonic Wars where brutal soldiery made hay in the cellars. It was not till 1850 that sweet champagne got a new foothold on the ladder to success which blossomed at the turn of the century when production could be counted in terms of a few million bottles. Having overcome various revolutions, *phylloxera*, and the First and Second World Wars, champagne started again and, by the 1970s, the sales reached 100 million bottles annually. The rise over the last fifteen years to something around 200 million bottles today is due to high technology: the *dégorgeur*, the *doseur*, the *boucheur* and the *ficeleur* are all automated. Where they are still employed, it is for the sake of tradition, for decoration, for PR and demonstration purposes. After all, it is always useful to have a few handymen around who know how to open a bottle of champagne with a firm twist of the wrist without spilling half of it on the deck.

Again, on the twenty-five- to thirty-year theory, one wonders how 200 million bottles of champagne could have been handled logistically without automatic labelling, packaging and freighting by container. For the record, this production, considering the unfavourable climate and the limited 25,000 hectares of AOC vineyards available, is a credit to French agronomists.

The 1983 edition of *Italian Wines*, over and above a full listing of DOC wines, dedicated a chapter to 'aged wines', taking them out of context for the purpose of setting them into relief. An aged wine costs more not only to the buyer but to the producer. The latter ties up money and has to maintain a cellar with suitable barrels and, in some cases, with air-conditioning. Logically, the producer does not put away in barrels of any dimensions, large or small, wines that he does not feel will justify the trouble: they are, therefore, wines that he is proud of. They may be 'noble' or they may be just 'quality' wines. In the following sections it is my purpose to be purely pragmatic and practical. I will add to the old list many new names of wines and producers who are working outside the DOC jurisdiction with general recognition and success, and something about the influence of limited grape-yields on the quality of wine.

The number of wines that, by DOC legislation, require five years of barrel-ageing is very limited:

Aglianico del Vulture Riserva (from Basilicata) (100 qu.)*
Barolo Riserva Speciale (from Central Piedmont) (80 qu.)
Brunello di Montalcino Riserva (from Tuscany) (100 qu.)
Marsala Vergine Riserva (from Sicily) (100 qu.)
Vin Santo Trentino Riserva (from Veneto) (120 qu.)

To this list can be added non-DOC wines such as Antinori's Solaia, and Giacomo Conterno's Monfortino, which are given over five years' ageing, and De Bartoli's ten-year-aged Vecchio Samperi Marsala.

The Aglianico del Vulture Riserva is a sort of ghost-wine that even Italian wine-lovers rarely come across. I have met it only a few times, always in the Winefood Company's well-made version: it is of course a big, mellow, full-bodied wine that answers all the

---

* The numbers in brackets represent the number of quintals per hectare, that is to say the hundreds of kilos of yield per 10,000 square metres of vineyards.

purposes of the best aged reds but even if its destiny is the same, it plainly has a different origin. It comes from the deep south, from the slopes of an extinct volcano, the Vulture.

Even the Italians tend to think that southern Italy is sub-tropical: it took the TV news cameramen's coverage of the earthquake disaster in the winter of 1980–81 to bring home to all that the hill-towns down there are as well snowed-in as the Highlands of Scotland. The summers, however, are long, warm and dry, which vines like. The producers of Aglianico find it difficult to sell their wine as it is little known, so the prices are consequently not unattractive; certainly a wine worth the trouble of seeking out. Most surprisingly, it is more available in London than in Rome.

Brunello and Barolo are, of course, the prime representatives of Tuscany and Piedmont: big, full-bodied, harmonious – all the flattering adjectives you wish to add. Wines that are good enough to withstand so long in the barrel, once bottled and properly cellared, should have a very long life, during which they should further develop their bouquet and delicacy, finally relaxing into a gentle old age, full of charm but with little vigour. In Italy, these wines are generally broached after ten years while they are still in the full flood of life but, depending on an infinite number of factors, they may have another two decades of muscle in them.

Marsala, after its early success as an English fortified wine, along with port, sherry and madeira, slowly declined from upstairs to downstairs, where it was used only for cooking and domestic tippling. In the last few years, it has seen a remarkable and surprising revival; this is perhaps because there has been no lack of funding for new plant and equipment. Sicily, and Marsala in particular, has had a renaissance of notable proportions over the last decade. Marsala's port is as great an exporter of bulk wines as Sète, near Marseilles, is an importer (we are, of course, talking about the same cargoes of wine in both cases), and all the wine companies of Marsala have grown and prospered. They have also set themselves to producing much finer wines than in the past and I have noted that even the best Marsalas are both stronger in taste yet more subtle in character than those of old. I suspect that the New Enology has had a lot to do with this.

The last on the list, the Vin Santo Trentino Riserva, is in the Tuscan tradition, and very good.

Four years' ageing before marketing is still a long haul and very expensive for the producer in terms of labour, space, barrels and tied-up capital. In fact, the list offers only one surprise; otherwise, the wines are among the conventionally recognized big wines of Italy:

Barbaresco Riserva Speciale (100 qu.)
Barolo Riserva (80 qu.)
Brunello di Montalcino (100 qu.)
Carema (80 qu.)
Gattinara (90 qu.)
Ghemme (90 qu.)
Taurasi Riserva (110 qu.)
Vin Nobile di Montepulciano Riserva Speciale (100 qu.)
Vin Santo Trentino (120 qu.)

Amongst the DOCs, we can include the Badia di Coltibuoni, which is sometimes aged more than the requirements. Antinori's Sassicaia and Lungarotti's San Giorgio, both non-DOCs, can be aged for four years. All are premium wines.

Italy's finest aged wines have never received the world accolade they merit and, to some extent, they are not easy to sell at home or abroad. This does rather explain why Italian producers are looking for other models, other trends. The above list of great aged wines is the essence of traditional Italian viticulture, along with a few more equally dignified wines that we find among the three year olds. They are all 'cru' wines made from grapes selected for their quality and to produce an extra degree of alcoholic content. What is instructive is the location of so many of these great wines from north to south of the country and the variety of vines employed.

The method of ageing is laid down precisely in some cases and equivocally or elastically in others. For example, the stipulated minima for a Barolo Riserva are two years in the barrel and three in the bottle, although a longer period in the barrel is not only permitted but probable. The Brunello, on the other hand, must have four years in the barrel by law and, by tradition, will most surely have a year in the bottle before leaving the winery. In all, it can be said that the wood- and bottle-aged wines are ready for drinking the day they are sold, though, in view of their high quality, they are capable of much more ageing in the bottle. Most of the wineries that invest in ageing do so because they are proud of the wines and seek recognition – I doubt that it is proportionately rewarding financially. Rather, it is a prestige act, like selling wines abroad at a lower profit margin than that normally earned in Italy. Both massage the producers' egos sufficiently to make up for the years of patience and hard work that go into producing fine wines, and rid them of the nagging thought that the effort was not worth the sacrifice of so many other pleasures of life.

To return to the four-year-old wines, the Barbaresco Riserva Speciale, the Carema, the Gattinara and the Ghemme are all made with the same varieties of the same vine, the Nebbiolo, which demonstrates different facets of its character according to its habitat – in these cases, Central Piedmont, the foothills of the Aosta Valley and the Novara Hills.

Tuscany is duly and with dignity represented by Brunello di Montalcino and Vin Nobile di Montepulciano, both Sangioveto varietals of great character. Plenty of Chianti Classicos are in fact aged four and more years, though this is not required by the discipline.

The surprise is the Taurasi, a big southern wine, that has none of the vices of the south. It is thought to have a Greek origin. Irrespective of where it came from, its current production is of such paramount quality that many denigrators of the south have had to drink their own words. The two whites (the Fiano and the Greco di Tufo) from the same area are sublime and they, too, like a modicum of ageing. Of these wines, only the Taurasi, the Vin Nobile and the Brunello must do all their four years in the wood; the Gattinara and Ghemme do three, the Barbaresco one, while the others split half and half in wood and bottle.

Moving to the three year olds, we find that the location of the vineyards extends to the Veneto, Emilia Romagna, Umbria, Puglia, Calabria and Sardinia and that the general rule is for the wine to be kept in the wood for at least a year, perhaps two, followed by a final period in the bottle. But here also one may find that these minima are simply those laid down by the law.

First, we have two Piedmontese wines:

Barbaresco Riserva (100 qu.)
Barolo (80 qu.)

These are 'big' wines to drink on important occasions or to cellar away for the future.

The Novara Hills wines are close competitors for the laurels with those of Central Piedmont. Gattinara's fame has encouraged others, so that now we have four DOC categories from those parts:

Boca (90 qu.)
Bramaterra Riserva (80 qu.)
Fara (100 qu.)
Sizzano (100 qu.)

If you include the non-DOC Spanna wines and the DOC two-year-old Lessona wines made from peripheral vineyards, you have a formidable group of man-size well-aged wines that is hard to rival, all offering 12–13 per cent of natural alcoholic content.

In Tuscany and Umbria, our list is:

Carmignano Riserva (80 qu.)
Chianti Classico Riserva (75–80 qu.) and Chianti Riserva (100 qu.)
Torgiano Rubesco Riserva (120 qu.)
Vin Nobile di Montepulciano Riserva (100 qu.)

All these wines, when acquired from the most reputable wineries, are of great stature: all of them can take a decade of bottle-age in their stride and profit immensely from it. They are all basically Sangioveto wines, though the Carmignano is blended with 10 per cent of Cabernet Sauvignon, which is more attractive. The three-year-old Vin Nobile di Montepulciano, of course, recalls the five year old while the Torgiano is an Umbrian cru and entirely to the credit of Giorgio Lungarotti who invented it, invested in it and nursed it over the years, till now his Rubesco is recognized as one of the best wines in Italy.

The Veneto and Emilia Romagna offer us a completely new horizon:

Cabernet di Pramaggiore Riserva (100 qu.)
Colli Berici Cabernet Riserva (120 qu.)
Colli Bolognesi Barbera Riserva (120 qu.)
Piave Cabernet Riserva (110 qu.)

Here is the first tangible sign of the total success of French vines in Italy. In the Veneto, one finds not only Cabernet Sauvignon and Cabernet Franc, but an abundance of Merlot which has equally acclimatized itself. The Bologna Hills DOC category has honoured its Barbera production with a Riserva, but I think it will not be long before the Merlots and Cabernets are also promoted and perhaps the Pinots and Rieslings will get a Superiore medal. To date, the DOC committee has accepted straight French varietals but rarely blends in claret style, which seems ungenerous, especially as some of Italy's best and long-established wines are precisely that: Fedrigotti's Fojenaghe, Loredan's Venegazzù and Baron Basetti's Roncade. Of recent years, Lungarotti has added his non-DOC San Giorgio which has 25 per cent Cabernet Sauvignon and up to four years in the wood.

To wind up the three year olds, we have seven from the south. The first two have already been mentioned in the earlier age-groups:

Aglianico del Vulture Vecchio (old) (110 qu.)
Taurasi (100 qu.)

They are followed by two dessert wines and six strong table wines:

Vernaccia di Oristane Superiore (80 qu.)
Aleatico di Puglia Riserva (80 qu.)
Cannonau di Sardegna (Oliena-Capo Ferrato) (110 qu.)
Cirò Reserva (115 qu.)
Regaleali Rosso del Conte (as a table wine, a non-DOC wine, the
    yield per hectare is not published)
Rosso Castel del Monte Riserva (80 qu.)
Rosso Canosa Riserva (80 qu.)
Rosso di Cerignola (80 qu.)

The dessert wines are made with grapes selected for their high sugar content and semi-dried to give a generous alcoholic content: the actual sweetness of the wine depends on how much of the sugar is converted into alcohol. In the case of the Puglia Aleatico, there is a total of 15 per cent potential of alcohol but only 13 per cent is actually turned into alcohol, the fermentation being halted in time to leave a 2 per cent residue of sugar: the Aleatico may also be fortified with wine alcohol up to 18.5 per cent, leaving 2.5 per cent as sugar. The Sardinian Vernaccia, on the other hand, has the same 15per cent (often much more) of potential alcohol which is fully converted, with a resulting bone-dry, sherry-type wine that has not been fortified.

The Cirò wines – particularly the old reds – have a colour, taste and velvety persuasiveness that is unique. They are redolent of the deep south, though one must watch out as they have a tendency to break up and oxidize without warning in the barrel and in the bottle. However, here also technology is raising its pretty head and changes in cultivation and processing methods are being made that will resolve this age-old problem of too low fixed acidity, too high temperatures during fermentation and ageing, and too much oxygen getting into the wine.

The Sardinian Cannonau is a very different kettle of fish. It is the red wine of Sardinia that turns up in a wide variety of forms ranging from an over-sweet, highly alcoholic, fortified Anghelu Ruju (Red Angel, the name of a Stone Age settlement in the vine-yards), port-like drink to being a mild and tamed Mandrolisai. It is at its greatest as Oliena and Capo Ferrato: these are formidable 15–18 per cent wines from the Barbagia Mountains and stern blacks of Cape Ferrato. They are mountain wines made to accompany a wild boar roasted on the spit over a bed of myrtle branches – you deserve it more if you have shot the beast yourself. Despite their high alcoholic content, the wines are fully harmonious and in no sense can be considered cutting wines. The best – Perda Rubia (Red Rock) – is made by Mario Mereu; the Oliena Co-operative and Mr Deana are close rivals and the Jerzu Co-operative does nicely, too. Not only is this bandit-land, but Mr Mereu him-self was held to ransom many years ago. Every wine-lover should drink a bottle of these wines once in his life, just to know that wine is not an involuted preciosity for aesthetes nor an extravagance for conspicuous spenders. They are austere, full-bodied, level-eyed wines, intolerant of criticism. After all, these wines stand alone – where can you find anything like them?

The market pressures to reduce Sardinia's wines to something that suits teenage palates are great. The Sardinians are dragging their feet in the hope that a new counter-trend – albeit a small one – will arise to keep their natural 15 per cent-plus wines in business; not even mainland Italians seem sufficiently aware of their exist-ence. Many wineries have already thrown down their blunder-busses, so to speak, and are making light, fresh, fruity and clean wines. But it would be a grave shame if we were to sacrifice all these remarkable wines on the altar of youth. To be added to this category is a distinguished non-DOC Riserva wine called Rosso del Conte from Regaleali in Sicily which is generous, strong and subtle.

The majority of the two-year-olds of Piedmont and Lombardy have to be kept in the wood for the full two years and some are half-and-half. In any event, two years either way – and, always in Italy, the tendency is to do more than the law requires – is a big invest-ment in a field where one-year ageing is considered a lot and is, in fact usually more than enough, especially if fresh barrels are used. The first batch is traditional Central Piedmont wine which, from the customary distinguished producers, is following close on Barolo's heels:

Barbera d'Alba (90 qu.)
Barbera d'Asti (90 qu.)
Barbera di Monteferrato (100 qu.)
Barbaresco (100 qu.)
Colli Tortonesi Barbera Superiore (90 qu.)
Lessona (90 qu.)

The Barbera vine is the source of the Piedmont-Lombardy jug wine. It is not the greatest of wines but, when cultivated with loving care and nursed like a Barolo through its fermentation to its ageing, becomes a big wine of character, comparable to the very best – and, incidentally, it should be much cheaper. The only new name here is Tortona Barbera; this is only an extension of the Barbera growing area which had not been legislated for.

Proceeding towards the Swiss frontier, north of Milan and Lake Como, we come to the Valtelline which has an established and solid reputation for its Nebbiolos, grown on hillsides at 2,000 feet, with a perfect southern aspect. It is perhaps, the only case in all Italy where a list of recommended producers is not necessary: there is no poorly made Valtellina. The wines are:

Grumello (100 qu.)
Inferno (100 qu.)
Sassella (100 qu.)
Sfursat or Sfurzat (non-DOC)

These go under the broad nomenclature of Valtellina Superiore.

The last, the Sfursat, is a maverick giant. It is a rich, dry, red wine made with some semi-dried grapes to offer a minimum of 14 per cent of alcoholic content. It is the same class as Verona's Amarone Recioto.

Near Bergamo in Lombardy, there is a new DOC category, Valcalepio, that is producing from French vines. It is an area that will be growing in importance and I will make greater mention of this lively area and others in Part Two.

Cabernet Sauvignon and Merlot are nowadays as much at home in north Italy as the Pinots and Chardonnays. The Bergamo area is noted for its fine wines and also for its champenois- and charmat-system sparkling wines. Most of them, however, are consumed locally in the wealthy cities of Milan, Brescia and Bergamo. Further south, a similar situation has surfaced in recent years:

Montello Cabernet Riserva (110 qu.)
Montello Merlot Superiore (110 qu.)
Gambellara Vin Santo (100 qu.)

This is further proof of the success of French vines. Though the French grape tends to be 'softer' than the traditional and hard Italian one (Nebbiolo, Sangiovese and Montepulciano), the former somehow takes on a slightly more positive character in Italy than at home and this has a considerable and unexpected charm. This trend towards the use of French vines may not be changing the face of Italian viticulture, but it is opening up a very large number of new options. The famous non-DOC Venegazzù comes from this area.

For the sake of convenience, I have put the three Venetos together: that is, the South Tyrol, the Veneto proper and Venezia Giulia on the Yugoslav border.

In this region, we find that the Alto Adige (South Tyrol) and the Trentino zone to its south have some novelties:

Alto Adige Cabernet Riserva (110 qu.)
Teroldego Rotaliano Superiore (130 qu.)
Trentino Cabernet Riserva (110 qu.)
Trentino Lagrein Riserva (120 qu.)
Trentino Marzemino Riserva (90 qu.)
Trentino Merlot Riserva (120 qu.)

Trentino Moscato Riserva (100 qu.)
Trentino Pinot Nero Riserva (110 qu.)

The Trentino area is great wine land. Ferrari and Equipe 5 are champenois-system wines made there, as are fine sparklers by the CAVIT, along with a huge range of fine aged reds, including Bossi-Fedrigotti's non-DOC Fojenaghe and the CAVIT's 4 Vicariati, both Cabernet blends.

Moving south to the Venetian wines and to those of Friuli Venezia Giulia we find:

Colli Orientali del Friuli Cabernet Riserva (110 qu.)
Colli Orientali del Friuli Merlot Riserva (110 qu.)
Colli Orientali del Friuli Picolit Riserva (40 qu.)
Colli Orientali del Friuli Pinot Reserva (110 qu.)
Colli Orientali del Friuli Refosco Riserva (110 qu.)
Merlot di Pramaggiore (130 qu.)
Piave Merlot Riserva (130 qu.)

This is surely enough to make the reader whose experience of Italian wines is limited to Chianti, Soave and Bardolino, raise his eyebrows. A year in *barriques*, eighteen months at the most, is certainly enough for a Cabernet, Merlot or Pinot Nero: any extra time served in the bottle can only be advantageous. Both areas (the Trentino and Friuli) are noted for their advanced wine-making expertise and their enological institutes (San Michele all'Adige and Conegliano), which have played a major role in the improvements in Italian wines. There are many producers from these parts who have gained international reputations as creators of new wines. This represents, however, only a small part of the great penetration of French vines into the whole Veneto and beyond to Bologna and even Tuscany.

The Marzemino, Teroldego Rotaliano and Refosco are local wines of which only the Teroldego is really outstanding: whilst the Picolit is the controversial nineteenth-century dessert wine – currently being kept alive and productive (it suffers from 'floral abortion') by highly skilled agronomists – that had its days of glory in Habsburgian times in Vienna. It is a fine subtle wine but, at its present price, I would prefer to settle for a Nasco from Cagliari which is in the best of health and the full vigour of life. The Trentino Moscato – an aromatic, amabile and full-bodied wine – is among the few fine whites that are still aged in the wood in Italy.

Central Italy, including Emilia Romagna, Tuscany and the Abruzzi, does not bring much by way of surprises:

Carmignano (80 qu.)
Chianti Classico Vecchio (80 qu.)
Montepulciano d'Abruzzo (140 qu.)
Morellino di Scansano Riserva (90 qu.)
Sangiovese di Romagna (110 qu.)
Vin Nobile di Montepulciano (110 qu.)

The Sangiovese di Romagna is a straight red varietal that has been under considerable pressure for improvement and launching on a larger market than its local one – along with its two white sisters, Albana and Trebbiano di Romagna – and it must be admitted that all three have gained a considerable degree of acclaim in Italy and abroad, though perhaps not on the highest levels. What, however, is remarkable is that the Albana is likely to be the first white DOC-Guaranteed. Thirty years ago, it was wryly regarded as a rather odd-ball wine, dry but with an amabile yet somehow bitter after-taste. Not everybody went for it and even some producers were a bit dubious. Over the years, it has been turned into a dry white that is acceptable to current taste. As for the Sangiovese, as a young wine, it marries with spiced and garlicked seafood to per-fection: aged, it admirably decorates the traditionally groaning tables of Emilia Romagna cuisine.

The other five wines on the list, from Carmignano to Montepul-ciano d'Abruzzo, are just less aged members of families we have met already: they are first pressings of very high quality that can still take further ageing in the bottle. The Morellino di Scansano is new; it is a Chianti-style wine from the Grosseto coastal area that is fast gaining a good reputation as wine land. Le Pupille is the name of a notable *barrique*-aged Morellino.

The south is well represented with seventeen aged wines:

Sardinia
Cannonau di Sardegna (110 qu.)
Carignano di Sulcis (100 qu.)
Malvasia di Bosa (80 qu.)
Malvasia di Cagliari Riserva (90 qu.)

Monica di Cagliari Riserva (90 qu.)
Monica di Sardegna Superiore (90 qu.)
Nasco di Cagliari Riserva (90 qu.)

Puglia
Castel del Monte (120 qu.)
Copertino (140 qu.)
Primitivo di Manduria (90 qu.)
Rosso di Barletta Invecchiato (150 qu.)
Rosso di Cerignola Riserva (140 qu.)
Salice Salentino Riserva (120 qu.)
Squinzano Riserva (140 qu.)

Calabria
Pollino Superiore (110 qu.)
Savuto Superiore (110 qu.)

Sicily
Marsala Superiore (100 qu.)

The Sardinian Cannonau can be and is processed in so many
different ways – even as a sparkling sweet red wine – that it is
impossible to make any overall judgement, except that it was wise
of the wine authorities to give Oliena and Capo Ferrato a sub-
DOC zone discipline of their own. The Monica di Sardegna Superiore is a table wine made from a grape that can be grown indis-
criminately almost anywhere on the island; it is a pleasing but not
outstanding wine. It is, however, remarkably, a wine that pleases
everybody. Grown on metre-high *alberelli* (vine bushes), as a cutting wine it used to give backbone as well as colour to some of
the finer and finest wines of Italy and Europe, without detracting
from – and possibly adding to – the traditional organoleptic
characteristics: a notable wine, therefore. The surprise from Sardinia is the new DOC Carignano di Sulcis, a red from the French
Carignano vine that is so full-bodied that the Sardinians say it is
a meal in itself.

The two Malvasias (malmseys) of Bosa and Cagliari are rich,
velvety white dessert wines that may also be fortified. The Monica
di Cagliari (to be distinguished from Monica di Sardegna which is
a table wine) has the same characteristics but is red. All are full-

bodied wines, sweet but with a dry after-taste that prevents all these remarkable dessert wines from being cloying. They are thus eminently drinkable at all hours and, of course, post-prandially. They are all made in relatively modest quantities – and ever less – since they cannot stand up to the international barrage of publicity for apéritifs, spirits and after-dinner drinks of all origins and colours. But, for the real wine-lover, they offer voluptuous depths that no gin and tonic or vodka martini will ever arouse; the dry (or almost dry) Nasco is a similar traditional wine of particular merit that I hope will not get lost in this age of automation.

Puglian wine-making is something of a lion-taming act – one cannot but admire the courage of the tamer and the brute strength of his wards. The results in this case are the first six wines mentioned above. They are all domesticated (perhaps castrated) versions of the great Puglia cutting wines. They are full-bodied, generous wines which, after a diet of meagre – if elegant, subtle and fragrant – wines of the north, come as a relief from an excess of prissiness. The tamest of the lions comes from Castel del Monte, while by far the most respected wine of the whole area is a well-aged Torre Quarto, a non-DOC but on the level of the best that Europe offers.

The two Calabrian offerings, the Pollino Superiore and the Savuto Superiore, are both made mostly with the same sturdy Gaglioppo and Greco Nero grapes in the hills of the Sila. The making and marketing of aged wines is not as easy as falling off a barrel but, like so many of the southerners, they are well on their way to succeeding. The vines, which are cultivated at around 2,000 feet, have no heavy southern characteristics; rather, they have the fragrant bouquet of Alpine wines. Unfortunately, because of the cost of agriculture in the hills, they are rather expensive.

In this two-year bracket there are many non-DOC reds of high repute, such as: Tenuta Caparzo's Ca' del Pazzo (Siena), Capannelle's Barrique Table Wine (Siena), Castello Volpaia's Coltassala (Siena), Castellare's I Sodi di S. Niccolò (Siena), Giacomo Bologna's Bricco dell'Uccellone (Piedmont), Tedeschi's Capitel San Rocco (Verona), Vigna dal Leon's Rosso dal Leon (Udine) and Monte Vertine's La Pergola Torta (Siena) and many more.

The one-year list does not simply reflect those of the previous sectors but opens up many new vineyards and puts more wines into this prime category of aged wines, thus also giving us a better opportunity to evaluate the wines in comparison with each other and in relation to the price asked for them. Particularly interesting is the Piedmont second line of defence – the Dolcettos, Barberas and Nebbiolos – which make excellent surrogates for the Piedmont big-reds at more contained prices. The Ligurian offerings are less inspiring.

Though a year of ageing may not seem a lot, it can have a profound effect on a wine, smoothing rough edges (if wine can be said to have edges) – and if you use fresh *barriques* for even six months, you may well have created a completely new wine. Many producers are doing precisely that.

Piedmont
Dolcetto d'Acqui Superiore (80 qu.)
Dolcetto d'Alba Superiore (90 qu.)
Dolcetto d'Asti Superiore (80 qu.)
Dolcetto di Dogliano Superiore (80 qu.)
Dolcetto d'Ovada Superiore (80 qu.)
Enfer d'Arvier (80 qu.)
Freisa d'Asti Superiore (80 qu.)
Nebbiolo d'Alba (90 qu.)

Liguria
Cinque Terre and Cinque Terre Sciacchetrà (90 qu.)
Rossese di Dolceacqua Superiore (90 qu.)

The Dolcettos and the Nebbiolos were once considered modest table wines. Given the attention that was previously reserved for Barolos, they have become the base of the traditionally generous and reliable reds of Piedmont. The Freisa d'Asti Superiore and of Chieri used to be made mostly frizzante and very slightly sweet but are now mostly traditional dry red wines, though pétillant versions with a trace of sweetness can still be found and are not without their charms. The Enfer d'Arvier is a wine of even smaller production that comes from well up the Aosta Valley. This and other mountain wines – Blanc de Morgex and Blanc de la Salle – are rarely available. They are either drunk on the snow-line or sold privately to regular subscribers on the plains.

In Liguria, perhaps I have been unlucky with the odd times I have drunk their Sciacchetrà, but it has failed to enchant me, whereas the table wines of the coast – Rossese di Dolceacqua included – are most agreeable though I doubt that ageing in the wood does them much good beyond rounding off some rough edges. They seem best drunk young and lively.

The Alto Adige (South Tyrol) offers four most pleasing wines. For climatic reasons, they are not alcoholically strong but they make up for this with a mountain freshness and a taste to satisfy the connoisseur. The alcoholic content is 'low' only vis-à-vis other Italian wines but it never drops below a natural 10 per cent which may be increased by licit methods. Nowadays, a lot of Pinot Nero is sold direct to the champenois- and charmat-system sparkling-wine producers all over north Italy.

Alto Adige Lagrein Scuro de Gries Riserva (100 qu.)
Alto Adige Merlot Riserva (130 qu.)
Alto Adige Sorni Scelto (100 qu.)
Alto Adige Pinot Nero Riserva (120 qu.)

The Lagrein is a local traditional vine widely used in the Adige Valley: it comes as Dunkel (dark) and Kretzer (rosé) and the best of it is from the Benedictine Kloster Kellerei where it is usually aged for two years. They also make the ethereal Santa Maddalena (or St Magdalener) which comes from higher up the mountains and, though DOC demands no barrel-ageing, I feel sure that the good Abbot gives it some, in view of the remarkable results.

The vintners have a very high reputation in these parts for avant-garde processing. However, their home production – on terraced mountain-sides – is insufficient for their order-books and, for their non-DOC wines, they find no difficulty in re-stocking their vats with Veneto wines.

Then come the world-famous wines of the Veneto:

Amarone Recioto della Valpolicella (120 qu.)
Bardolino Classico Superiore (80 qu.)
Valpantena Superiore (120 qu.)
Valpolicella Rosso Superiore (120 qu.)

These require only one year's ageing. They are not austere, tannic wines that need a long softening in the barrel: in fact, Bardolino is noted mostly as a wine to be drunk as young as possible. Italian wine-lovers, over the last decade, have been able to enjoy the greatly improved quality of Valpolicella and Valpantena which has come about largely as a result of the demand from abroad for Superiore quality wines. However, one of the greatest of aged wines of the Veneto, and perhaps of Italy, is the non-DOC Amarone Recioto della Valpolicella which, after a *ripasso* therapy, is suitably aged at the discretion of the vintner to reach over 14 per cent of alcoholic content and to become a full-bodied, yet elegant and exceedingly stable and harmonious wine, fit to honour the table of the most exacting gourmet.

The Euganean Hills, near Padua, have gained repute in the last thirty or so years for their light spumantes and their Colli Euganei Superiores, both red and white. The red is a rare DOC-approved blend of Cabernet Sauvignon and Merlot with additions of Barbera and Verona Rabosa: the white has 25 per cent Sauvignon. The most distinguished winery in the district is that of the famous Luxardo Company which, long, long ago, invented Maraschino, the cherry liqueur, when its winery was sited in Austro-Hungarian Dalmatia (now Yugoslavia) and, after the Second World War, decided that the economic climate was better in Italy and that cherry trees would grow just as well in the Veneto. Luxardo is noted also for its Cabernet-Merlot aged wine, called St Elmo.

The wines for one year's ageing from central Italy are conventional and reliable:

La Parrina (110 qu.)
Rosso Piceno Superiore (140 qu.)
Vernaccia di San Gimignano (100 qu.)

Vernaccia di San Gimignano, at my last tasting of it, had not undergone the New Enology and had retained its old characteristics – or defects, as they are more correctly called today. However, defects have their charms and we would not like to lose all of them. It is like praying for the virtues of continence and chastity – but not yet. Most of us prefer to hang on to a few of our more endearing faults and so it can be with wine. However, Vernaccia di San Gimignano is currently represented by a newcomer with already a big reputation: it is a briefly *barrique*-aged wine called Terre di Tufo. In all events, Vernaccia di San Gimignano is a most highly respected wine with a lively vinous bouquet and a harmonious body in good Tuscan country spirit. La Parrina is a post-Second World War enterprise on the Tuscan Seaboard near

Argentario; slowly, the wine has built up its quality and reputation. This whole Tuscan coastal strip, including Pisa and the Lucca hills, is now beginning to demonstrate its vocation for vineyards, especially recalling the great Sassicaia Cabernet that is now being produced not far from Leghorn.

The last five wines in this one-year class are a mixed bunch from the south, two of which I admit I have never tasted, the Trani and the Vulture; they are probably rich, honest wines with a tendency to oxidize.

Sardinia
Cannonau di Sardegna (110 qu.)
Moscato di Cagliari Riserva (90 qu.)

Puglia
Moscato di Trani (80 qu.)

Basilicata (Lucania)
Aglianico del Vulture spumante (100 qu.)

Pantelleria Island
Moscato Passito di Pantelleria Extra (70 qu.)

The Sardinian wines are sweet dessert wines that also come in a fortified form: this goes for the Moscato di Trani, too. Even less available, surely, is the sparkling Aglianico del Vulture (or perhaps this all finishes up in London!). In any case, if it reflects its dry edition, it should be formidable. I would like to do a little flag-wagging for the last on the list, the white, or rather, amber-coloured, Passito, from the little island of Pantelleria that lies half-way between Sicily and Tunis. It is an endangered species. Like the warm wines of Cagliari, it is a voluptuous, velvety, strong and fragrant wine that also might disappear because its small production does not justify full-page ads in the press and fifteen-second nationwide TV commercials.

The panorama of aged Italian wines, then, runs from Pantelleria up to the snow-line in the Aosta Valley and the South Tyrol, with dozens of stops in specific and distinct wine-producing areas on the way. With vines originating in at least half a dozen countries

(Italy, France, Germany, Spain, Greece and the Lebanon), it is scarcely an entity that one can facilely dub 'Italian wine', as though there were some common denominator.

This enormous variety is, however, not an advantage: it disperses too much energy. Not even Italian experts are able to keep tabs on all the changes and chances of mortal life, even with the well-established companies, let alone the burgeoning new ones demanding recognition. In the first edition of this book, the recommendations were all specifically known to me over the years. In the 1983 edition, I had to turn to one or two highly competent advisers to help me out, particularly for the lesser-known new zones, since personally updating the whole range of Italian wines and their variations from winery to winery would have been too great a physical effort and I should have fallen by the wayside too often.

A difference between French and Italian aged wines, I would hazard, is that the former, with relatively brief ageing in the wood, gain their stature in the bottle: however, when bought young, there is something of a gamble as to how the wine will turn out. With the longer ageing carried out by the Italians, the wine should be ready to drink on marketing, with its characteristics well defined: with further ageing, the wines will be enhanced but they will not evolve. The risk, to the wine-lover, as to the outcome of the wine, has been absorbed by the producer. However, this traditional viewpoint is not as valid as it used to be since the Italians are making wide use of Californian-style short-ageing techniques, which muddles the issue.

This leads to the question of vintages, which I find unrewarding. Certainly, there were great years like 1964 which spread over all Italy and there were poor ones like 1980 which did not spread over all Italy. Bad years, in a mountainous country like Italy, where the barometer spends most of its time sticking upright on 'variable', are never definitive, even regionally. The poor harvest of 1980 was not poor all over (the Lambrusco crop, for example, was quite unharmed), though there was a tendency for the harvest to be a couple of weeks late.

The classic scenario regarding the unreliability (and often meaninglessness) of vintage charts is that half-way through the harvest it rains cats and dogs and then snows. Half the crop is gathered in perfect condition, the other half is 'saved' by the enologist but at a far more modest quality: equally, there could well be totally different weather conditions in vineyards only twenty miles apart, say, in Tuscany, yet the vintage chart will still give an overall figure or qualification for the region and the wine. Furthermore, the better wineries are often better because they own the sunniest hillsides and, therefore, during the poor years, find that they still have enough sugar alcohol in their grapes to make a Riserva whilst their next-door neighbour must sell his wine in bulk.

The question of how long an aged wine will last in the cellar brings up the same old question regarding the length of a piece of string. This morning, a friend told me over the telephone that he had drunk ninety-five-year-old Lessona which was faded but still full of subtle delights. But this wine had been in a cellar only five miles from the winery during all that period. I have drunk twenty-year-old white Trebbiano with Dr Lungarotti at Torgiano: again, the wine had never been moved from the dry, cold, dark, vibration-less and silent cellar under his house. The nearer you can get to such conditions, the longer a wine will last. The best of the Piedmont and Tuscan aged wines are generally reckoned to be able to rival anything that the French wines can do; but I would not like to push many of the others beyond the decade, which is a good ripe old age for a wine.

Ageing does not depend only on the characteristics of the wine and the cellaring: the bottling method and the cork are also very important. During very long ageing, the wine may well have to be decanted and re-corked more than once, and by skilled professionals.

Aside from the biggest and best wines, which might be allowed to age appreciably for no better reason than that they can, the Italian thinking is to drink wines in the full flood of mature virility rather than to await that inevitable, delicate, gentle and long decline, fascinating though it may be. This means, broadly speaking, opening bottles at between four and fourteen years of age, according to the grape. A fair guide-line to the ageing of wines is that the longer they have been aged in the wood within the DOC limitations for the various types of wine (one to five years), the longer they are likely to last in the cellar. For this reason, I would encourage putting the date of bottling as well as the vintage date on the label.

7

The Age of the Ageless

Perversely, the exports of Italian wines are increasing, but only those of Villa Banfi and RIUNITE: the others, broadly speaking, are declining. Added to that, the general sales per capita in Italy are declining, too, and Villa Banfi does not try to sell very hard in Italy: it does not even have its own sales-force. And yet it must be admitted that a goodly number of producers (many already listed and others to be mentioned in Part Two) have improved their wines beyond measure and many have outstripped the traditionals with fine new wines, new blends, new varietals, new processing, new ageing and much else. We have, in fact, the unacceptable situation by which the wine – Sassicaia, for example – that could be considered the best produced in Italy comes into the lowliest quality bracket, 'Table Wine', with no mention on the label that it is made from Cabernet Sauvignon and Cabernet Franc and is long-aged in *barriques*. There are dozens of new-blend fine red wines that come into this Table Wine category for which the Italian Board of Trade prohibits a proper and precise presentation to the public. But, looking at the issue a trifle cynically, it doesn't matter because, even if Antinori got an order for a container-load, they would not be able to fill it.

In the south, there are other forms of misinformation caused by DOC regulations: for example, looking for a bottle of white wine in a Sardinian supermarket, I bought a table wine from Sant'Antioco Island but noticed that it had a 16.5 per cent alcohol content which is nearly sherry strength and too high for a luncheon wine. I bought it and, when I tasted it, it was a delicious, sweet muscat wine which, since chaptalization is neither permitted nor necessary in Sardinia, had also a percentage of sugar in it to bring it up to the maximum that Nature's chemistry permits a fermented grape to reach. The only two clues to the wine being a sweet dessert wine, rather than a modest table wine, was the 16.5 per cent alcoholic content printed in small type and the price which was, say, 25 per cent more than that of a standard DOC white. This is, of course, stupid, as has already been mentioned, as is the category for the Sassicaia which once won the *Decanter* magazine award for the best Cabernet in the world. To make things worse, by Common Market rules the Sardinian wine would be a '*vin tout court*' and 'suitable for making into table wine', which means a poor wine with a very low alcoholic content which, chaptalized, might become a table wine. Our Sardinian wine, on the other hand, has too much alcohol, not too little. Perhaps it is best to look the other way and think about other things, as the Italians do when bureaucracy gets too infuriating.

Then there is the equally perverse situation by which most *vini novelli* are presented as table wines. If you look at the label, you cannot necessarily discover that they are made by the Beaujolais *nouveau* system; nor will you be permitted to know that they are made with, perhaps, the noblest of grapes and, being without a vintage or bottling date (presumably illegal, too), you cannot know the date by which they should be consumed. A year and a bit from bottling time is reckoned to be the maximum cellaring period, after which a *nouveau* should either be drunk or used for making vinegar.

All labels have to be approved by the Board of Trade – many famous and antique ones have been disqualified and contemporary graphic artists are driven up the wall fitting the size of the lettering (terribly important) and general design to bureaucratic rules and, in particular, to the interpretation of the Food Section of the Board of Trade.

The fact is that only people like Villa Banfi can overcome the problem of bureaucracy, not by getting anything changed but because, subsequently, in the States, they have their salesmen who reach up to the American carriage trade in Fifth Avenue and further up the road to Harlem, where they can explain the quirks of the Italian civil service to their clients personally. For example, why Santa Costanza and Centine Brunello are described as table wines when they are premium wines. And, for that matter, how the billion two hundred million bottles of Lambrusco, imported over the last twenty years into the States, are non-DOC.

In this field, there are probably thousands of table wines of which hundreds are made regularly with specific quality varietals or blends and which should have the right to get out of the enforced anonymity in which they live. DOC legislation has come and nearly gone. I wrote in the 1974 edition of *Italian Wines*:

> The DOC system is good but it is not definitive. There are plenty of wineries that have always worked on altogether higher levels than those required by the law: wineries that own better land, have more skilled employees and enologists, cooler cellars and better vats, casks and equipment and mature their wines better than the law specifically demands: and there are wines that, due to the traditional modes of production, cannot insert themselves into the DOC orbit and producers who do not wish to vitiate their reputations by joining their neighbours and prefer to stand alone.

This pretty well describes the situation fourteen years later, extended to dozens if not hundreds of wineries and with a versatility that reflects the Italians' low threshold of patience with Dullsville and their inventiveness as soon as they get out of the crippling grip of personal economic problems. It might be said that Italy started to get out of that grip for the first time only two decades ago, and now a considerable well-being is felt throughout the Republic. There is a long way to go to reach the comforts and security of other Common Market countries but enough for a lot of the more fortunate Italians to risk doing their own thing on a small business or industrial level.

There is a sector of Italian wines that has very little to do with the rest of the world: it was always there. It is mostly DOC nowadays, not because DOC had any influence on it but because it has been there since the fourteen-year old Catherine de' Medici took her rosolio wine-makers to Paris from Florence along with her cooks when she became Queen of France.

These strong rosolio wines are called dessert wines nowadays, but scarcely anybody drinks them post-prandially any more. In Italy, spumante has taken their place at the end of a dinner. Italians have a tendency to decry their own products in favour of what comes from abroad. Some years ago, to balance this negative publicity, copy-writers started calling dessert wines 'meditation wines' or 'contemplation wines' but this is falling off, probably because you don't drink much wine contemplating or meditating: at most a solitary mysanthropic consumption of half a bottle. Recently, I note that the ad-men have moved on and now call dessert wine 'seduction wine' which, perhaps, is nearer the mark: at least there are two drinkers. I once wrote that Orvieto Amabile was an ideal seduction wine to share with a lady, since it was not too sweet for man's palate. But current philosophy tosses into the ring all sweet wines from Asti Spumante to Virgin Marsalas. It has not yet taken the step to distinguish between seducing men and seducing women: it will do so by 1990. There is a goodly number of fine dry seduction wines that ladies should know about and keep hidden at a warm room temperature.

In the main, starting in the north, we have Sfursat, a strong, thought- and action-producing red wine from 4,000 feet up in the Alps in the Valtellina; there is Verona's Amarone which warms the blood; there are many Vin Santos that are bone-dry and turn one's thoughts towards the more attractive aspects of contemporary life; and, not to be forgotten, there is Brusco dei Barbi, a super-Brunello from Montalcino. In the south, one can find the rare, pure Marsala of Vecchio Samperi, also an aged wine that warms the cockles of a man's heart.

These seduction wines are sweet or dry but always with a naturally high alcoholic content (not as high as fortified sherry but getting on for it). If you see 'liquoroso' on the bottle, it will have a wine-alcohol additive bringing it up to sherry strength. These travel best and oxidize least.

Each winery has its own way of making Vin Santo, though all appear to agree that it is made with aromatic white grapes. For the rest, the secret is passed down from father to son over the centuries. They say it is not all that easy to make and that amateurs can make the most expensive vinegar in the world doing it wrong.

Vin Santo is said to be made, roughly speaking, by taking a small fifty-litre Vin Santo barrel, called a *caratello*, in which there is a little wine left which, through evaporation, has reached an alcohol content of 18–20 per cent. This is then filled up with a good strong Passito wine (made with dried grapes), of Malvasia and Greco and, if wanted, a little concentrated must. The barrel is well sealed and stowed away, not in the cellar but in the attic, under the roof. Here, for five or six years, it lies forgotten: it heats up in summer and perhaps ferments a little and it lies dormant in winter, precipitating various trace elements of sediment that have served their purpose. Then, after all this benign neglect, this quite astonishing wine is ready. It is one of the mysteries of the world why this small production is not snapped up by wine-lovers with prices spiralling as they did for Alba truffles which have risen from £25 a lb. in 1974 to £300 a lb. in 1988, a price that can only in part be accountable to inflation, and has been attained without the help of exports. In fact the world prefers Périgord black truffles, which is just as well. Italy is a great consumer of its own luxuries as well as those of other countries, and the premium wines of Italy are almost all consumed in Italy. Surprisingly, on the other hand, Italy imports 29 per cent of the total production of Scottish single-malt whisky (against 21 per cent for the UK), all of which is from the most qualified and authentic pot-still sources.

The other antique wines are chiefly from Sardinia. It is thought that they are mostly a legacy from the 300 years or so of Spanish rule which finished after the Treaty of London, when Queen Anne gave Sardinia to the House of Savoy, whose Dukes became Kings of Sardinia. Some of the wines may hark back to Byzantine and even Phoenician times.

Sardinia has an important place in this bracket, with its muscular Vernaccia di Oristano (this should have been amongst the men's seduction section), a wine that can arouse a man to higher things. It is made much like a Vin Santo and has the driest of after-tastes. The Malvasia (malmsey) of Bosa is a rich southern wine of which little is available nowadays: the same can be said of the seduction wines of Cagliari. As urban sprawl eats up vineyards, they are never replaced. The varying dry to sweet wines go under the names of Girò, Monica, Malvasia, Nasco and Moscato, all of which are produced also as fortified wines with a circa 17 per cent alcoholic content.

Then there are the formidable black wines from the mountains on the east coast (Ogliastra and Dorgali) which run up to 16–17 per cent of alcohol and can oxidize into a mellow delight: these, too, are getting harder to find. The best known is a sweet wine, the Anghelu Ruju (Red Angel) of Alghero. It is a port-like wine, well-aged and with a strong bouquet, that offers 17 per cent of alcohol and 7 per cent of sweetness. This has the best chance of survival because it is produced by Sella & Mosca, a Piedmontese company that knows all about marketing, publicity and the New Enology: but Anghelu Ruju is not truly a Sardinian tradition.

None of these wines sells enough to justify an advertising budget and they will, therefore, except for Anghelu Ruju, get rarer and rarer as the younger generation grows up dedicated to beer and Coca-Cola. It is a lost cause.

For the rest, you may find Ceratti's Greco di Tufo in Calabria, which is so good you might not wish even to share it: a true meditation wine! Amongst the new varieties are the Torcolato of the Maculan winery in the Veneto, the Ramandolo of the Dri Winery in Friuli, the Verduzzo Friulano by Ronchi di Fornaz and, to wind up, a Malvasia delle Lipari (Malmsey of the Lipari Islands), Tanit from Pantelleria Island, half-way to Tunis, which comes from the fabulous Zibbibo grape and, as special choices, the Avignonesi Vin Santo from Montepulciano and Giacomo Conterno's Monfortino, a super-Barolo that stands on its own.

I have no interest in whether anybody drinks Italian wine (or, for that matter, that of any other country), but I am fond of this sector of strong wines which is tending to disappear and seems to me to be irreplaceable. Other wines are produced with brains, fantasy, technology and efficiency and can become what market-survey people call 'the product'. Seduction wines are not a 'product', an appellation that is nauseous.

8

The Age of International Legislation

My memories sometimes make me feel like a walking history book: that is perhaps why I noticed that the world moved into top-gear by the time I was forty – and not only in the wine field. In no time, we had TV, colour TV, avionics, transistors, computers, electronics, automation, robots, men on the moon, lasers, plastics, nuclear energy, intercontinental flights, satellite communications and how much more: all in twenty-five to thirty years. The New Enology and Ezio Rivella were very little in comparison with all that, though they first made use of many of these inventions: one can, justly I think, speak of pre-Rivella and post-Rivella wine-making.

I drank, in the Cadet's Mess bar at Sandhurst at the beginning of the Second World War, a lot of the last French wine they had – white Graves. It must have been many years before they had any more. Returning to London some years later, I found that Chilean wine was *à la mode* for lack of anything else, though it was remarkably good. The only other wine (other than palm-wine I had found in the East, chiefly Bombay) was South African, which was also remarkably good considering the climate and the rudimentary stabilizing techniques then available; while their brandy and that of Portugal, acquired in Goa, saved the day. Both Bombay and Calcutta gins were more than just drinkable, they were quite good; the only bottle to avoid was that containing Arak which could send you blind for ever.

Less than ever do most people, nowadays, live permanently within the delivery range of their favourite supplier of wine and spirits. We travel and stay in distant lands where we have to discriminate and ask for local counsel as to what is best among the unfamiliar offerings, though this circumstance can arise even

66

at home when confronted with a new range of wines – say New Zealand, Upper State New York or Tunisian.

On the whole, except for certain infrastructures, quality controls and the like, the less bureaucrats involve themselves with wine and so much else, the better it is. However, wine is, so to speak, a very fluid product that is hard to nail down and legislate for. The US BATF (Bureau of Alcohol, Tobacco and Firearms) – remarkably open-minded and reasonable gentlemen from such of their texts I have read, even if their name sounds like an anti-bootlegging and anti-gun-running division of the FBI – have had their 'Partial Ingredient Labelling of Wine' legislation on the *tapis* for many years. Chiefly, they seem concerned with too much sulphur-dioxide being used during and, even more, after processing. This is criticism of German wines mostly, less so of French wines and not at all of Italian ones.

In brief, a very small amount of sulphur-dioxide is essential at the present state-of-the-art of fermentation to 'disinfect' the must. However, if you have a fragile wine, you need much more: that is to say, the further you go north to where the grapes ripen with difficulty, the more sulphur you are going to need at fermentation time; and, often, in these chilly areas, more is added as a stabilizer at bottling time.

The BATF does not consider this a health hazard, but they don't like it: the World Health Organisation, on the other hand, takes a dimmer view. In all events, the BATF wants this sulphur-dioxide and all the other additives in a wine clearly stated on the bottle or, at least, available on request from the suppliers. Ironically, it is often said that there is greater bureaucratic quality-control over cans of dog food than for wines and food for human consumption. At this time, no producer or *négociant* is required to explain himself or to list his ingredients.

To their irritation, the enologists have not yet found an economic substitute for the initial dose of sulphur, essential for stabilizing the musts. The American Food and Drug Administration claim that sulphur-dioxide has never been found to be harmful and that its use is self-limiting due to its unpleasant smell and taste: chilling the wine, however, reduces this unpleasantness. For all that, there is a great deal of difference between an input of 225 milligrams per litre for red wine and 300–400 milligrams for white permitted by the EEC and the residual 10 milligrams of trace elements to be found in Italian wines. The question seems to be divided into two issues: sulphur added to the must is consumed by its work fighting wild yeasts, whereas the sulphur used just before bottling time remains intact. In Italy, it is not used for this second stage. Both issues must be resolved on a European level quickly or they will be decided for us by the BATF. So far, nobody has yet taken any action.

Several years ago, there was a lot of talk about a new, agro-economic formula, Euro-wines. These were to be blends of wines from Common Market countries and all to be legislated for and labelled accordingly. This had a nice protectionist aura about it: a bureaucrat's joy. It turned sour, however, when it was pointed out that Euro-wines had already existed for a long time: tanker cargo boats loaded with Sicilian wine sail from Marsala to Sète, others from Sardinia to Germany and yet others from Brindisi in Puglia to who knows where. Italy's contribution to Euro-wine is historic, even if scarcely documented. I tend to be on the side of the BATF and another American institution, 'the right to know'. I recently asked a Sardinian dealer in bulk wines if he knew their destination: he replied that he knew the name of the port where the wines were unloaded but that afterwards the wines changed hands and were lost in the mists. Italy is equally caught up in this secrecy. I recall, years ago, at a noted winery in Piedmont, being told laughingly by a young enologist how some local producers, having had a poor-quality harvest, had freighted by train all their 'fine' wines over the border to France to have them chaptalized and then bought them back as 'fine' French wines. No self-respecting enologist would put his signature to such trickery. In fact, the wine may well have been good but that does not prescind from the fact that it was fraudulent. Fraud, nowadays, is not so much that you are sold 'undrinkable' wine (made with chemicals and fermented banana skins, as they used to say twenty and more years ago) in the name of one of repute. The wine you are sold in every probability is good state-of-the-art wine made with good grapes but not what you are paying for. My pious hope is that producers publish ever more information about their wines and their origins; not only because this is important in evaluating them but because such information also makes an educational conversation-piece.

Many wine-drinkers do not understand the many forms that a grape juice can take on, thinking, for example, that a Pinot Noir is either the source of a good Burgundy or, magically, can be transformed into champagne – and that is that.

A good enologist can make, from a Pinot Noir, a red champagne and a pink champagne as well. It depends only on how long the black grape-skins stay in contact with the must during fermentation. He can also make them a 2 atmosphere frizzante wine and a little sweet, too, if he halts the fermentation at the right time. All these can be by the champagne or the charmat method. He can make a light white or rosé table wine if he runs the must off the lees fairly quickly, and if he bottles with a little CO_2 it will be a delicately pétillant wine, though this effect should, more correctly, be reached by abbreviating the fermentation. He can, with his various still wines, age them in big barrels or small barrels, new barrels or old barrels, each with a different result. If he has a poor crop, he can de-colourize his red wine, turning it into paper-white *tout court* wine. He can take advantage of all the Common Market regulations that permit him to chaptalize. He can also make a strong 'dessert' wine by drying the grapes (either on the vine or after harvesting) before crushing them. He can, finally, also make marc or brandy. Ringing the changes is therefore an enologist's privilege. Yet all this started with some black Pinot grapes and, equally, could happen with Nebbiolo, Sangiovese or Cannonau grapes in Italy. The right-to-know, then, is not an extravagant request, particularly as I forgot to include in the list the making of a *vin nouveau*.

Vine-dressing is equally an obscure subject for wine-lovers, and it is often just as long as a piece of string. What you do in, say, champagne country, if done in Sardinia has completely different results and with many combinations and permutations available.

In the pages that tell of aged wine (see Chapter 4), after each of the DOC categories, I give the number of quintals per hectare (the hundreds of kilos of yield per each 10,000 square metres of vineyard). A small yield is considered better in quality and these figures vary mostly between 80 and 120 which can be considered good for Italy: above 150 is a trifle over-abundant whereas 50 is a very low yield. In certain areas of southern Italy you can get a crop of over 300 quintals per hectare with the right vine-dressing, due to the very favourable climate. There would be nothing 'wrong' with wine made with such super-abundant grapes, but it just would not be the sort to lay down in your cellar.

The Chianti Classico growers have, however, of recent years by joint accord reduced their yields from 100 to 75–80 quintals. The reader will immediately ask how: here comes the length of a piece of string again.

Supposing you have long vines in Chianti-land that climb over a pergola, you will have a big yield, not too much sugar and a high total acidity. Prune these back to, say, eight-foot long branches and you get less yield, more sugar and less total acidity – and, one hopes, higher quality. Prune back to four-foot high bushes and you get a further reduction of yield but much more sugar (probably too much), giving more alcohol and insufficient total acidity. You obviously settle for something in the middle. All these considerations are also relative to where you are planting your wine. If you plant it, not in Tuscany, but in Bordeaux-land over pergolas, your must will be rather thin, lacking sugar and with a good acidity, though you might get quite a large crop in good years: Champagne is said to yield up to 70 quintals per hectare, despite its cold climate, whereas if you vine-dress champagne-style in Sicily, your yield will be far greater, very sweet but lacking acidity. Both require the gentle hand of the enologist and the agronomist to put them on the right track. If you look at oil-paintings of the Roman or Neapolitan countryside of a hundred or two hundred years ago, you will see vines strung out fifteen feet from the ground between poplar trees some ten yards apart: one can only assume they harvested when the grapes were over-mature and full of sugar to counter-balance the inevitable excess acidity. It cannot have been a very good way of making wine as nobody does it any more save in the Minho, in Portugal, for vinho verde; and harvesting on ladders was plainly dangerous and scarcely a brain-wave of time-and-motion study.

A fine Bordeaux yields an average of 40 quintals a hectare whereas Brunello gives 100 quintals: at first sight, the claret grapes are better, but the incidence of climate has to be taken into account. Also, some vines are more fruitful than others, some vineyards are more generous than others, and some are much warmer than others, being further south and on the plains rather than in the hills or in mountain valleys. These have a greater number of 'degree days' of heat. Some vines prefer the cold, some the heat. Others are broad-minded and like both but, generally speaking, the greater the number of degree days, the greater the yield, especially remembering the two crops a year of Barbera in tropical Brazil.

A degree day is a novelty to me and perhaps to others: it is the summation of the hours, over a period of twenty-four hours, that are above 50°F during the growing season from 1 April to 31 October. Temperatures under 50°F (10°C) do not permit growth. Region One in California (which would seem to be the origin of this evaluation system) has less than 2,500 degree days: i.e. just enough for growth at 62°F. Region Five, at the other end of the scale, has over 4,000, a warm average of 69°F and more. This system of evaluating climates and micro-climates might well be absorbed into Italian (and European) thinking for judging, with a greater precision, both vines and vineyards.

Here I would like to mention briefly the European zoning arrangements, which nobody seems to mention, but which reflect, very roughly, the thinking behind the degree day principle. The Common Market has already divided itself up into zones, some of which are permitted chaptalizing privileges, according to the prevailing climate, to produce a satisfactorily alcoholic wine. This classification is instructive: it shows that the natural sugar content is below requirements in northern Europe and increases, going south, till – in the Midi of France and central and north Italy – the optimum is reached where no chaptalization should be needed. In the case of southern Italian wines, the problem is not to get them to reach the minimum but to prevent their going over the top. This is a tricky legal matter, as wines with natural 15–17 per cent alcohol content are not recognized as being within the scope of the Common Market arrangements if there is any sugar content still not turned into alcohol during fermentation; and there are plenty of these sweet, dessert wines. For the Common Market, dessert wines must have over 17 per cent alcohol, which means that either they must be chaptalized or have wine alcohol added. Such wines, incidentally, also come into the higher bracket of excise duties for Great Britain and pay as though they were fortified wines, such as sherry and port, irrespective of whether they have been fortified. The correction of this anomaly is said to be under consideration in Brussels – but the years pass. Equally, the Italians are horrified by the way the Germans increase the alcoholic content of their wines but, rather than make a fuss, they look the other way and pretend it isn't happening. After all, German wines are not in direct rivalry with those of Italy. But, as the reader will see, the problem of meeting requirements is not simple.

To return to the argument, the Italian wine-producer, bearing in mind the wine he is aiming to produce, will prune and dress his vineyard suitably to give the right yields, the amount of sugar necessary to make, let us say, a standard luncheon wine of 11.5 per cent alcohol and enough acidity to balance things out. He then has to pray that it won't rain all summer: and he also has to pray that the weather won't be too good.

In Italy, with DOC rules, if you get too great a yield, you have to degrade the surplus to table wine status to teach you a lesson and force you to dress your vines 'correctly' for the following year. In France, if there is a bumper crop, the producers can fairly easily get permission from the provincial wine board to bottle and sell: after all, there is no reason to punish a vintner just because the sun shines more than usual. With such conditions of work, one can well understand why so many Italian producers prefer to stay out of the DOC system and retain as much flexibility in their processing as God has in his meteorology. This has become all the more important with the new fashion for light wines, such as Tuscan Galestros, Lambruscos and many more.

However, it would be useful to know the number of quintals per hectare of table wines: if overly high they might be avoided. If they are in the best DOC bracket (80–120 qu.), they become interesting and worthy of further investigation for their other characteristics. In fact, to know the quintals per hectare is more important with table wines than with DOC wines. For example, with the fine non-DOC table wines nowadays available, such as Sassicaia and Solaia, their high quality can, in all probability, be recognized by their having a very low yield. This, however, we shall never know – for bureaucratic reasons and also because few producers feel that this important information can be of interest to the public. They are probably right today but, in the future, wine-lovers will also like to know the yield – after all, a contained yield is a real and demonstrable mark of merit. I am always interested in facts on which to base my opinion. I do not want to know from wine-experts that a certain wine has a 'buttery nose', a 'bouquet of crushed nettles' or an 'after-taste of tar and violets'.

Sugar in wine-making is an important ingredient. In Italy, it is not permitted, not because it is in any way harmful but because politics, very early in this century, decided that cutting wines and/or concentrated must should be used instead. The purpose of this legislation was to sop up some of the surplus strong wines in the south, thus supporting the agricultural economy (a sort of con-science money) of those parts which had had a poor economic deal after the destitution of the Bourbon King of the Two Sicilies and the uniting of Italy under the Kingdom of Sardinia, which was run by the northern Piedmontese. A good part of the population of Sicily and Naples wisely upped sticks and settled in the Bronx, while the legislation favouring the production of cutting wine remains to this day. No consideration was taken then or now of the fact that Germany and most of France could use sugar to enhance their wines at a much lower cost than Italy, thus making Italian wines less competitive on a world market, because the legislators were not thinking of a world market that didn't exist. They had only a political ploy in mind, and little has changed since then. Nowadays, there is a pressure to change the regulations to permit, with poor harvests only, the use of a little sugar in Italy, though this is most unlikely to occur.

The only new element thrown into the pot recently is the theory that chaptalization should be permitted nowhere in the Common Market, forcing all cold-weather producers, at great expense, to dry their grapes (either on the vine or after harvesting) to make a standard 11 per cent wine or to make the light-weight wines of Lambrusco style that are currently so popular. This would cause such an earthquake that it will never be turned into law.

Another trial balloon, seen occasionally flying above wine fairs, is that of converting surplus wine into sugar instead of industrial alcohol. This sugar, processed from grapes of southern France and southern Italy, would be used for Germany's and France's chaptalization and for Italy's, too, should a permissive law be approved. This would save the Common Market millions of pounds sterling in distilling and storage of vast quantities of indus-trial alcohol that nobody wants. Though the sugar-beet industry might not see this initiative in the same friendly light, it would logically and obviously be better if chaptalization, where permitted, was done with a wine-based sugar, just as the alcohol added to fortify sherry must be a wine-alcohol: though even here, some years ago, a sherry company found itself unwittingly using industrial spirit, and not wine-alcohol, acquired in Yugoslavia. You just can't be too careful.

It is also proposed that this wine-sugar, being a more natural product than cane- or beet-sugar, should be marketed to the food industry and as an alternative in domestic use. I can almost see the fancy upmarket packages of wine-sugar and bottled wine-syrup on the supermarket gourmet shelves. For all that, something must be done about surplus wine.

PART TWO

9
Piedmont

THE LANGHES (MOORS) OF CENTRAL PIEDMONT

Thirty years ago, everybody agreed that Barolo was Italy's finest wine; today, Brunello has stolen the honours. Gattinara and Barbaresco were considered, then, almost in the same breath as Barolo. Has Brunello improved? Barolo has certainly not deteriorated, but perhaps its producers have not kept up with the times. They are accused of being mentally rigid but that is not a novelty. The Piedmontese are given the credit of founding modern Italy and then driving all the other Italians up the wall with their un-Italian inflexibility, which characteristic they passed to the Italian State they founded. However, there are plenty of exceptions; amongst them, Ezio Rivella, who is the prime example of open-mindedness and innovation.

A reputation for producing fine wine is best made by producing fine wine. But if nobody talks about it, nobody chooses it for special occasions, nobody writes articles and poems about it, and the producer does little to make his wine better known, that wine is, I fear, not likely to stay in the top ten for very long. The other Italians are self-critical, ever searching for improvement, while the Barolo-makers seem convinced that their wines are the best and that there's nothing much left to do. Perhaps other fine reds are as good or better; perhaps they are only dancing a minuet which draws more attention than the rumbling grandeur of the huge black barrels of Piedmont Barolo. Wherever the truth may lie, the big wines of Piedmont are losing their share of the market. To the drinker, at home and abroad, this can only mean that the prices are unlikely to spiral as was the fear ten years ago. I recall then noting the improvement in quality of all the other Nebbiolo-based wines which I considered substitute Barolos for when the price went up, just as a Brunello Vineyards can substitute for a Brunello DOCG. These 'poor man's' Barolos included the Barbaresco, the Dolcettos, all the wines of the Novara Hills, including Gattinara and Ghemme, many of which have been worked on with great care, but I doubt with enormous financial gains. There are now five DOC Barberas, also designed to take the pressure off disproportionately rising prices which have never in the event risen disproportionately. Perhaps this trouble in Paradise is due to the producers not looking to the future; but, perhaps, in a wine paradise you don't look to the future, you expect the future to look to you.

However, not all the producers are strumming old favourites on their harps: Angelo Gaia has been in California and is making *barrique*-aged Barbaresco and Chardonnay. Amongst other innovators, we can count Renato Ratti (Abbazia dell'Annunziata), Bruno Ceretto, Pio Cesare, Giacomo Bologna, Castello di Neive, Giacomo Conterno, Bruno Giacosa, Cordero di Montezemolo, Riccardo Cerretto, Fratelli Oddero, Alfredo Prunotto, Aldo Conterno, Giulio Mascarello, Vietti, I Paglieri, Fontanafredda, Franco Fiorina and Massimo Oddero: a short rather than a long list and all names that are the essence of wine-making in Piedmont.

Being adjacent to France, the Piedmont population is French-speaking even today to a considerable extent: the capital of the Duchy of Savoy was first Chambéry and only later Turin. It is, then, no surprise to find a passion for fine food and wine there.

When France, in the last century, got into the technological lead in wine-making, it was mostly the Piedmontese who went to France to learn how to catch up and engaged French agronomists and enologists to improve their own wines. Not only were the Barolo and Barbera vines brought to their fine state-of-the-art but the muscat grape was experimented with, particularly by Carlo Gancia (founder of the famous winery of the same name), and it was brought to perfection as Asti Spumante. At the same time, Antonio Carpénè, in the Veneto, did the same and produced Prosecco sparkling wines. Of course, in the last twenty years, all these have again been improved on with new cuve-close methods. The Asti Spumante was the first sweet sparkling wine, a style that was only to become more popular with the passing of the decades, and as much loved abroad as at home.

The only other major Piedmont white is the Cortese di Gavi (or just Gavi), vinified as a bone-dry and hard wine by most producers. Though its reputation (and price) is ever rising, it seems that it would be better employed as the base for a champenois-system brut, while Ezio Rivella, in his Principessa Gavia version, has made it an entrancing, soft and pétillant wine. To Ezio Rivella's credit must be added the re-creation of the Brachetto d'Acqui, a medium-aged red with a trace of sweetness and an 'Argusto' Dolcetto d' Acqui, a *barrique* red of traditional body but greater complexity – both DOC gourmet wines. Acqui is a few miles only from the Villa Banfi Cellars and was well known as a health spa in Roman times, as it is still today.

All the reds of Piedmont should be treated with profound respect, from the cellaring through to the serving. Most require to be opened well before serving and at a warmish room-temperature. They repay generously all courtesies extended to them. I should add that the Grignolino red, a lighter wine of great breeding which, because it is getting rare, should be kept aside and broached with the most subtle of gourmet fare rather than a robust roast. Sediment is less of a problem than in the past: however, with old vintages, it is as well to decant with due ceremony.

The reader will note in the listings that the 'big' names of Piedmont repeat themselves: it should be made clear that, though their names are big, the production and their acreage is small, and is often divided up into a few crus of different wines, according to the lie of the land. But, in all cases, the issue is availability. These producers are not going to ring your doorbell – you must ring theirs, even if their present and their future are not as rosy as they deserve to be.

Piedmont is the most orthodox region of Italy and its producers aim to make ever finer wines within their traditions rather than experiment as so many are doing in Italy. However, in Piedmont, Ezio Rivella is also producing some excellent non-DOC sparkling muscat and sparkling Pinot brut wines. There are the generous DOC-style Nebbiolos, called Spanna, of Antonio Vallana in Gattinara land, of no inconsiderable clout, which should not be ignored. Wines like the strong red Monfortino and the unusual resuscitated Arneis white are wines to remember and, if possible, acquire.

(The numbers after the name of each DOC wine refer to the issue of the *Italian State Gazette* in which the DOC discipline was promulgated and through which all modifications can be traced.)

Barbaresco (145: 14.6.66 and 244: 26.9.70)

The subspecies Michet, Lampia and Rosé of the Nebbiolo vine produce a dry red wine with a minimum alcoholic content of 12.5%. Two years' ageing are obligatory. If three are in the wood, the wine may be called Riserva; if four, Riserva Speciale. The wine is due to be categorized as DOCG.

Producers
Bersano, Nizza Monferrato (Asti)
Giacomo Borgogno, Barolo (Cuneo)
Luigi Bosca, Canelli (Asti)
Luigi Calissano, Alba (Cuneo)
Parroco di Neive, Neive (Cuneo)
Castello di Neive, Neive (Cuneo)
Giorgio Carnevale, Rocchetta Tanaro (Asti)
Pio Cesare, Alba (Cuneo)
Giacomo Conterno, Monforte d'Alba (Cuneo)
Giuseppe Contratto, Canelli (Asti)
Franco Fiorina, Alba (Cuneo)
Angelo Gaja, Barbaresco (Cuneo)
Bruno Giacosa, Neive (Cuneo)
Marchesi di Barolo, Barolo (Cuneo)

Alfredo Prunotto, Alba (Cuneo)
Fratelli Oddero, La Morra (Cuneo)
Francesco Rinaldi, Alba (Cuneo)
Renato Ratti, La Morra (Cuneo)
Fontanafredda, Serralunga d'Alba (Cuneo)
Paolo de Forville, Barbaresco (Cuneo)
Cantina Produttori del Barbaresco, Barbaresco (Cuneo)
Az. Agr. 'Le Colline' dei Conti Ravizza, Gattinara (Vercelli)
Paolo Cordero di Montezemolo (Cuneo)
I Paglieri (Cuneo)
Bruno Ceretto (Cuneo)

Barbera d'Alba (228: 9.9.70 and 15: 16.1.78)

This dry red wine is obtained exclusively from the Barbera grape. It must have a minimum alcoholic content of 11.5%; if this is 12% and the wine has been aged for at least two years, one of which must be in the bottle, it may be called Superiore.

Producers
Renato Ratti (Cuneo)
Bersano, Nizza Monferrato (Asti)
Giacomo Borgogno, Barolo (Cuneo)
Parroco di Neive, Neive (Cuneo)
Cavallotto, Castiglione Falletto (Cuneo)
Riccardo Ceretto, Alba (Cuneo)
Pio Cesare, Alba (Cuneo)
Giacomo Conterno, Monforte d'Alba (Cuneo)
Eredi di Luigi Einaudi, Dogliani (Cuneo)
Dogliani 7 Cascine, La Morra (Cuneo) – formerly Kiola
Marchesi di Barolo, Barolo (Cuneo)
Fratelli Oddero, La Morra (Cuneo)
Mario Savigliano, Diano d'Alba (Cuneo)
Vietti, Castiglione Falletto (Cuneo)
Alfredo Prunotto, Alba (Cuneo)
Cantina Sociale Govone, Govone (Cuneo)
Cantina Sociale Castiglione Falletto (Cuneo)
Bruno Ceretto, Barbaresco (Cuneo)
Paolo de Forville, Barbaresco (Cuneo)

Angelo Gaia (Cuneo)
Aldo Conterno (Asti)

Barbera d'Asti (73: 23.3.70 and 9: 10.1.78)

A Barbera that produces a dry red wine with a minimum alcoholic content of 12%. If aged for two years, of which one must be in the wood, and with 12.5% alcohol, the wine may be labelled Superiore.

Producers
Pietro Barbero, Moasca (Asti)
Bersano, Nizza Monferrato (Asti)
Giacomo Bologna, Rocchetta Tanaro (Asti)
Luigi Bosca, Canelli (Asti)
Luigi Calissano, Alba (Cuneo)
Ferruccio Nicolello (Asti)
Cantina Sociale Co-operative di Canelli (Asti)
Cantina Sociale di Casorzo, Casorzo (Asti)
Giorgio Carnevale, Cerro Tanaro (Asti)
Giuseppe Contratto, Canelli (Asti)
Amilcare Gaudio, (Alessandria Margarino, Porto Comaro d'Asti
   (Asti)
Scarpa Antica Casa, Nizza Monferrato (Asti)
Luigi Trinchero, San Martino Alfieri (Asti)
G. L. Viarengo, Castello d'Annone (Asti)
Villa Banfi Cellars, Strevi (Alessandria)

Barbera del Monferrato (72: 21.3.70 and 162: 14.6.79)

The Barbera grape, with a blend of Freisa, Grignolino and Dolcetto (up to 15%), produces a dry red wine with a minimum alcoholic content of 12%. With two years' ageing and 12.5% alcohol, it may be labelled Superiore.

Producers
Lorenzo Bertolo, Turin (Torino)
Villa Banfi Cellars, Strevi (Alessandria)
Luigi Calissano, Alba (Asti)

Amilcare Gaudio, Bricco Mondalino, Vignale Monferrato
(Alessandria)
Livio Pavese, Podere Sant'Antonio, Treville Monferrato
(Alessandria)
Tenuta Cannona (Dr Nicola Cassone), Carpeneto (Allesandria)

Barolo (146: 15.6.66; 244: 26.9.70)

This dry red wine is derived from the three subspecies of the
Nebbiolo vine called Michet, Lampia and Rosé. It must offer a
minimum alcoholic content of 13% and three years' ageing of
which two must be in the wood. If matured for over four years, it
may be called Riserva; if for more than five years, Riserva Speciale.
It is one of the first wines to be included in the DOC-G category.

Producers
Bersano, Nizza Monferrato (Asti)
Giacomo Borgogno, Barolo (Cuneo)
Luigi Bosca, Canelli (Asti)
Bruzzone, Strevi (Alessandria)
Luigi Calissano, Alba (Cuneo)
Olivio and Gildo Cavallotto, Castiglione Falletto (Cuneo)
Pio Cesare, Alba (Cuneo)
Giacomo Conterno, Monforte d'Alba (Cuneo)
Giuseppe Contratto, Canelli (Asti)
Eredi Luigi Einaudi, Dogliani (Cuneo)
Fontanafredda, Serralunga d'Alba (Cuneo)
Marchesi Fracassi, Nazzole (Cuneo)
Franco Fiorina, Alba (Cuneo)
Angelo Germano, Barolo (Cuneo)
Bruno Giacosa, Neive (Cuneo)
Istituto Agrario Enologico di Alba, Alba (Cuneo)
Giuseppe Marcarini, La Morra (Cuneo)
Marchesi di Barolo, Barolo (Cuneo)
Giulio Mascarello, La Morra (Cuneo)
Cordero di Montezemolo, La Morra (Cuneo)
Fratelli Oddero, La Morra (Cuneo)
Alfredo Prunotto, Alba (Cuneo)
Francesco Rinaldi, Alba (Cuneo)
Scarpa Antica Casa, Nizza Monferrato (Asti)

Renato Ratti, La Morra (Cuneo)
Vietti, Castiglione Falletto (Cuneo)
Terre del Barolo (Cuneo)
Rocche dei Manzoni-Migliorini
Bruno Ceretto (Cuneo)
Aldo Conterno (Asti)

Bracchetto d'Acqui (282: 7.11.69)

A Bracchetto grape, with a blend of Aleatico and Moscato Nero (up to 10%), produces a sweet red wine that is pétillant if bottled young. It has a minimum alcoholic content of 11·5%.

Producers
Marchesi di Barolo, Barolo (Cuneo)
Bersano, Nizza Monferrato (Asti)
Giacomo Bologna (Asti)
Cantina Sociale Maranzana, Maranzana d'Asti (Asti)
Giorgio Carnevale, Cerro Tanaro (Asti)
Villa Banfi Cellars, Strevi (Alessandria)

Colli Tortonesi (68: 13.3.74)

Two wines are covered by this legislation: a white and a red. The former is a Cortese with 10% alcoholic content. The red is Barbera with a blend of Freisa, Bonarda Piedmontese and Dolcetto (up to 15%) and a minimum alcoholic content of 11·5%. If the alcohol content is 12·5% and the wine aged for two years, one of which is in the wood, it may be labelled Superiore.

Producers
Sergio Borasi, Villaromagnano (Alessandria)
Cantina Sociale di Tortona, Tortona (Alessandria)
Cantina Volpi, Tortona (Alessandria)

Gavi or Cortese di Gavi (294: 12.11.74)

The Cortese produces a dry white wine with a minimum alcoholic content of 10%. It may be used to make a sparkling wine.

Producers
Bersano, Nizza Monferrato (Asti)
Luigi Bosca, Canelli (Asti)
Villa Banfi Cellars, Strevi (Alessandria)
La Battistina, Novi Ligure (Alessandria)
La Piacentina, Gavi (Alessandria)
La Scolca, Rovereto di Gavi (Alessandria)
Olivari Pastorino, La Giustiniana, Rovereto di Gavi (Alessandria)
Pinelli-Gentile, Tagliolo Monferrato (Alessandria)
Raggio d'Azeglio, Gavi (Alessandria)
Tenuta San Pietro di Gazzaniga, Gavi (Alessandria)
Villa Banfi Vineyards, La Richella–Novi Ligure (Alessandria)
Pio Cesare (Cuneo)
La Giustiniana (Alessandria)

Cortese dell'Alto Monferrato (322: 26.11.79)

A dry white Cortese with a minimum alcoholic content of 10%. It may be transformed into a sparkling wine.

Producer
Villa Banfi Cellars, Strevi (Alessandria)

Dolcetto d'Acqui (308: 27.11.72)

A Dolcetto dry red wine with a minimum alcoholic content of 11·5%. With a minimum of 12·5% and one year's ageing, the wine may be labelled Superiore.

Producers
Villa Banfi Cellars, Strevi (Alessandria)
Cantina Sociale Canelli, Canelli (Asti)

Dolcetto d'Alba (276: 23.10.74)

A Dolcetto dry red wine with a minimum alcoholic content of 11·5%. With a minimum of 12·5% and one year's ageing, the wine may be labelled Superiore.

Producers
Giacomo Borgogno, Barolo (Cuneo)
Luigi Bosca, Canelli (Asti)
Luigi Calissano, Alba (Cuneo)
Parocco di Neive, Neive (Cuneo)
Riccardo Ceretto, Alba (Cuneo)
Giacomo Conterno, Monforte d'Alba (Cuneo)
Fontanafredda, Alba (Cuneo)
Franco Fiorina, Alba (Cuneo)
Bruno Giacosa, Neive (Cuneo)
Renato Ratti, Abbazia Annunziata, La Morra (Cuneo)
Bersano, Nizza Monferrato (Asti)
Casa Vinicola Cevetto, Barbaresco (Cuneo)
Paolo de Forville, Barbaresco (Cuneo)
Vietti (Cuneo)
Prunotto (Cuneo)

Dolcetto d'Asti (269: 15.10.74)

A Dolcetto dry red wine with a minimum alcoholic content of
11·5%. It may be labelled Superiore with one year's ageing and
12·5% alcohol.

Producers
Bersano, Nizza Monferrato (Asti)
Dante Borgogno, Cascina Boidi, Calosso (Asti)
Cantina Sociale Canelli, Canelli (Asti)
Cantina Sociale Maranzana, Maranzana (Asti)

Dolcetto di Diano d'Alba (269: 15.10.74)

A Dolcetto dry red wine with a minimum alcoholic content of
12%. With a minimum of 12·5% and one year's ageing, the wine
may be labelled Superiore.

Producers
Mario Savigliano, Diano d'Alba (Cuneo)
Colue di Massimo Oddero (Cuneo)

Dolcetto di Dogliani (299: 16.11.74)

A Dolcetto dry red wine with a minimum alcoholic content of
11·5%. With a minimum of 12·5% and one year's ageing, the
wine may be labelled Superiore.

Producers
Cantina Sociale del Dolcetto, Cuneo (Cuneo)
Eredi Luigi Einaudi, Dogliani (Cuneo)
Chionetti, Dogliani (Cuneo)

Dolcetto delle Langhe Monregalesi (276: 23.10.74)

A Dolcetto dry red wine with a minimum alcoholic content of
11%. It may be labelled Superiore with one year's ageing and 12%
alcohol.

Producers
Giacomo Borgogno, Barolo (Cuneo)
Giuseppe Contratto, Canelli (Asti)
Marchesi di Barolo, Barolo (Cuneo)

Dolcetto d'Ovada (311: 30.11.72)

A Dolcetto dry red wine with a minimum alcoholic content of
11·5%. With a minimum of 12·5% and one year's ageing, the
wine may be labelled Superiore.

Producers
Agostino Pestarino, Silvano d'Orba (Alessandria)
Giuseppe Luigi Ratto, Cascina Oliva, Ovada (Alessandria)
Terra del Dolcetto Cantina Sociale, Presco (Alessandria)
Aldo Conterno (Asti)

Erbaluce di Caluso, Caluso Passito, Caluso Liquoroso (203: 14.8.67)

The Erbaluce grape, blended with Bonarda (5%), produces a sweet
dessert wine with a minimum alcoholic content of 13·5% through
the use of semi-dried grapes. Five years' ageing in the wood is

obligatory. It is also made as a white table wine with an 11% alcoholic content, and as a fortified wine.

Producers
Renato Bianco, Caluso (Torino)
Luigi Ferrando, Ivrea (Torino)
Mattia Thione, Caluso (Torino)
Istituto Carlo Ubertini, Caluso (Torino)
Maria Passera Boux, Caluso (Torino)

Freisa d'Asti (311: 30.11.72)

A Freisa makes both a dry and a sweet red wine with a minimum alcoholic content of 11%. With 11·5% alcohol and one year's ageing, the wine may be labelled Superiore.

Producers
Pietro Barbero, Moasca (Asti)
Bersano, Nizza Monferrato (Asti)
Biletta, Casorzo (Asti)
Dante Borgogno, Cascina Boidi, Calosso (Asti)
Luigi Calissano, Alba (Cuneo)
Alfredo Prunotto, Alba (Cuneo)

Freisa di Chieri (27: 29.1.74)

Freisa di Chieri is both a dry and a sweet red wine with a minimum alcoholic content of 11%. Both may be re-fermented naturally to produce a sparkling wine. With 11·5% alcohol and one year's ageing, the wine may be labelled Superiore.

Producers
Melchiorre Balbiano, Andezono (Torino)
Lorenzo Bertolo, Via del Carmine 32, Turin (Torino)

Grignolino d'Asti (218: 24.8.73)

Grignolino, blended with Freisa (10%), produces a dry red wine with a minimum alcoholic content of 11%. This wine is customarily aged, though it is not required by DOC legislation.

Producers

Bersano, Nizza Monferrato (Asti)
Giacomo Bologna, Braida, Rocchetta Tanaro (Asti)
Luigi Bosca, Canelli (Asti)
Cantina della Porta Rossa, Diano d'Alba (Cuneo)
Cantina Sociale di Canelli, Canelli (Asti)
Cantina Sociale di Casorzo, Casorzo (Asti)
Giorgio Carnevale, Cerro Tanaro (Asti)
Bruno Giacosa, Neive (Cuneo)
Scarpa Antica Casa, Nizza Monferrato (Asti)
G. and L. Viarengo, Castel di Annone (Asti)
Paolo Biggio, Migliandolo (Asti)

Grignolino del Monferrato Casalese (266: 11.10.74)

Grignolino produces a dry red wine with a minimum alcoholic content of 11%. This wine is customarily aged for one year.

Producers

Amilcare Gaudio, Bricco Mondalino, Vignale Monferrato
  (Alessandria)
Livio Pavese, Podere Sant'Antonio, Treville Monferrato
  (Alessandria)
Vietti, Castiglione Falletto (Cuneo)

Malvasia di Casorzo d'Asti (267: 19.10.68)

The Malvasia di Casorzo, blended with Freisa, Grignolino and Barbera (10%), produces a sweet red wine with a minimum alcoholic content of 10·5%. It is usually a frizzante wine.

Producers

Cantina Sociale di Casorzo, Casorzo (Asti)
Livio Pavese, Podere Sant'Antonio, Treville Monferrato
  (Alessandria)

Malvasia di Castelnuovo Don Bosco (26: 28.1.74)

A Malvasia di Schierano produces a light red aromatic sweet wine at a minimum alcohol level of 10·5%. This may be made into a sparkling wine by natural methods.

Producers
Cantina Sociale di Castelnuovo, Castelnuovo (Cuneo)

Moscato Naturale d'Asti (199: 9.8.67)

This wine, which is used for making Asti Spumante, is no longer marketed as a still wine in bottles.

Moscato d'Asti, Asti Spumante, Asti (199: 9.8.67; 201: 7.8.69; 38: 12.2.70; 192: 25.7.72; 155: 18.6.73; 20: 7.1.78)

The Moscato produces a sweet white wine which is subjected to the charmat process to make it sparkling. It has a minimum alcoholic content of 11·5%.

Producers
Luigi Bosca, Canelli (Asti)
Villa Banfi Cellars, Strevi (Alessandria)
Luigi Calissano, Alba (Cuneo)
Cantina Sociale di Canelli, Canelli (Asti)
Giorgio Carnevale, Rocchetta Tanaro (Asti)
Francesco Cinzano, Turin (Torino)
Cora, Turin (Torino)
Giuseppe Contratto, Canelli (Asti)
Fontanafredda, Serralunga (Cuneo)
Fratelli Gancia, Canelli (Asti)
Dogliani Sette Cascine, La Morra (Cuneo) ex Kiola
I Vignaiuoli Sanstefanesi, Santo Stefano Belbo (Asti)
Martini e Rossi, Pessione (Torino)
Riccadonna, Canelli (Asti)

Nebbiolo d'Alba (228: 9.9.70)

The Nebbiolo red wine, when young, is dry but with ageing becomes slightly sweet. The minimum alcoholic content is 12% and one year's ageing is required. It is also made as an amabile sparkling wine.

Producers
Luigi Bosca, Canelli (Asti)
Cavallotto, Castiglione Falletto (Cuneo)
Giacomo Conterno, Monforte d'Alba (Cuneo)
Franco Fiorina, Alba (Cuneo)
Bruno Giacosa, Neive (Cuneo)
Marchesi di Barolo, Barolo (Cuneo)
Fratelli Oddero, La Morra (Cuneo)
Alfredo Prunotto, Alba (Cuneo)
Terre del Barolo, Castiglione Falletto (Cuneo)
Casa Vinicola Ceretto, Barbaresco (Cuneo)
Paolo de Forville, Barbaresco (Cuneo)
Bruno Ceretto (Cuneo)

Rubino di Cantavenna (71: 20.3.70)

Barbera, with a blend of Grignolino and Freisa (up to 25%), produces a dry red wine with a minimum alcoholic content of 11·5%.

Producers
Cantina Sociale di Cantavenna, Cantavenna (Alessandria)

Some non-DOC recommendations

ARNEIS

A traditional dry, white wine that is being 'resuscitated': currently it is non-DOC and therefore has no discipline to follow. However, it seems to be finding its own way to the market-place and the smart magazines.

Producers
Bruno Ceretto (Cuneo)
Bruno Giacosa (Cuneo)
Castello di Neive (Cuneo)
La Cornerea (Cuneo)
Roero (Cuneo)

PIEDMONTESE CHARDONNAY

A non-DOC, *barrique*-aged still dry wine.

Producer
Angelo Gaja (Cuneo)

MONFORTINO

A very long barrel-aged (ten years plus) wine, made with Barolo and given a *ripasso* therapy to stabilize it at over 14 degrees of alcoholic content.

Producer
Giacomo Conterno (Cuneo)

Some non-DOC wines from Villa Banfi Cellars

MOSCATO DI STREVI

A sweet white sparkling wine.

BELL'AGIO FRIZZANTE

A sweet white sparkling wine.

PRIMA VERA

A dry, light wine.

MOSCATO DI STREVI

An Asti Spumante-style wine.

THE AOSTA VALLEY

The Aosta Valley leads up to the St Bernard's Pass into Gaul: it was overrun by barbarian Burgundians in Roman times who succeeded in civilizing themselves but never got round to speaking either Latin or Italian correctly. Though it would clearly have been easier to buy their wine in barrels and from the plains (they were, and are still, the heaviest wine-drinkers in Italy), they obstinately insisted on planting vines well over 3,000 feet up the mountainsides. Various theories have been advanced regarding this ethnic autarky *vis-à-vis* wine production, the most probable being, as always, that barrels coming from the plains on mule-back were taxed, whereas what was vinified and drunk at home, and on the snow-line, dodged the excise-man.

These wines are mostly mountain Barolos; less alcoholic and with less body, but with an attractive bouquet. The well-aged Carema can be come by even in London in modest quantities; Donnaz, no; while the Enfer d'Arvier Petit Rouge, the Blanc de Morgex and the Chambave malmsey are rarities. If offered a glass or a bottle of any of these, accept with alacrity as it may be long time before you are offered another. The few names to remember here are Luigi Ferrando, Cantina dei Produttori Nebbiolo di Carema, Caves Cooperatives de Donnaz, Les Riboteurs and the Association Viticolteurs.

It is quite a challenge cultivating vines where snow can fall after the vines have budded and where snow may be lying when the harvest is brought in. There must be a lot of ethnic pride involved in the production of these wines as their price can scarcely justify the hard work in harsh conditions that is required

Carema (199: 9.8.67)

A Nebbiolo (Picutener, Pugnet, Nebbiolo-Spanna) dry red wine with a minimum alcoholic content of 12%. It requires at least four years' ageing, of which two in the wood are obligatory.

Producers
Luigi Ferrando, Ivrea (Torino)
Cantina dei Produttori Nebbiolo di Carema, Carema (Torino)

Donnaz (87: 5.6.71)

A Nebbiolo dry red wine with a minimum alcoholic content of 11·5%. It requires at least three years' ageing, two in the wood being obligatory.

Producers
Caves Cooperatives de Donnaz, Donnaz (Aosta)
Luigi Ferrando, Ivrea (Torino)

Enfer d'Arvier (112: 10.8.72)

The Petit Rouge vine produces a dry red wine with a minimum alcoholic content of 11·5%. One year's ageing in the wood is obligatory.

Producers
Luigi Ferrando, Ivrea (Torino)
Les Riboteurs, La Salle (Aosta)
Association Viticolteurs, Aosta (Aosta)

THE NOVARA HILLS

The Novara Hills wines are comparable to the best that Italy – or anywhere else you may select – produces. A lot of them (Lessona and Bramaterra) form part of the liquid assets and patrimony of the Sella Bank, ageing and increasing in value. One member of that family, an old friend, Conte Paolo Sella, an eccentric barrister and scholar rather than a wine-maker or banker, liked to deride his banker-vintner cousins for their centuries-long penny-pinching banking habits and pointed out to me that they made some of the best wine in the world and used the cheapest label they could squeeze out of the local printer. I recount this if only to demonstrate that, in an impossible country like Italy, the slickest logo does not necessarily guarantee the best wine, just as the best wine proverbially requires no 'bush', which is also true I am assured in the Friuli area where wine-makers sell their wine by the glass or jug in the evenings to save the trouble of bottling it and paying taxes on it. Vine bush or no vine bush exhibited on their threshold, word quickly gets round regarding the availability and quality of the wine.

Boca (226: 5.9.69)

A Nebbiolo (45–70%), with some Vespolina (20–40%) and Bonarda (20%), produces a dry red wine with a minimum alcohol content of 12%. It must be aged for at least three years, two of which must be in the wood.

Producers
Cantina Sociale de Fara, Fara Novarese (Novara)
Ermanno Conti, Maggiora (Novara)
Vallana e Figlio, Maggiora (Novara)
Podere ai Valloni, Boca (Novara)

Bramaterra (285: 18.10.79)

A Nebbiolo, with a little Cabernet and Bonarda, produces a dry red wine with a minimum alcoholic content of 12%. With 13% and three years' ageing in the wood, it may be labelled Riserva.

Producer
Az. Sella Bramaterra, San Girolamo, Biella (Vercelli)

Ghemme (292: 19.11.69)

The Nebbiolo, with some Vespolina (10–30%) and Bonarda (up to 15%), produces a dry red wine with a minimum alcoholic content of 12%. Ageing for four years is obligatory, three of which must be in the wood.

Producers
Brugo, Ghemme (Novara)
Cantina Sociale di Sizzano e Ghemme, Sizzano (Novara)
Guido Ponti, Ghemme (Novara)
G. and F. Sebastiani, Ghemme (Novara)

Lessona (58: 2.3.77)

The Nebbiolo grape (with up to 25% of Vespolina and Bonarda) produces a dry red wine with a minimum alcoholic content of

11·5%. The wine must be aged for two years, one of which must be in the wood.

Producer
Azienda Sella, Lessona (Vercelli)

Sizzano (225: 4.9.68)

A Nebbiolo, with some Vespolina (15–40%) and Bonarda (25%), produces a dry red wine with a minimum alcoholic content of 12%. Three years' ageing is obligatory, two of which must be in the wood.

Producers
Cantina Sociale di Sizzano e Ghemme, Sizzano (Novara)
Giuseppe Bianchi, Sizzano (Novara)
Guido Ponti, Ghemme (Novara)

Fara (279: 5.11.69)

The Nebbiolo (locally called 'Spanna'), with Vespolina (10–30%) and Bonarda (up to 40%), produces a dry red wine with a minimum alcoholic content of 12%. Three years' ageing are obligatory, of which two must be in the wood.

Producers
Cantina Social Colli Novaresi, Fara Novarese (Novara)
Luigi Dessilani, Fara Novarese (Novara)

Gattinara (200: 10.8.67)

The Nebbiolo alone produces a dry red wine with a minimum alcoholic content of 12%. It requires four years' ageing, two in the wood.

Producers
Mario Antoniolo, Gattinara (Vercelli)
Consorzio del Gattinara, Gattinara (Vercelli)
E. Conti, Maggiora (Novara)
L. and F. Nervi, Cattinara (Vercelli)

Ugo Ravizza, Gattinara (Vercelli)
Giancarlo Travaglini, Gattinara (Vercelli)
Antonio Vallana, Gattinara (Vercelli)
Luigi Dessilani (Vercelli)
Le Colline (Vercelli)

Some non-DOC Novara Hills wines

SPANNA

Spanna is the local name for the Nebbiolo vine and is used chiefly
in reference to Gattinara-style wines produced just outside the
DOC area. Though without a discipline, it can usually be relied
upon to be a fine, big wine in the Piedmont tradition.

Producers
Luigi Dessilani (Novara)
Cantina Sociale Sizzano (Novara)
Raimondo Vallana, Maggiora (Novara)

10

Lombardy

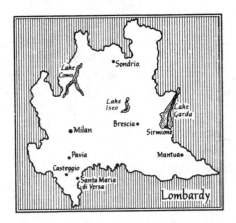

THE OLTREPÒ PAVESE

Lombardy brings to mind Milan and Milan brings to mind industry rather than agriculture or even agri-business. In fact, twenty years ago, though there was ample wine production, it was mostly drunk close by and in the major cities – Milan, Bergamo, Brescia and Pavia – rather than making a national or international reputation. This has all changed. No longer does the Barbera–Bonarda blend dominate – good though it was and is (thanks to the lively ideas of Giovanni Ballabio and Giorgio Odero who made it as a well-aged wine).

The great growing area was that of the Oltrepò Pavese, which means 'south of the River Po in the Pavia area' which, in turn, means the extension of the Piedmontese moors that produce the fine Nebbiolos in all their forms, and others, into Lombardy. Twenty years ago, Milan wines were San Giorgio, Gran Cru, La Vigna, and others with unusual names such as Barbacarlo, Buttafuoco, Sangue di Giuda, Balastiere and Clastidium. All these local wines lost ground when faced with DOC regulations, and the Oltrepò area became Italy's greatest Pinot, Chardonnay and Riesling growing area, supplying its own great co-operative (Santa Maria della Versa) and dozens of other wineries with fine raw products for sparkling wines. The sheer wealth of this growing area, for quantity and quality, cannot be exaggerated: while the co-operative, directed by Duke Antonio Denari, is a great vinifier of sparkling wines.

In the last decade, the entrepreneurial spirit of Milan seems to have gobbled up the provincial spirit of yore – agri-business has set in. Though plenty of the old-style (and, I must say, *simpatico*) Milan wines are still available, several of the great creators of these wines have passed to another vineyard in the sky. The vacuum they left was filled by the two sisters Fugazza, who are very much alive and creating wines worthy of the local traditions.

The agri-business, however, probably supported by Milan stock-exchange Investment Funds as a gilt-edged hedge, is the production of Pinot, Riesling and Chardonnay which are likely to be swiftly vinified by the Santa Maria della Versa winery and delivered, refrigerated and protected from the elements by a blanket of inert nitrogen, to the many specialized sparkling-wine makers of the North. Santa Maria della Versa is the major champenois-system and charmat producer in the zone: other noted ones are Riccadonna, Anteo of Pavia, the historic Ballabio winery with its Clastidio, Fontanachiara and Duke Antonio Denari's Il Casale Estate.

Oltrepò Pavese (273: 27.10.70; 300: 13.11.75; 9: 10.1.78)

When not otherwise qualified, Oltrepò Pavese refers to a dry red wine produced from Barbera (up to 65%), Croatina (minimum 25%), Uva Rara and Vespolina (up to 45%) grapes and with a minimum alcoholic content of 11.5%.

Producers
Azienda Alberici, Castana (Pavia) BUTTAFUOCO
Bagnasco, Santa Maria della Versa (Pavia)
Balestriere, Casteggio (Pavia)
Lino Maga, Proni (Pavia) BARBACARLO
Carlo Boatti, Monsupello, Torricella Verzate (Pavia)

Giorgio Odero, Casteggio (Pavia) FRECCIAROSSO
Luigi Valenti, Callescoropasso (Pavia) SANGUE DI GIUDA
Cantina Sociale Santa Maria della Versa (Pavia)
Antonio Denari (Pavia)
M. & G. Fugazza (Pavia)
Edmondo Tronconi (Pavia)

Barbera dell'Oltrepò Pavese (Gazette reference as above)

Barbera, with a blend of Uva Rara and Croatina (up to 20%), produces a dry red wine with a minimum alcoholic content of 11·5%.

Producers
Carlo Boatti, Monsupello, Torricella Verzate (Pavia)
Cantina Sociale, Santa Maria della Versa (Pavia)
Edmondo Tronconi, Rovescala (Pavia)
Villide, Stradella (Pavia)   SANGUE DI GIUDA

Bonarda dell'Oltrepò Pavese

Bonarda, with a small percentage of Uva Rara and Barbera (10%), produces a dry red wine with a minimum alcoholic content of 11%.

Producers
Giovanni Agnes, Rovescala (Pavia)
Balestriere, Casteggio (Pavia)
Cantina Sociale Santa Maria della Versa, S. M. della Versa (Pavia)
Cantina Sociale Casteggio, Casteggio (Pavia)
Edmondo Tronconi, Rovescala (Pavia)

Cortese dell'Oltrepò Pavese

A Cortese produces a dry white wine with a minimum alcoholic content of 11%.

Producer
Cantina Sociale, Santa Maria della Versa (Pavia)

Moscato dell'Oltrepò Pavese

Moscato produces a sweet white wine with a minimum alcoholic content of 10·5%; it is used mostly for making sparkling wines.

Pinot dell'Oltrepò Pavese

The legislation permits the making of three Pinots – red, rosé and white – each with 11% alcoholic content. They are mostly used for the production of sparkling wines.

Producers

Reds
Cantina Sociale, Santa Maria della Versa (Pavia)
Balestriere, Casteggio (Pavia)
Maga Lino, Brioni (Pavia)
Carlo Boatti, Monsupello, Torricella Verzate (Pavia)

Rosé
Mairano, Le Fracce, Casteggio (Pavia)
Carlo Boatti, Monsupello, Torricella Verzate (Pavia)

White
Cantina Sociale, Casteggio (Pavia)
Cantina Sociale, Santa Maria della Versa (Pavia)
Giorgio Odero, Casteggio (Pavia)   FRECCIAROSSA

Riesling dell'Oltrepò Pavese

A Riesling Italico or Riesling Renano (or both) make a dry white wine with a minimum alcoholic content of 11%.

Producers
Balestriere, Casteggio (Pavia)
Cantina Sociale Casteggio, Casteggio (Pavia)
Cantina Sociale, Santa Maria della Versa (Pavia)
Antonio Denari, 'Il Casale', Santa Maria della Versa (Pavia)

THE VALTELLINA

The English have known about the Valtellina and Lake Garda wines for generations, since the days of Mr Thomas Cook when he invented the guided tour of beautiful places where sipping the wines was part of the excitement of being abroad. This was before the holiday fashion moved down to the Mediterranean, to San Remo, to Santa Margherita, Alassio and other little towns on the Italian Riviera such as Portofino and Ravello.

The Valtellina wines were always well recognized for their quality (basically the same grape as used for Barolo), especially by the Swiss, who preferred them (at least in terms of imports) to the equally nearby Burgundy vineyards. I recall that the Valtellina wines were among the first to be remembered by English vintners immediately after the Second World War, but they would seem to have lost their place in the affections of the British, whereas the various wines from around Lake Garda – the Bardolinos, the Valpolicellas and the Soaves – have not.

The Valtellina has a great seduction wine, the Sfurzat (or Sforzato), similar to, though not as good as, the Amarone Recioto of Valpolicella, neither of which, curiously enough, were mentioned fifty and more years ago. Were they made and drunk privately? This is most probable. Many Italians, even today, think that foreigners would not like the things they like best and offer a bland multinational alternative.

Perhaps the Valtellina has lost its English market (there seem to be no importers) through lack of innovation, *barriques* and New Enology. Basically, the Valtellina is an ideal producing area, cool at 3,000 feet in the mountains which protect it from foul weather, and with a sunny southern aspect warm enough to make a 12 per cent wine for ageing. It is curious. Reports have it that the Swiss, whose frontier is close by, drink the lot. This could be an explanation.

Valtellina and Valtellina Superiore (244: 25.9.68)

The Nebbiolo grape (locally called Chiavennasca) for 70%, blended with Pinot Nero, Merlot, Rossola, Pignola Valtellinese and Prugnola (30%), produces a dry red wine with a minimum alcoholic content of 11%.

The same Nebbiolo vine with only 5% of the other varietals produces the Superiore at 12% alcohol content. However, both Valtellina and Valtellina Superiore must be aged, the former for one year, the latter for two.

If the wine is made from semi-dried grapes, has an alcoholic content of over 14·5%, and is suitably aged, it may be called Sfurzat. The use of the old cru names, Grumello, Inferno, Sassella and others, is frowned upon by officialdom, though the reputation of Valtellina wines was made with them.

Producers
Fratelli Bettini, San Giacomo di Teglio (Sondrio)
Enologica Valtellinese, Sondrio (Sondrio)
Pellizzatti, Sondrio (Sondrio)
Tona 1892, Villa di Tirano (Sondrio)
Rainoldi e Figlio, Chiuro (Sondrio)
Nino Negri, Sondrio (Sondrio)
Triacca, Villa di Tirano (Sondrio)

BRESCIA AND LAKE GARDA

Twenty years ago, Botticino, Cellatica and Franciacorta were 'names' in the north: these, too, have given way to innovation and new names, though that of Guido Berlucchi was even then top of the list with his Franciacorta reds and whites. Today, Berlucchi means, with the collaboration of enologist Ziliani, the production of champenois-system Cuvée Imperiale; Ca' del Bosco (also of Brescia) means champenois system too, but with avant-garde sparkling-wine expert Maurizio Zanella. To add to these distinguished names is the Cuvée Bellavista, a sparkling Spumante Classico Metodo Champenois.

This activity in the Brescia-Franciacorta-Valcalepio-Bergamo area includes the planting and vinification of Chardonnays and Cabernets. Brains and money have been invested in this area extensively and, in consequence, the wine-lover, importer and stockist are counselled to take good note of what has happened here in recent years. The Valcalepio white is a Pinot Bianco with some Pinot Grigio. The Franciacorta red is half Cabernet Franc with the balance of Barbera, Nebbiolo and Merlot: the whites are Pinots that mostly go to making sparkling wines. It is all a long way from Mussolini's days of autarky: Italy has rethought its economic philosophies and the results are more than just interesting.

Brescia has become a centre of innovation. The names Bellavista, Ca' del Bosco and Berlucchi mean not only champenois-system sparkling wines made with all the right materials – the three Pinots and Chardonnay in various blends, from their own vineyards – but also helped out by wine from the Oltrepò, the Trentino and the South Tryol.

Ca' del Bosco, over and above its various sparklers, produces a fine red, classified as a table wine since it is a claret blend of Cabernet Sauvignon 35 per cent, Cabernet Franc 30 per cent and Merlot 35 per cent. It is called Maurizio Zanella after its distinguished creator. Franco Ziliano, an equally distinguished enologist, is producing *barrique*-matured Chardonnay and many other fine wines through four subsidiary estates of the Berlucchi holding of which wine-writers are also approving. His customers seem to be satisfied, too, as his gross turnover is around £10 million. This is a far cry from what I wrote unenthusiastically about 'Franciacorta' (as they are officially called) wines in the 1974 edition of *Italian Wines* – 'the white is drunk young when dry, fresh and lively ... the red, obtained from a mixture of Cabernet Franc, Barbera, Nebbiolo and Merlot, ages well ...' – though, by the 1983 edition, I wrote of the 'nationwide success of Ca' del Bosco's and Berlucchi's "champagnes" '. However, now the Franciacorta DOC wines are flourishing with New Enology.

Two new DOC wines are Capriano del Colle, with a Sangioveto base (the most northerly presence of this Chianti-Brunello vine in Italy) and the Valcalepio which is also something of a novelty – a two-year aged Merlot-Cabernet wine that is slowly meeting with something of a welcome. The white Capriano del Colle Trebbiano is a well-made wine, but not outstanding.

The lake wines – Riviera del Garda, Lugana, Tocai di San Martino, Valcalepio and Colli Morenici – are most pleasing whites while the reds often have an unexpected richness of personality that is quite different from the lively Bardolinos that come from the other side of the lake in the Veneto. At all events, like the Bardolino, they are mostly wines to drink and enjoy young.

Botticino (140: 3.6.68)

Produced from the Schiava Gentile (35–45%), Barbera (25–30%), Marzemino and Terzi Hybrid (10%) grapes, the Botticino is a dry red wine with a minimum alcoholic content of 12%.

Producers
Pietro Bracchi, Botticino Sera (Brescia)
Contessa Cazzago, Botticino (Brescia)
Emilio Franzoni, Botticino Sera (Brescia)

Capriano del Colle or Capriano del Colle Trebbiano (315: 17.11.80)

The former is a 10·5% dry red wine made with Sangiovese (40–50%), Marzemino (35–45%) and Barbera (3–10%): the latter is a dry white made from Trebbiano di Soave.

Cellatica (141: 4.6.68)

The Cellatica is a dry red made from Schiava Gentile (35–45%), Barbera (25– 30%), Marzemino (20–30%) and Terzi (10–15%) vines. It must have a minimum alcoholic content of 11·5%.

Producers
Cooperativa Vitivinicultura Cellatica-Gussago, Cellatica (Brescia)
Fratelli Tonoli, Tenuta Santella, Cellatica (Brescia)

Colli Morenici Mantovani del Garda (224:25.8.76)

A dry white wine made from a broad range of grapes (Garganega (20–25%), Trebbiano (20–25%), Trebbiano dei Castelli Romani and/or Soave (10–40%) or Pinot Bianco, Malvasia di Candia and Riesling Italico) and with a minimum alcoholic content of 10·5%. There is also a red and a rosé; both dry 11% wines (a blend of Molinara (30–60%), Rondinella (20–50%) and Negrara Trentina (10–30%)).

Producer
Cantina Sociale dell'Alto Mantovano, Ponti sul Mincio (Mantua)

Franciacorta Pinot (209: 21.8.67)

The white Pinot produces a dry white wine with a minimum alcoholic content of 11·5%; it is much used for making champenois- and charmat-method sparkling wines.

Producers
Guido Berlucchi, Borgonata di Cortefranca (Brescia)
Ca' del Bosco, Erbusco, Franciacorta (Brescia)
Cooperativa Vitivinicultura Cellatica-Gussago, Cellatica (Brescia)
Giacomo Ragnoli, Colombaro di Cortefranca (Brescia)
Gualberto Ricci Curbastro, Capriolo (Brescia)
Bellavista (Brescia)

Franciacorta Rosso (209: 21.8.67)

The Cabernet Franc grape (40–50%), with some Barbera (20–30%), Nebbiolo (15–25%) and Merlot (10–15%), produces a dry red wine with a minimum alcoholic content of 11%. It is suitable for ageing but this is not required by legislation.

Producers
Guido Berlucchi, Borgonata di Cortefranca (Brescia)
Ca' del Bosco, Erbusco, Franciacorta (Brescia)
Cooperativa Vitivinicultura Cellatica-Gussago, Cellatica (Brescia)
Giacomo Ragnoli, Colombaro di Cortefranca (Brescia)
Gualberto Ricci Curbastro, Capriolo (Brescia)

Lugana (210: 22.8.67; 201: 7.8.69; 38: 12.2.70)

The Trebbiano di Lugana vine offers a dry white wine with a minimum alcoholic content of 11·5%.

Producers
Aziende Agricole del Lugana, Pozzolengo (Brescia)
Santi (Verona)
Fratelli Zenato (Brescia)

G. Frassine, Moniga (Brescia)
Lamberti, Lasize del Garde (Verona)
Premiovini, San Grato, Brescia (Brescia)
Pietro dal Cero, Lugana di Sirmione (Brescia)
Az. Agr. 'Tassinara', Rivoltella del Garda (Brescia)

Riviera del Garda Bresciano (282: 15.10.77)

A red and a rosé (Chiaretto) are included in this legislation. The former is a dry red wine produced from the Gropello vine (50–60%), with smaller proportions of Sangiovese (10–20%), Barbera (10–20%) and Marzemino (5–15%). The minimum alcoholic content is 11%, but with 12% and one year's ageing, the wine may be labelled Superiore.

The Chiaretto is made from the same grapes but small quantities of Trebbiano, Nebbiolo, Schiava and Cabernet Franc may also be included. The Chiaretto has no ageing legislation, but has a minimum alcoholic content of 11·5%.

Producers
Francesco Bertelli, Raffa del Garda (Brescia)
Fabio Bottarelli, Picedo di Polpenazze (Brescia)
Azienda Bertanzi, Moniga (Brescia)
Gerardo Cesari, Quinzano (Brescia)
Frassine, Moniga del Garda (Brescia)
San Grato – Selezione Premiovini (Brescia)

Tocai di San Martino della Battaglia (131: 27.5.70)

The Friuli Tocai vine here produces a dry white wine with a minimum alcohol content of 12%.

Producers
Prandell, San Martino della Battaglia (Brescia)
Ercole Romano, San Martino della Battaglia (Brescia)
Zenato (Brescia)
Ca' del Bosco (Brescia)

Valcalepio (308: 18.11.76)

The Merlot vine, with the support of some Cabernet Sauvignon, produces the Valcalepio red with not less than 12% alcoholic content. Two years' ageing in the wood is obligatory. The Valcalepio white is made mostly with Pinot Bianco and some Pinot Grigio, with a resulting minimum alcoholic content of 11%.

Producer
Cantina Sociale Bergamasca, San Paolo d'Argon (Bergamo)

Recommended non-DOC Brescia wines

CABERNET MAURIZIO ZANELLA

This has a claret blend with up to a year's ageing in small fresh oak barrels.

Producer
Ca' del Bosco (Brescia)

BRESCIA CHARDONNAY

A *barrique*-aged dry white.

Producer
Guido Berlucchi (Brescia)

Liguria

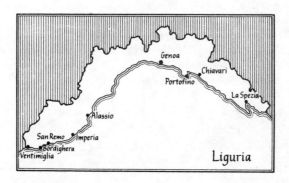

THE ITALIAN RIVIERA

Liguria is said to have sixty-four different varieties of wine, almost all produced in very small quantities and consumed privately, with no assistance required from outsiders, foreign or native. Only two are widely known and available.

Liguria is a sunny strip of land, more commonly known as the Italian Riviera, that stretches from San Remo to Genoa and to just after Portofino. Behind this narrow coastal strip of flat land, hills rise and lead back to the great wine-producing areas of Piedmont. On the hills overlooking the sea, farmers have for centuries built terraces on which to grow vines and fruit and olive trees. The value of land has rocketed since the Second World War, both on the coast and in the hills. The towns have doubled and tripled in size and new trunk roads and corniche autostradas have been built, also eating up agricultural land. This evolution led smallholders to change their profession and become townsmen, abandoning their patches of terraced land. Those that stayed often changed profession, too, taking to growing flowers for an ever larger European market.

Wine production has, inevitably, been dropping and there is little doubt that much of the wine labelled as Ligurian used to fly under false colours. This credibility gap has at last been closed by two major wines – the Rossese and the Cinque Terre – getting their DOC recognition. Wines with a long history, such as the Polcevera and the Coronata, unless something is done to resuscitate them, will soon be part of that same history.

As with the wines of Capri and Ischia, which are equally redolent of sunshine and sea-breezes, the Ligurian wines are light and fresh to taste, but one should drink with prudence as they all have a larger alcoholic content than one initially thinks and can sometimes make driving, let us say, hazardous.

At all events, the red Rossese, saved by the gong, is now available in fair quantities – the Croesi winery has the best reputation. The white Cinque Terre is less attractive than the beautiful countryside it comes from, and the Sciacchetrà, a dessert wine made from the same grape, but semi-dried, is even less so.

Cinque Terre and Cinque Terre Sciacchetrà (21: 23.9.73)

Both of these white wines are produced from the Bosco grape (60%) and either the Albarolo (also called Erbarola) or Vermentino vines (40%), with a minimum alcohol content of 11% for the table wine. The Sciacchetrà dessert wine is customarily fortified to 17%, of which 13% is developed into alcohol, making an amabile wine after one year's ageing in the cask.

Producers
Cantina Crespi, Imperia (Imperia)
Cooperativa Cinqueterre, Riomaggiore (Imperia)
Asaldo, San Pier d'Arena (Genoa)
Cantina Callera, Salea d'Albenga (Savona)

Rossese di Dolceacqua or Dolceacqua (125: 15.5.72)

The Rossese vine produces a dry red wine with a hint of sweetness and a minimum alcoholic content of 12%. With 13% alcohol and one year's ageing, it may be labelled Superiore.

Producers
Cantina del Rossese Crespi, Dolceacqua (Imperia)
Croesi, Salea di Imperia (Imperia)
Enzo Guglielmi, Soldano (Imperia)
Michele Guglielmi, Soldano (Imperia)
Giuseppe Viale, Soldano (Imperia)
Cantina Callera, Salea d'Albenga (Savona)

12

Trentino – Alto Adige (South Tyrol)

Trento, capital of the Trentino province, is on the road that leads up the Adige Valley from Verona to Bolzano (locally also called Bozen) and then over the Brenner Pass to Austria and Germany. The hillsides along the whole valley are covered with vines and every town, large or small, seems to have a winery or two. It is a land that has many elegant wines of international style, partly because Trento and all points north, up until the First World War, belonged to the Austro-Hungarian Empire and have not yet forgotten it. Depending on where you go, a knowledge of German varies from being useful to being essential.

At San Michele all'Adige there is one of Italy's major enological colleges (the others are at Conegliano in the Veneto and Asti in Piedmont) which also makes and sells Riesling, Traminer, Pinot Bianco, Moscato Rosa, Pinot Nero, Teroldego Rotaliano, Cabernet

Sauvignon and Merlot and has, inevitably, made a profound impression on the quality of both the vine-dressing and the processing of the grapes throughout the area.

There are a lot of not very interesting wines, too – mostly light reds which have a declining market in Germany and Austria. For all that, it is hard to say whether the whites or the reds are better. The only world-class wine from the region is from the Trentino, the champenois-system Pinots and Chardonnays made famous by Gino Lunelli, owner of the Ferrari winery. These are followed, at a distance, by sparklers from Equipe 5, Cesarini Sforza and the big CAVIT co-operative, all of whose Pinots and Chardonnays come from the vineyards in the nearby foothills. André Simon, way back, gave Ferrari his blessing – and that should be recommendation enough.

Even to the Italians the names of the wines are unfamiliar – Veltliner, Teroldego Rotaliano, Sylvaner, Marzemino, Schiava, Lagrein, Lagrein Dunkel, Casteller, Sorni and Traminers, some of which may be bottled and labelled German-style to make them even more unfamiliar; even old friends like Pinot Nero turn up as Blauburgunder and Pinot Grigio as Ruhländer: rosé becomes *kretzer* and white muscat turns into Goldenmuskasteller: but there are also Rieslings, Rhine and Italic to be found, though they, too, may be printed in Gothic script.

The exaggerated number of DOC wines is an added confusion to the point that one should, perhaps unjustly, just pick out those (DOC or otherwise) which have got their heads above the crowd.

After the sparkling wines, we can find a number of fine reds in the Trentino. Two non-DOCs I think are outstanding: the Fojenaghe 'claret' blend by Conte Bossi Fedrigotti (I believe you have to join a long queue for a few crates of the 60,000 bottles made), and the CAVIT's Cabernet-Merlot 4 Vicariati, a highly civilized wine for the wine-lover who recognizes quality. Names such as San Michele all'Adige (the enological college), Barone de Cles, Endrizzi, Hofstatter and Gonzaga should also be borne in mind. However, the local varietal that rises head and shoulders above the others is the Teroldego Rotaliano (with the assistance of Foradori, chiefly) and is made by all the more important Trentino wineries including Donati, Zeni, Conti Martini and the Mezzacorona Co-operative.

Historically, the South Tyrol has been a red-wine land (with exports to North Europe since the time of Charlemagne) but today Italy has become a burgeoning market with a lot of clout, causing completely new trends for the South Tyrolese. Today, whites – Pinots, Rieslings and Chardonnays – have been planted out extensively for the ever-growing champenois- and charmat-system production.

Herbert Tiefenbrunner has made a lot of headway recently with his innovative ideas: so, too, has Franco Kettmeir, who was amongst the first into the New Enology. I have always had a soft spot for the ethereal Santa Maddalena, a red from higher up the mountain, and hope it is still as good as it was once upon a time. It should be remembered that the Trentino–South Tyrol does not have a Mediterranean climate, but an Alpine micro-climate with enormous variations of temperature: it can be, in winter or summer, both the hottest or the coldest area of all Italy during the course of twenty-four hours. The temperature can drop to 0°C at night with a sunny warm midday, warmer than Capri.

In the South Tyrol, Alois Legader (with a fine mountain Chardonnay), Conti Martini and Cantine Bellendorf (both with a notable Pinot Bianco), Klosterkellerei and Vaja, amongst others, should be remembered.

TRENTINO

Casteller (275: 3.10.74)

This is a composite dry red wine made up of Schiava Grossa and Schiava Gentile (at least 30%) and Merlot (not more than 20%), with a balance of Lambrusco (40%) and 10% of other approved grapes. It has an alcoholic content of not less than 11%.

Producers
CAVIT, Ravina di Trento (Trento)
Liberio Todesca, Mattarello 1 (Trento)

Sorni (280: 13.10.79)

A Schiava, with some Lagrein and Teroldego, produces this dry red wine. Its minimum alcoholic content is 10·5%, but with 11% and one year's ageing, it may be labelled Scelto (selected).

Producer
Cantina Sociale Lavis Sorni, Salorno (Trento)

Teroldego Rotaliano (139: 3.6.71)

Made entirely from grapes of the Teroldego vine, this wine has an alcoholic content of 11·5%. A dry red Teroldego, with 12% alcohol and at least two years' ageing in the wood, may be called Superiore.

Producers
Barone de Cles, Maso Scari, Mezzolombardo (Trento)
Bossi-Fedrigotti, Rovereto (Trento)
Cantina Sociale Mezzocorona, Mezzocorona (Trento)
CAVIT, Ravina di Trento (Trento)
Pierfranco Donati, Mezzocorona (Trento)
Foradori, Mezzolombardo (Trento)
Istituto Agrario San Michele all'Adige (Trento)
Zeni (Trento)
Conti Martini (Trento)
Endrizzi (Trento)
Gonzaga (Trento)

Vini del Trentino (221: 2.9.71 and 324: 28.11.79)

TRENTINO CABERNET

This wine is made from Cabernet (90%) and has a minimum alcoholic content of 11%. A wine for ageing; with two years in the wood and 11·5% alcoholic content, it may be considered Riserva.

Producers
CAVIT, Ravina di Trento (Trento)
Endrizzi, San Michele all'Adige (Trento)
Guerrieri Gonzaga, Borghetto all'Adige (Trento)
La Vinicola Sociale, Aldeno (Trento)
Pisoni, Pergolese (Trento)
Diberio Todesca, Mattarello Trento (Trento)
Bossi-Fedrigotti, Rovereto (Trento)

TRENTINO LAGREIN

A light red wine with a minimum alcoholic content of 11%. There is also a rosé called Lagrein Kretzer from Mezzocorona at 12·5%, produced by Dorigati. It may be considered Riserva after two years' ageing.

Producers
Barone de Cles, Maso Scari, Mezzolombardo (Trento)
Dorigati, Mezzolombardo (Trento)
Bossi-Fedrigotti, Rovereto (Trento)
Cantina Sociale Mezzocorona, Mezzocorona (Trento)

TRENTINO MARZEMINO

A dry red wine with a minimum alcoholic content of 11%: with 12% and two years' ageing, the wine may be called Riserva.

Producers
Bossi-Fedrigotti, Rovereto (Trento)
Cantina Sociale Nomi, Nomi (Trento)
CAVIT, Ravina di Trento (Trento)
Endrizzi, San Michele all'Adige (Trento)
La Vinicola Sociale, Aldeno (Trento)

TRENTINO MERLOT

A ruby red wine made entirely from Merlot grapes and with a minimum alcoholic content of 11%. If aged for two years, it may be labelled Riserva.

Producers
Baron de Cles, Mezzolombardo (Trento)
Bossi-Fedrigotti, Rovereto (Trento)
Endrizzi, San Michele all'Adige (Trento)
Guerrieri Gonzaga, Borghetto all'Adige (Trento)

TRENTINO MOSCATO

A sweet white wine produced from semi-dried grapes to give a minimum alcoholic content of 13%. Aged for two years it becomes Riserva.

Producers
CAVIT, Ravina di Trento (Trento)
Bossi-Fedrigotti, Rovereto (Trento)
Endrizzi, San Michele all'Adige (Trento)

TRENTINO PINOT NERO

A dry red wine with 11·5% alcohol content. After two years' ageing it may be labelled Riserva.

Producers
Cantina Sociale Lavis Sorni Salorno, Lavis (Trento)
CAVIT, Ravina di Trento (Trento)
Endrizzi, San Michele all'Adige (Trento)
Gaierhof (Trento)

TRENTINO PINOT

A dry white wine with an alcoholic content of 11%. It may also be made as a sparkling wine.

Producers
Cantina Sociale Lavis Sorni Salorno, Lavis (Trento)
Cantina Sociale Nomi, Nomi (Trento)
CAVIT, Ravina di Trento (Trento)
Barone de Cles, Mezzolombardo (Trento)
Dorigati, Mezzocorona (Trento)
Endrizzi, San Michele all'Adige (Trento)
Equipe 5, Trento (Trento)
Ferrari, Trento (Trento)
SAV Cantina, Nogaredo (Trento)

TRENTINO RIESLING

A dry white wine with a minimum alcoholic content of 11%.

Producers
CAVIT, Ravina di Trento (Trento)
Endrizzi, San Michele all'Adige (Trento)

TRENTINO TRAMINER AROMATICO

A dry but aromatic wine with a minimum alcohol content of 12%.

Producers
Rudolf Carli, Nalles (Bolzano)
Bossi-Fedrigotti, Rovereto (Trento)
Abbazia di Novacella, Bressanone (Bolzano)
Instituto Agrario Provinciale, San Michele all'Adige (Trento)
Cantina dei Benedettini di Muri, Gries (Bolzano)

TRENTINO VIN SANTO

A sweet white wine made from semi-dried grapes to reach a total alcohol content of 16% after ageing.

Producer
CAVIT, Ravina di Trento (Trento)

Recommended non-DOC Trentino Chardonnay

Producer
CAVIT, Ravina di Trento (Trento)

ALTO ADIGE

Alto Adige (190: 18.7.75)

Sixteen different types of wine are permitted under this legislation. Their labelling may be either in the Italian language or in German – the German names for the various wines are given in brackets.

ALTO ADIGE CABERNET

Cabernet produces a dry red wine with an alcoholic content of 11%. If aged for two years, the wine may be labelled Riserva.

Producers
Carli, Nalles (Bolzano)
G. Kettmeir, Bolzano (Bolzano)
Vaja, Egna-Neumarkt (Bolzano)
Hoffstatter, Termeno (Bolzano)

ALTO ADIGE LAGREIN ROSATO (Lagrein Kretzer)

The Lagrein Rosato is made from the Lagrein grape with a minimum alcoholic content of 11%. If produced within the Comune limits of Bolzano, the wine may be called Grieser Lagrein or Lagrein de Gries.

Producers
Carli, Nalles (Bolzano)
G. Kettmeir, Bolzano (Bolzano)
Vaja, Egna-Neumarkt (Bolzano)

ALTO ADIGE LAGREIN SCURO (Lagrein Dunkel de Gries or Griester)

The Lagrein grape in this case is used to produce a dark red dry wine with an alcoholic content of not less than 11%. With one year's ageing, this wine may be labelled Riserva. It may also be called Lagrein de Gries or Grieser Lagrein, if produced in the Comune of Bolzano.

Producers
Cantina Sociale Gries, Gries (Bolzano)
Klosterkellerei, Muri-Gries (Bolzano)
Cantina dei Benedettini di Muri, Gries (Bolzano)

ALTO ADIGE MALVASIA (Malvasier)

The Malvasia produces a dry white wine with an alcoholic content of not less than 11%.

Producers
Cantina Sociale Gries, Gries (Bolzano)
G. Kettmeir, Bolzano (Bolzano)

ALTO ADIGE MERLOT

The Merlot produces a dry red wine with an alcoholic content of not less than 10·5%. If aged one year, the wine may be qualified as Riserva.

Producer
G. Kettmeir, Bolzano (Bolzano)

ALTO ADIGE MOSCATO GIALLO (Sudtiroler Goldenmuskateller)

Moscato produces a sweet white wine with a minimum alcoholic content of 10·5%.

Producers
Brigl, Cornaiano (Bolzano)
Carli, Nalles (Bolzano)
Walch, Termeno (Bolzano)
Hofstatter, Termeno (Bolzano)
G. Kettmeir, Bolzano (Bolzano)
Kupelwieser, Bolzano (Bolzano)
Vaja, Egna-Neumarkt (Bolzano)
Alois Lageder (Bolzano)
Tiefenbrunner Schloss Turmhof (Bolzano)

ALTO ADIGE MOSCATO ROSA (Rosenmuskateller)

The Moscato Rosa is a sweet rosé wine with a minimum alcoholic content of 12%.

Producers
Brigl, Cornaiano (Bolzano)
Carli, Nalles (Bolzano)

ALTO ADIGE PINOT GRIGIO (Ruländer)

The Pinot Grigio produces a dry white wine with a minimum alcoholic content of 11%.

Producers
Kupelwieser, Bolzano (Bolzano)
Lun, Bolzano (Bolzano)
G. Kettmeir, Bolzano (Bolzano)
Vaja, Egna-Neumarkt (Bellermont Wangen)
Schloss Kehlburg, Appaiano (Bolzano)
Alois Lageder (Bolzano)

ALTO ADIGE PINOT NERO (Blauburgunder)

The Pinot Nero produces a dry red wine with a minimum alcoholic content of 11%. If aged for one year, the wine may be qualified Riserva. It may also be used for making sparkling wine.

Producers
Brigl, Cornaiano (Bolzano)
Hofstatter, Termeno (Bolzano)
G. Kettmeir, Bolzano (Bolzano)
Lun, Bolzano (Bolzano)
Schloss Kehlburg (Bellermont Wangen), Appaiano (Bolzano)
Tiefenbrunner Schloss Turmhof (Bolzano)
Vaja, Egna-Neumarkt (Bolzano)
Walch, Termeno (Bolzano)

ALTO ADIGE RIESLING ITALICO (Welchriesling)

This Riesling Italico is a dry white wine with a minimum alcoholic content of 10·5%.

Producer
G. Kettmeir, Bolzano (Bolzano)

ALTO ADIGE RIESLING X SYLVANER (Müller-Thurgau)

The Müller-Thurgau produces a dry white wine with a minimum alcoholic content of 10·5%.

Producers
Cantina Sociale Isarco, Chiusa (Bolzano)
Abbazia Novacella (Neustift), Bressanone (Bolzano)

ALTO ADIGE RIESLING RENANO (Rheinriesling)

The Riesling Renano is a very dry white wine with a minimum alcoholic content of 10·5%.

Producers
Brigl, Cornaiano (Bolzano)
G. Kettmeir, Bolzano (Bolzano)
Kupelwieser, Bolzano (Bolzano)
Lun, Bolzano (Bolzano)
Schloss Kehlburg (Bellermont Wangen), Appaiano (Bolzano)
Tiefenbrunner Schloss Turmhof (Bolzano)

ALTO ADIGE SAUVIGNON

The Sauvignon produces a dry white wine with a minimum alcoholic content of 11·5%.

Producers
Cantina Sociale Terlano, Terlano (Bolzano)
Abbazia Novacella, Chiusa (Bolzano)

ALTO ADIGE SCHIAVA (Vernatsch)

This Schiava is a dry red wine with a minimum alcoholic content of 10%.

Producers
Brigl, Cornaiano (Bolzano)
Hofstatter, Termeno (Bolzano)
G. Kettmeir, Bolzano (Bolzano)
Lun, Bolzano (Bolzano)
Nuova Cantina Sociale di Caldaro, Caldaro (Bolzano)
Walch, Termeno (Bolzano)

ALTO ADIGE SYLVANER

The Sylvaner produces a dry white wine with a minimum alcoholic content of 10·5%.

Producers
Abbazia Novacella, Bressanone (Bolzano)
Cantina Sociale Isarco, Chiusa (Bolzano)

ALTO ADIGE TRAMINER AROMATICA (Gewürztraminer)

The Traminer makes a dry white wine with a minimum alcoholic content of 11%.

Producers
Hofstatter, Termeno (Bolzano)
Walch, Termeno (Bolzano)
G. Kettmeir, Bolzano (Bolzano)
Brigl, Cornaiano (Bolzano)
Kupelwieser, Bolzano (Bolzano)
Lun, Bolzano (Bolzano)
Schloss Kehlburg (Bellermont Wangen), Appaiano (Bolzano)
Tiefenbrunner Schloss Turmhof (Bolzano)
Vaja, Egna-Neumarkt (Bolzano)

Caldaro or **Lago di Caldaro** (Kalterersee) (115: 9.5.70)

This wine may be made from any of the following or a blend of all three: Schiava Grossa, Schiava Gentile and Schiava Grigia; locally these vines are called Grossvernatsch, Kleinvernatsch and Grauvernatsch. There may be up to 15% of Pinot Nero (Blauburgunder) and Lagrein to result in a dry red wine with an alcohol content that must not be less than 11%; should it be above 11%, the wine may be labelled Scelto or Auslese.

Producers
Brigl, Cornaiano (Bolzano)
Cantina Sociale San Michele, Appiano (Bolzano)
Carli, Castel Schwanburg, Nalles (Bolzano)
CAVIT, Ravina di Trento (Trento)
Karl Schmid, Merano (Bolzano)
G. Kettmeir, Bolzano (Bolzano)
Anton Lindner, Appaiano (Bolzano)
Vaja, Egna-Neumarkt (Bolzano)
Walch, Termeno (Bolzano)

Colli di Bolzano (Bozner Leiten) (291: 3.11.75)

A dry red wine obtained from the Schiava (Vernatsch) grape (90%) with Lagrein and Pinot Nero (10%). It has minimum alcoholic content of 11%.

Producers
Maloyer, Bolzano (Bolzano)
Rotensteiner, Bolzano (Bolzano)

Meranese or Meranese di Collina (Meraner or Meraner Hugel) (188: 26.7.71)

This wine is made with the Schiava Grossa (Grossvernatsch), Ledia (Mittervernatsch), Piccola or Gentile Schiava (Kleinvernatsch), Schiava Grigia (Grauvernatsch) and the Tschaggele (Tschaggelevernatsch): no percentages are specified. In view of the high altitude in the Alps in which these are cultivated, 15% of cutting wines may be added. This dry red wine has a 10.5% alcohol content, it may also be labelled Burgravio or Burggrafler.

Producers
Cantina Sociale di Merano, Merano (Bolzano)
G. Kettmeir, Bolzano (Bolzano)

Santa Maddalena (Maddalener) (245: 28.9.71)

Made from four varieties of the Schiava grape, this dry red wine must have an alcoholic content of 11·5%.

Producers
Brigl, Cornaiano (Bolzano)
Carli, Castel Schwanburg, Nalles (Bolzano)
Hofstatter, Termeno (Bolzano)
G. Kettmeir, Bolzano (Bolzano)
Klosterkellerei (Bolzano)
Anton Lindner, Appaiano (Trento)
Vaja, Egna-Neumarkt (Bolzano)
Walch, Termeno (Bolzano)

Terlano (Terlaner) (177: 17.6.75)

The Terlano legislation offers seven white wines, with varying alcoholic contents: Terlano (11·5%); Terlano Pinot Bianco (11%); Terlano Riesling Italico (10·5%); Terlano Riesling Remano (11·5%); Terlano Sauvignon (12%); Terlano Sylvaner (11·5%); Terlano Müller-Thurgau (11%). A 5% in volume use of cutting wines is permitted. The Pinot Bianco is called Weissburgunder locally.

Producers
Brigl, Cornaiano (Bolzano)
Carli, Castel Schwanburg, Nalles (Bolzano)
G. Kettmeir, Bolzano (Bolzano)
Walch, Termeno (Bolzano)
Cantina Sociale Colterenzio-Cornaiano (Bolzano)
Cantina Sociale San Michele, Appaiano (Bolzano)

Valdadige (Etschtaler) (194: 23.7.75)

Two wines, a Valdadige red and a Valdadige white of a very eclectic nature, are permitted under this legislation.

VALDADIGE BIANCO

This white must be made up of more than 20% of one of or a blend of Pinot Bianco, Pinot Grigio, Riesling Italico and Müller-Thurgau. The difference must be made up from one of or a blend of Bianchetta Trevigiana, Trebbiano Toscano, Nosiola, Vernaccia, Sylvaner and Veltliner. The modest result must be a wine made with a minimum alcoholic content of at least 10·5%. A 15% in volume use of cutting wines is permitted.

VALDADIGE ROSSO

The red wine must be made up of Schiava (at least 20%) and Lambrusco (10%). The difference may be made up with Merlot, Pinot Nero, Lagrein, Teroldego and Negrara as required. The minimum alcoholic content must not be less than 11%, and 15% by volume use of cutting wine is permitted.

Producers
Brigl, Cornaiano (Bolzano)
G. Kettmeir, Bolzano (Bolzano)
Walch, Bolzano (Bolzano)

Valle Isarco (Eisacktaler) (299: 16.11.74)

The DOC legislation allows for the production of five dry white wines with varying varietal grapes and minimum alcoholic contents: Traminer Aromatica (Gewürztraminer) (11%); Pinot Grigio (Rulander) (11%); Veltliner (10·5%); Sylvaner (10·5%); Müller-Thurgau (10·5%). At all events, 10% by volume of cutting wines may be added. The wines may be given the geographical denomination of Bressanone or Brixner.

Producers
Abbazia di Novacella, Novacella, Bressanove (Bolzano)
Cantina Sociale Valle (Eisacktaler Kellereigenossenschaft), Chiusa
   (Bolzano)

Recommended South Tyrol non-DOC wines

NON-DOC PINOT BIANCO

Producer
Tiefenbrunner Schloss Turmhof (Bolzano)

NON-DOC CHARDONNAY

Producers
Alois Lageder (Bolzano)
Viticoltori Alto Adige (Bolzano)
Tiefenbrunner Schloss Turmhof (Bolzano)
R. Zeni, San Michele (Bolzano)

Much of the Pinots, Chardonnays, Rieslings etc. is transformed into sparkling wines of the highest quality by Giulio Ferrari, Equipe 5 and CAVIT locally and much is 'exported' to Lombardy and Piedmontese sparkling-wine makers, both of charmat and champenois systems.

13

Veneto

THE VERONA–VICENZA HILLS

Despite all the controversy and harsh words about Verona wine,
it flourishes: the English importers are well represented with the
top quality wines from the best producers. Over the last decade,
these have been growing in quality and I would like to say in
sophistication, but sophistication has a different and pejorative
meaning – adulteration – in the wine field. What I wish to say is
that the various Amarones, in particular, have been worked on,
bringing them to an affluent state-of-the-art, and are justly called
conversation wines, rather than dessert, meditation or seduction
ones. These super-Valpolicellas are made with dried grapes, and
Masi, with his Campo Fiorin, gives his a second *ripasso* fermentation, similar to the historic Chianto *governo* process. These
wines have a body, aroma and after-taste that would be wasted
on teenage palates. Today, these great wines are considered rep-

resentative of Verona wines rather than the Superiore table wines; and incidentally, they travel without risk of spoilage.

The producers, once referred to as 'artisan' vintners, are especially respected in Verona and one might mention a few names – Masi, Allegrini, Quintarelli, Tedeschi, Santa Sofia, Guerrieri-Rizzardi, Santi, Anselmi, Piropan, Galli and Speri, who all make the whole range of Classico and Superiore Valpolicellas, Soave, Bardolinos, Amarones and sweet Reciotos. There is even a strong, sweet, red sparkling version (notably made by Le Ragose which makes only the super-Valpolicella wines) which could, judiciously offered, serve to gain one an amnesty in sore circumstances. Two famous producers, Bolla and Bertani, have specialities: the former its Amarone, the latter, its new cru Castellaro, a classic white Soave.

The old grumble about Verona wines and Soave in particular was caused by commonplaces: the swift and pressurized industrialization of Italy after the Second World War caused a lot of things to be done, unwisely in the long run, as long as they produced both cheap goods and labour-intensive employment immediately – Soave did both. However, twenty years ago, chiefly owing to big exports to the States of Superiore, the whole situation changed. That is, at first there was, say, 20 per cent of Superiore made by the private (artisan) vintners. This quickly became 60 per cent through increased production while the remainder, made by the co-operatives, remained plonk, and was sold locally or distilled as surplus wine. The processing of the Superiore was handled from vineyard to bottle by the (artisan) producer whereas the ordinary wine was bought in bulk from the co-operatives. Despite improvements in the wine from the co-operatives the general system is unaltered today.

All this is only to stress the importance of reputable names, qualifying adjectives such as Superiore, Classico, Riserva etc., rather than DOC which can be manipulated to include almost anything except, perversely enough, the finest of crus. Only now, in this last decade, have so many élite producers caused a further chaos by making 'non-DOC table wines' which are, in fact, often the finest crus of Italy and aged in *barriques*, but cannot yet fit into a DOC category.

I think most experts agree that the Bardolinos, Valpolicellas, Valpantenas and Soaves, even when Superiore Classicos, should be drunk young. Look for the vintage date only to ensure that it is very recent: not more than two years old for reds and last year's wine for the whites. Exceptions should be made for Tedeschi's Capitel San Rocco red, Le Ragose's Le Sassine red and Guarnieri-Rizzardi Classico Superiore Valpolicella, all of which can age from three to six years. Amarone can also take five and perhaps more years of ageing in the bottle.

In the 1974 and 1983 editions of *Italian Wines*, the Verona wine zone's secondary and nearby wine-producing areas existed but had made little headway. Today, there is something to say about them: in 1973, I wrote:

> The DOC white of Custoza is something of a mystery . . . I have never managed to trace it . . . this DOC white is alleged to come from between Verona and Lake Garda, next to the Bardolino zone.

It turns out that the Arvedi family has been living there and making top-quality wine for 500 years and still does so with the New Enology. They, too, recommend that their distinguished dry white wine should be drunk within a year. Other nearby vineyards, also producing in the Verona spirit, are those of Gambellara, the Berici Hills and Breganze, all of them to the east, towards Padua and Venice. The Gambellara zone encompasses the Zonin winery which is a large and serious producer of a wide range of wines from other zones as well; amongst them are two excellent charmats, one Pinot, the other Durello.

On the Berici Hills we find Alfredo Lazzarini, who has made a reputation with his Pinot Nero: in this zone, there is a lot of Merlot and Cabernet being produced, if not yet making its mark.

In the Breganze zone, also empty ten to twenty years ago, there is the Maculan winery which has recently made a big name with its white, sweet Torcolato, fortified to 15 per cent, and by its skill in *barrique*-ageing it. Maculan has a wide range of DOC and non-DOC wines: amongst the more distinguished ones are a *barrique*-aged DOC Tocai called Prato di Canzio; a *barrique*-aged Breganze red (Cabernet and Merlot blend); a non-DOC Amarone and a well-respected Pinot Bianco DOC.

Here starts the rise of the dry, white Tocai di Lison, a wine that was famous and well-loved thirty years ago, went into a decline and now is rising on a new wave of public affection and esteem.

It is found right through Friuli to the Yugoslavian frontier, reborn with the New Enology. Maculan makes a good one.

Bardolino (186: 23.7.68 and 324: 4.12.76)

A blend of the grapes – the Corvina Veronese (50–65%), Rondinella (10–30%), Molinara (10–20%) and Negrara (10%) – produces a dry red wine with a minimum alcoholic content of 10·5%. It may be labelled as Classico when made with grapes coming from the original limited growing area. If aged for a year and reaching 11·5% of alcohol, it may be called Superiore.

Producers
G. B. Bertani, Verona (Verona)
Fratelli Bolla, Soave (Verona)
Cantina Sociale della Valpantena, Quinto Valpolicella (Verona)
Cantina Sociale di Soave, Soave (Verona)
Colle dei Cipressi, Calmasino di Bardolino (Verona)
Lamberti, Lazise Sul Garda (Verona)
Masi, Cantina di Affi, Marano Valpolicella (Verona)
Pasqua, Verona (Verona)
Pegaso Premiovini, Brescia (Brescia)
A. and G. Piergriffi, Bardolino (Verona)
Portalupi (Verona)
Santi, Illasi (Verona)
Fratelli Tedeschi, Verona (Verona)
Sterzi, San Martino della Battaglia (Verona)

Bianco di Custoza (142: 5.6.71)

A composite wine made from grapes from the following vines: Trebbiano, Garganega, Friuli Tocai, Cortese, Tuscan Malvasia and Riesling Italico. It is dry and white and has a minimum alcoholic content of 11%.

Producers
Balcamin, Bussolengo (Verona)
Santa Sofia, Valpolicella (Verona)
Conte da Schio, Lungara (Vicenza)
Fratelli Tedeschi (Verona)

Arvedi d'Emilei (Verona)
Bertani (Verona)
Le Tende (Verona)
Pasqua, Verona (Verona)
Portalupi (Verona)

Breganze (235: 4.9.69)

This DOC legislation permits six different types of wine to be made under the Breganze label.

BREGANZE BIANCO

A dry white wine made with at least 85% Tocai grapes and a minimum alcoholic content of 11%.

BREGANZE ROSSO

A dry red wine made from Merlot grapes and with a minimum alcoholic content of 11%.

BREGANZE CABERNET

Made from Cabernet grapes, this dry red wine must have a minimum alcoholic content of 11·5%. If with 12% and suitably aged it may be called Superiore.

BREGANZE PINOT NERO

This dry red wine is made from 100% Pinot Nero grapes and has a minimum alcoholic content of 11·5%. If with 12% and suitably aged, it may be called Superiore.

BREGANZE PINOT BIANCO

Pinot Bianco (40–60%) and Pinot Grigio (60–40%) grapes, processed together, produce a dry white wine with a minimum alcoholic content of 11·5%. If 12%, the wine may be labelled Superiore.

BREGANZE VESPAROLO

The Vesparolo is a local white grape which produces a dry white wine with a minimum alcoholic content of 11·5%.

Producers
Cantina Sociale Beato Bartolomeo da Breganze, Breganze (Vicenza)
Maculan (Vicenza)
Zonin, Gambellara (Vicenza)

Colli Berici (32: 4.2.74)

This legislation permits the making of seven different wines under the Colli Berici label.

BERICI GARGANEGO

A dry white wine made from the Garganego Trebbiano di Soave (10%) and a minimum alcoholic content of 10%.

BERICI MERLOT

A dry red wine made entirely with Merlot provides an alcoholic content of 11%.

BERICI PINOT BIANCO

A dry white wine made with Pinot Bianco and 15% Pinot Grigio provides an alcoholic content of 11%.

BERICI SAUVIGNON

A dry white wine made entirely with Sauvignon grapes to produce a minimum alcoholic content of 11%.

BERICI TOCAI BIANCO

A dry white wine made from Tocai (90%) and Garganego (10%) grapes with an alcoholic content of 11%.

BERICI TOCAI ROSSO

A dry red wine made of Tocai (85%) and Garganego (15%) with an alcoholic content of 11%.

BERICI CABERNET

A dry red wine, made with Cabernet Franc and/or Cabernet Sauvignon to provide a minimum alcoholic content of 11%. If with 12·5% and three years' ageing, the wine may be labelled Riserva.

Producers
Conte da Schio, Custozza (Vicenza)
Alfredo Lazzarini, Villa dal Ferro (Vicenza)
Zonin, Gambellara (Vicenza)

NON-DOC BERICI HILLS CABERNET

Producer
Alfredo Lazzarini, Villa dal Ferro (Vicenza)

Colli Euganei (281: 6.11.69)

Three diverse wines are permitted under this discipline.

COLLI EUGANEI WHITE

This is a blended wine – Garganega (30–50%), Serpina (20–40%) and Tocai and/or Sauvignon (20–30%) grapes – with a minimum alcoholic content of 10·5%. If with more than 12% (11% for sweet wine) and aged suitably, it may be called Superiore. This wine may be processed to make a sparkling wine.

COLLI EUGANEI ROSSO

This is a blended wine – Merlot (60–80%), Cabernet, Barbera and Verona Raboso (20–40%); with a minimum alcoholic content of 11%. With a year's ageing and more than 12% of alcohol this wine may be labelled Superiore.

COLLI EUGANEI MOSCATO

This is a sweet white wine with a minimum alcoholic content of 10·5%. It is much used for making of spumante.

Producers
Consorzio Vini DOC, Abano Terme (Padova)
Cantina Sociale Euganei Vò, Padua (Padova)
Luxardo, Torreglia (Padova)

Gambellara (132: 29.5.70)

This DOC legislation covers three wines, each based on the Garganega grape (80–90%), blended with a little Trebbiano di Soave.

GAMBELLARA BIANCO

A dry white wine with an alcoholic content of 11%, but if with 11·5%, it may qualify as Superiore.

GAMBELLARA RECIOTO

Produced by the semi-dried grape method to reach a minimum alcoholic content of 12%, this wine is customarily processed to be both sweet and sparkling.

GAMBELLARA VIN SANTO

Also produced from semi-dried grapes, this wine, which reaches an alcoholic content of over 14%, must be aged for two years in the wood.

Producers
Cantina Sociale di Gambellara, Gambellara (Vicenza)
Zonin, Gambellara (Vicenza)

Soave and **Recioto di Soave** (269: 22.10.68; 227: 27.8.76; 72: 14.3.75)

SOAVE

Garganega (approximately 80%) and Trebbiano di Soave (approximately 20%) form the Soave dry white wine to give an alcoholic content of 10·5%. This wine may be qualified as Superiore if with an alcoholic content of 11·5%, and Classico if produced in the original delimited area of Soave.

RECIOTO DI SOAVE

This wine is made with semi-dried grapes to reach an alcoholic content of at least 14%; it is customarily sweet, often sparkling and may be fortified.

Producers
G. B. Bertani, Verona (Verona)
Biscardo, Bussolengo (Verona)
Fratelli Bolla, Soave (Verona)
Cantina Sociale della Valtramigna, Cazzano di Tramigna (Verona)
Cantina Sociale di Soave, Soave (Verona)
Lamberti, Lazise sul Garda (Verona)
Pasqua, Verona (Verona)
Pegaso Premiovini, Brescia (Brescia)
Piropan, Soave (Verona)
Pietro Sartori, Negrar (Verona)
Tenuta Masi, Cantina di Soave, Marano (Verona)
Santi, Illasi (Verona)
Anselmi (Verona)
Serego Aligheri (Verona)
Le Ragose (Verona)
Portalupi (Verona)

Valpolicella and **Recioto della Valpolicella** (268: 21.10.68; 72: 14.3.75; 271: 11.10.76)

VALPOLICELLA

This wine is made up from Corvina Veronese (85%), Rondinella (25–30%) and Molinara (5–15%), while Rossignola, Negrara,

Barbera and Sanigovese contribute the remaining 10%. The minimum alcoholic content is 11% but, with 12% and two years' ageing, the wine may be labelled Superiore. Wines from the original Valpolicella growing area may be labelled Classico.

RECIOTO DELLA VALPOLICELLA AND AMARONE

This wine is made by semi-dried grapes to reach an alcoholic content of at least 14%. The Recioto is usually made as a sweet dessert wine, sometimes sparkling, but more usually as a full-bodied, dry table wine.

Producers
Arturo Allegrini, Fumane Valpolicella (Verona)
G. B. Bertani, Verona (Verona)
Fratelli Bolla, Verona (Verona)
Cantina Sociale di Soave, Soave (Verona)
Cantina Sociale di Illasi, Illasi (Verona)
Pasqua, Verona (Verona)
Pegaso Premiovini, Brescia (Brescia)
Giuseppe Quintarelli, Ciriè di Negrar, Negrar (Verona)
Pietro Sartori, Negrar (Verona)
Tenuta Masi, Marano, Valpolicella (Verona)
Cantina Sociale della Valpantena, Quinto Valpantena (Verona)
Fratelli Tedeschi, Verona (Verona)
Santi, Illasi (Verona)
Cantina Sociale di Negrar, Negrar (Verona)
Marta Galli, Az. Ag. Le Ragose, Arbizzano di Valpolicella del Negrara (Verona)

THE VENETIAN HINTERLAND

The Venetians, and their fellow-countrymen ashore, are among Italy's best drinkers, and they have some excellent products. If one moves to the Venetian Hinterland and to the obscure Montello DOC zone, one finds the Venegazzù, a wine well known to Italian wine-lovers for thirty and more years, chiefly due to its being regularly recommended by the various *maîtres d'hôtel* of the special gourmet restaurants of the CIGA hotels (the Grands and Excelsiors of Italy), confident that nobody can easily fault them. Venegazzù was then and is today a magnificent wine based on Cabernet Sauvignon, Cabernet Franc, Malbec and Merlot, which may have a familiar ring to many readers.

Here, there is a treasure house of excellent wines. There are plenty of reds, chiefly Cabernets and Merlots, a noted one being that of Castello di Roncade; but there is a cascade of names that are part of the local history – Bianchi Kunkler, Antonio Falzacappa, Conti di Porcia, Santa Margherita di Portogruaro, Italo Maccari and, of course, the Conti Loredan of Venegazzù fame. Good wines comes from the little-known Pramaggiore area (La Braghina and Sant'Anna wineries) especially the Tocais and the Prosecco di Conegliano Valdobbiadene.

This last is a little masterpiece: it is an amabile (and one might say amiable, too) charmat sparkler which does not insist on being taken too seriously. It comes also in baby-bottles and is, therefore, an ideal pick-me-up, a late breakfast beverage, a stirrup-cup or what you will to make a friendly gesture. It is not of a cloying sweetness and can be drunk throughout a light meal, whereas the Cartizze Classico Prosecco is a more serious proposition, being champenois-system and made with 80 per cent Pinot grapes.

Vini del Piave or Piave (242: 24.9.71)

PIAVE CABERNET

This wine is dry, red and with an alcoholic content of 11·5%; with 12·5% and three years' ageing, it may be labelled Riserva.

Producers
Cantina Sociale di Campodipietra, Campodipietra di Salgareda (Treviso)
Cantina Sociale di San Dona, San Dona di Piave (Venezia)
Castello di Roncade Basetti, Roncade (Treviso)
Antonio Verga Falzacappa, San Vendemiano (Treviso)
Leone Agnolotti Giavera del Montello (Treviso)
Ivan Cescon, Cessalto (Treviso)

PIAVE MERLOT

This wine is red and dry with an alcoholic content of 11%. With 12% and two years' ageing, it qualifies as Riserva.

Producers
Bianchi di Kunkler, Mogliano Veneto (Treviso)
Castello di Roncade Basetti, Roncade (Treviso)
Cantina Sociale di Campodipietra, Campodipietra di Salgareda (Treviso)
Cantina Sociale di San Dona, San Dona di Paive (Treviso)
Liasora, Ponte di Piave (Treviso)
Antonio Verga Falzacappa, San Vendemiano (Treviso)
Italo Maccari, Visna di Vazzola (Treviso)
Ivan Cescon, Cessalto (Treviso)

PIAVE TOCAI

A dry white wine with a minimum alcoholic content of 11%.

Producers
Cantina Sociale Colli del Soligo, Farra di Soligo (Treviso)
Cantina Sociale di San Dona, San Dona di Piave (Venezia)
Liasora, Ponte di Piave (Treviso)
Italo Maccari, Visna di Vazzola (Treviso)
Bianchi-Kunkler, Mogliano Veneto (Treviso)

PIAVE VERDUZZO

A dry white wine with a minimum alcoholic content of 11%.

Producers
Cantina Sociale di Campodipietra, Campodipietra di Salgareda (Treviso)
Marcello del Majno, Fontanelle di Oderzo (Treviso)

Tocai di Lison (220: 1.9.71)

The Friuli Tocai vine providing 95% of the grapes, with the balance unspecified, produces a dry white wine with an alcoholic content of 11·5%. There is a Classico zone which offers a Superiore wine at 12%.

Producers
G. G. Conti di Porcia, Pordenone (Pordenone)
La Braghina, Lison di Portogruaro (Venezia)
Santa Margherita, Fossalta di Portogruaro (Treviso)
Tenuta S. Anna, Loncon di Annone Veneto (Venezia)

Cabernet di Pramaggiore (244: 27.9.71)

A dry red wine made from Cabernet (90%) and Merlot (10%) with a minimum alcoholic content of 11·5%. With 12% minimum and three years' ageing in the barrel, it may be called Riserva.

Producers
G. G. Conti di Porcia, Pordenone (Pordenone)
La Braghina, Lison di Portogruaro (Venezia)
Tenuta S. Anna, Loncon di Annone Veneto (Venezia)

Merlot di Pramaggiore (244: 27.9.71)

Made with Merlot (90%) and Cabernet (10%), it has a minimum alcoholic content of 11·5%. If the wine is aged for at least two years and reaches not less than 12% alcoholic content, it may be qualified as Riserva.

Producers
La Braghina, Lison di Portogruaro (Venezia)
Tenuta S. Anna, Loncon di Annone Veneto (Venezia)
Santa Margherita, Fossalta di Portogruaro (Treviso)
Cantina Sociale di Portogruaro, Portogruaro (Venezia)

Montello e Colli Asolani (304: 8.11.7)

CABERNET DI MONTELLO

This dry red wine is produced from Cabernet (85%) with the addition of Cabernet Franc, grown in the same vineyards. An alcoholic content of 11% is required; if 12%, and with two years' ageing, the wine may be qualified as Superiore.

MERLOT DI MONTELLO

This is produced from Merlot (85%) with the addition of a suitable blend of Malbec, Cabernet Franc and Sauvignon which must come from the same vineyards. A 10·5% alcoholic content is required; if more than 11·5% and with two years' ageing, the wine may be labelled Superiore.

PROSECCO DI MONTELLO

This is produced from Prosecco (85%) with permitted blending of Pinot Bianco, Pinot Grigio, Riesling Italico, Verduzzo Trevigiano and Bianchetto Trevigiano coming from the same vineyards. An alcoholic content of 10% is required.

Producer
Cantina Sociale Montelliana dei Colli Asolani, Montebelluna (Treviso)

Recommended non-DOC Montello red

Producer
Conti Loredan, Villa Gasparini, Venegazzù di Montello (Treviso)

Prosecco di Conegliano–Valdobbiadene (141: 7.6.69)

This legislation deals with the Prosecco both as a still and as a sparkling wine, as well as in its dry, amabile and sweet characteristics. It also distinguishes between Prosecco and Cartizze, the classic zone.

The Prosecco is made from Prosecco (90%) grapes with additions of Verdiso to reach a minimum alcoholic content of 10·5% – the Cartizze 11%.

In the case of bruts made by the champenois method, Pinot grapes are the major ingredient.

Producers
Cantina Sociale di Valdobbiadene, Valdobbiadene (Treviso)
Cantina Sociale di Soligo, Soligo (Treviso)
Carpene Malvolti, Conegliano (Treviso)
De Bernard, Conegliano (Treviso)
Valdo Vini Superiore, Valdobbiadene (Treviso)
Pino Zardetto, Conegliano (Treviso)
Casa Bianca (Treviso)

14

Friuli – Venezia Giulia

The vineyards of this area were destroyed not only by *phylloxera*, but by two World Wars. At last, some great wines are being produced there with continuity: they are mostly whites. There are fifty-three DOC disciplines which is rather more than most people can cope with, so I will stress the names of the distinguished producers and the best varietals they use. I note that there are a few English importers: not many, but they stress Pinot Grigio, whose reputation in Italy exploded like a fireworks display some ten or so years ago; plainly, these pyrotechnics were also noted in London.

In brief, Friuli–Venezia Giulia had a little renaissance on its own that impressed everybody. Manlio Collavini led the way, followed by Mario Schiopetto; they both offered the most elegant of white wines. Marco Felluga, from his Russiz Superiore winery, extended this new reputation which, in turn, was further amplified by the Abbazia di Rosazzo. A full list of noted producers is in the next section.

A few special wines to note are: Ronco del Gnemiz's Chardonnay; Pinot Bianco and Pinot Brut 'Mus' from Marina Danieli

Fisdan (whose winery has a long tradition of female owner-management); a Pinot Bianco by Russiz Superiore; a Pinot-Tocai blend (Ronco delle Acacie) by the Abbazia di Rosazzo; a Sauvignon by Collavini as well as a variety of charmat- and champenois-system sparklers (see 'Applause Cremant') and Tocai Friulana by Schiopetto, which are just a few of the unusual wines that the great experts of this area have literally created out of nothing – or, rather, out of one-time battlefields.

One red stands out particularly: it is a 'claret', made with Cabernet Sauvignon, Cabernet Franc and Merlot and aged in *barriques*. This Vigne dal Leon comes from the winery of the same name and, despite its pedigree, is catalogued as table wine.

The seaport of Trieste, the capital city of this zone, is odd, yet most pleasing to visit. It is a blend of Mitteleuropa and the Mediterranean. The food is substantial – a sort of Italianized Viennese cuisine where the goulash is much better, but more than anything, the seafood is supreme and worthy to accompany the great white wines created there.

As a tailpiece, the local Verduzzo, not overly praised in the past, has been New-Enologized by Giovanni Dri as a sweet wine, made with lightly dried grapes, in which case it is called Ramandolo and is gaining a reputation. Surely, this wine has been inspired by Picolit, the centuries-old dessert wine of the Austro-Hungarian Empire which currently is very expensive (and not entirely satisfactory) as it suffers from a vine-disease called Floral Abortion and consequently has a very poor yield.

THE GORIZIA HILLS

Collio Goriziano or Collio (178: 15.7.68; 153: 6.6.79)

COLLIO

A dry white and slightly sparking wine made from the Ribolla, Istrian Malvasia and Tocai grapes produced in the same vineyards to reach an alcoholic content of 11%.

Producers
Conti Formentini, San Floriano del Collio (Gorizia)
La Viticoltori, San Floriano del Collio (Gorizia)

COLLIO CABERNET FRANC

A dry red wine made solely from Cabernet Franc with an alcoholic content of 12%.

Producers
Attems, Lucinico (Gorizia)
Collavini (Udine)
Livio Felluga, Cormons (Gorizia)
Marco Felluga, Gradisca d'Isonzo (Gradisca d'Isonzo)
Gradmir Gradnik, Cormons (Gorizia)
Conte Michele Formentini, San Floriano del Collio (Gorizia)
Rocca Bernarda (Udine)
Roncada, Cormons (Gorizia)
Russiz Superiore, Capriva del Friuli (Gorizia)
Giovanni Scolaris, San Lorenzo Isontino (Gorizia)
Mario Schiopetto, Spessa di Capriva (Gorizia)

COLLIO MALVASIA

A dry white wine with an alcoholic content of 11·5%.

Producers
Azienda Agricola Roncada, Cormons (Gorizia)
Attems, Lucinico (Gorizia)
Barone Codelli, Mossa (Gorizia)
Formentini, San Floriano del Collio (Gorizia)
Russiz Superiore, Capriva del Friuli (Gorizia)
Valle Azienda Vitivinicole, Buttrio (Udine)

COLLIO MERLOT

A dry red wine with an alcoholic content of 12%.

Producers
Attems, Lucinico (Gorizia)
Azienda Agricola Roncada, Cormons (Gorizia)
Paolo Caccese, Cormons (Gorizia)
Cantina Produttori Vini del Collio e dell'Isonzo, Cormons
  (Gorizia)
Enofriulia, Capriva del Friuli (Gorizia)
Livio Felluga, Cormons (Gorizia)
Marco Felluga, Gradisca d'Isonzo (Gorizia)
Formentini, San Floriano del Collio (Gorizia)
Ercole Pighin, Risano (Udine)
Russiz Superiore, Capriva del Friuli (Gorizia)
Subida di Monte, Cormons (Gorizia)
Valle Aziende Vitivinicole, Buttrio (Udine)

COLLIO PINOT BIANCO

A dry white wine with an alcoholic content of 12%.

Producers
Azienda Agricola Roncada, Cormons (Gorizia)
Cantina Produttori Vini del Collio e dell'Isonzo, Cormons
  (Gorizia)
Collavini (Udine)
D'Attimis Maniago, Cormons (Gorizia)
Enofriulia, Capriva del Friuli (Gorizia)
Marco Felluga, Gradisca d'Isonzo (Gorizia)
Livio Felluga, Cormons (Gorizia)
Formentini, San Floriano del Collio (Gorizia)
Gradmir Gradnik, Cormons (Gorizia)
Mario Schiopetto, Capriva (Gorizia)
Giovanni Scolaris, San Lorenzo Isontino (Gorizia)
Russiz Superiore, Capriva del Friuli (Gorizia)

COLLIO PINOT GRIGIO

A dry white wine with an alcoholic content of 12·5%.

Producers
Attems, Gorizia Lucinico (Gorizia)
Azienda Agricola Roncada, Cormons (Gorizia)
Livio Felluga, Cormons (Gorizia)
Formentini, San Floriano del Collio (Gorizia)
Ercole Pighin, Risano (Udine)
Giovanni Scolaris, San Lorenzo Isontino (Gorizia)
Russiz Superiore, Capriva del Friuti (Gorizia)

COLLIO PINOT NERO

A dry red wine with an alcoholic content of 12·5%.

Producers
Livio Felluga, Cormons (Gorizia)
Marco Felluga, Gradisca d'Isonzo (Gorizia)
Gradmir Gradnik, Cormons (Gorizia)
Russiz Superiore, Capriva del Friuli (Gorizia)
Mario Schiopetto, Spessa (Gorizia)
Giovanni Scolaris, San Lorenzo Isontino (Gorizia)

COLLIO RIESLING ITALICO

A dry white wine with an alcoholic content of 12%.

Producers
Attems, Lucinico (Gorizia)
Marco Felluga, Gradisca d'Isonzo (Gorizia)
Giovannia Scolaris, San Lorenzo Isontino (Gorizia)
Mario Schiopetto, Spessa (Gorizia)
Russiz Superiore, Capriva del Friuli (Gorizia)
Angoris Sacta, Cormons (Gorizia)

COLLIO SAUVIGNON

A dry white wine with an alcoholic content of 12·5%.

Producers
Livio Felluga, Cormons (Gorizia)
Attems, Lucinico (Gorizia)

Azienda Agricola Roncada, Cormons (Gorizia)
Marco Felluga, Gradisca d'Isonzo (Gorizia)
Formentini, San Floriano del Collio (Gorizia)
Ercole Pighin, Risano (Udine)
Valle Azienda Vitivinicole, Buttrio (Udine)
Russiz Superiore, Capriva del Friuli (Gorizia)

COLLIO TOCAI

A Tocai white wine with a minimum alcoholic content of 12%.

Producers
Attems, Lucinico (Gorizia)
Paolo Caccese, Cormons (Gorizia)
Livio Felluga, Cormons (Gorizia)
Formentini, San Floriano del Collio (Gorizia)
Ercole Pighin, Risano (Udine)
Produttori del Collio e dell'Isonzo, Cormons (Gorizia)
Giovanni Scolaris, San Lorenzo Isontino (Gorizia)
Valle Aziende Vitivinicole, Buttrio (Udine)
Russiz Superiore, Capriva del Friuli (Gorizia)
Volpe-Pasini (Udine)
Abbazia dei Rosazzo (Corno di Rosazzo)
Borgo Conventi (Gorizia)
Princic (Gorizia)

COLLIO TRAMINER

A dry white wine with an alcoholic content of 12%.

Producers
Gradmir Gradnik, Gradisca (Gorizia)
Angoris Sacta, Cormons (Gorizia)
Mario Schiopetto, Spessa (Gorizia)

THE EASTERN FRIULI HILLS

Colli Orientali del Friuli (424: 30.9.70; 166: 19.6.79)

COLLI ORIENTALI CABERNET

A dry red wine with an alcoholic content of 12%. If aged for two years, the wine may be labelled Riserva.

Producers
Angoris Sacta, Cormons (Gorizia)
Conti di Maniago, Soleschiano (Udine)
D'Attimis Maniago, Buttrio (Udine)
Valle Aziende, Buttrio (Udine)
Volpe-Pasini, Togliano di Torreano, Cividale (Udine)

COLLI ORIENTALI MERLOT

A dry red wine with an alcoholic content of 12%. If aged for two years it may be labelled Riserva.

Producers
Colutta, Bandut, Manzano (Udine)
D'Attimis Maniago, Buttrio (Udine)
Livio Felluga, Cormons (Udine)
Ronchi di Manzano, Manzano (Udine)
Valle Aziende, Buttrio (Udine)
Volpe-Pasini, Togliano di Torreano, Cividale (Udine)
Colli di Manzano, Ronchi di Manzano (Udine)
Conti di Maniago, Soleschiano (Udine)

COLLI ORIENTALI PICOLIT

An amabile dessert wine with an alcoholic content of 15% made by the semi-dried grape method. If aged for two years, it may be labelled Riserva.

Producers
Angoris Sacta, Cormons (Gorizia)
Antonio Furchin, Felettis di Bicinicco (Udine)

Collavini (Udine)
Conti di Maniago, Soleschiano (Udine)
Florio Maseri, Buttrio (Udine)
Livio Felluga, Cormons (Gorizia)
Rocca Bernardo, SMOM, Ipplis (Udine)
Valle Aziende, Buttrio (Udine)
Volpe-Pasini, Togliano di Torreano, Cividale (Udine)

COLLI ORIENTALI PINOT BIANCO

A dry white wine with a minimum alcohol content of 12%.

Producers
Livio Felluga, Cormons (Gorizia)
Ronchi di Manzano, Manzano (Udine)
Valle Aziende, Buttrio (Udine)
Volpe-Pasini, Togliano di Torreano, Cividale (Udine)

COLLI ORIENTALI PINOT GRIGIO

A dry white wine with an alcoholic content of 12%.

Producers
Colli di Manzano, Ronchi di Manzano (Udine)
Conti di Maniago, Soleschiano (Udine)
Livio Felluga, Cormons (Gorizia)
Florio Maseri, Buttrio (Udine)
Volpe-Pasini, Togliano di Torreano, Cividale (Udine)
Collavini (Udine)
Russiz Superiore (Gorizia)

COLLI ORIENTALI PINOT NERO

A dry red wine with an alcoholic content of 12%. If aged for two years, the wine may be labelled Riserva.

Producers
Ronchi di Manzano, Manzano (Udine)
Volpe-Pasini, Togliano di Torreano, Cividale (Udine)

COLLI ORIENTALI REFOSCO

A dry red wine with an alcoholic content of 12%. If aged for two years, the wine may be labelled Riserva.

Producers
Colutta, Bandut, Manzano (Udine)
Conti di Maniago, Soleschiano (Udine)
Valle Aziende, Buttrio (Udine)

COLLI ORIENTALI RIBOLLA

A dry white wine with a minimum alcoholic content of 12%.

Producers
Gradmir Gradnik, Cormons (Gorizia)
Valle Aziende, Buttrio (Udine)
Mario Schiopetto, Spessa (Gorizia)

COLLI ORIENTALI RIESLING RENANO

A dry white wine with an alcoholic content of 12%.

Producers
Livio Felluga, Cormons (Udine)
Ronchi di Manzano, Manzano (Udine)
Valle Aziende, Buttrio (Udine)

COLLI ORIENTALI SAUVIGNON

A dry white wine with an alcoholic content of 12%.

Producers
Angoris Sacta, Cormons (Gorizia)
Colli di Manzano, Ronchi di Manzano (Udine)
D'Attimis Maniago, Buttrio (Udine)
Marco Felluga (Gorizia)
Rubini Cantina, Spessa di Cividale del Friuli (Udine)
Bandut-Colutta, Manzano (Udine)

Mario Schiopetto (Gorizia)
Collavini (Udine)
Attems (Gorizia)
Formentini (Gorizia)

COLLI ORIENTALI TOCAI

A dry white wine with an alcoholic content of 12%.

Producers
Colli di Manzano, Ronchi di Manzano (Udine)
Colutta, Bandut, Manzano (Udine)
Conti di Maniago, Soleschiano (Udine)
D'Attimis Maniago, Buttrio (Udine)
Livio Felluga, Cormons (Gorizia)
Florio Maseri, Buttrio (Udine)
Rocca Bernarda, SMOM, Ipplis (Udine)
Ronchi di Manzano, Manzano (Udine)
Valle Aziende, Buttrio (Udine)
Volpe-Pasini, Togliano di Torreano, Cividale (Udine)

COLLI ORIENTALI VERDUZZO

A dry white wine with an alcoholic content of 12%. When made
as a sweet wine it is called Ramandolo.

Producers
Colutta, Bandut, Manzano (Udine)
Livio Felluga, Cormons (Gorizia)
Ercole Pighin, Risano (Udine)
Rocca Bernarda, SMOM, Ipplis (Udine)
Ronchi di Manzano, Manzano (Udine)
Colli di Manzano, Ronchi di Manzano (Udine)
Giovanni Dri (Udine)
Ronchi di Fornaz (Udine)
Ronco del Gnemiz (Udine)

Recommended non-DOC

CHARDONNAY SPUMANTE CHARMAT

Producers
Ronco del Gnemiz (Udine)
Abbazia di Rosazzo
Collavini 'Il Grigio' (Udine)

THE WESTERN FRIULI HILLS

Grave del Friuli (244: 26.9.70; 166: 19.6.79)

GRAVE CABERNET

A dry red wine with an alcoholic content of 11·5%.

Producers
Cantina Sociale Casarsa, Casarsa della Delizia (Pordenone)
Antonio Furchir, Felettis di Bicinicco (Udine)
Arcangelo Pavan, San Quirino (Pordenone)
Fratelli Pighin, Risano (Udine)
Valle Aziende, Buttrio (Udine)

GRAVE MERLOT

A dry red wine with an alcoholic content of 11%.

Producers
Cantina Sociale Casarsa, Casarsa della Delizia (Pordenone)
Conti G. G. di Porcia, Pordenone (Pordenone)
Antonio Furchir, Felettis di Bicinicco (Udine)
Arcangelo Pavan, San Quirino (Pordenone)
Fratelli Pighin, Risano (Udine)
Collavini (Udine)

GRAVE PINOT BIANCO

A dry white wine with an alcoholic content of 11·5%.

Producers
Cantina Sociale Casarsa, Casarsa della Delizia (Pordenone)
Fratelli Pighin, Risano (Udine)

GRAVE PINOT GRIGIO

A dry white table wine with an alcoholic content of 11%.

Producers
Cantina Sociale Casarsa, Casarsa della Delizia (Pordenone)
Plozner, Spilimbergo (Pordenone)
Villa d'Arco, A. Pavan, San Quirino (Pordenone)

GRAVE REFOSCO

A dry red wine with an alcoholic content of 11%.

Producers
Friulvini, Porcia (Pordenone)
Antonio Furchir, Felettis di Bicinicco (Udine)
Plozner, Spilimbergo (Pordenone)

GRAVE TOCAI

A dry white wine with an alcoholic content of 11%.

Producers
Cantina Sociale Casarsa, Casarsa della Delizia (Pordenone)
Conti G. G. di Porcia, Pordenone (Pordenone)

GRAVE VERDUZZO

A dry white wine with an alcoholic content of 11%.

Producers
Cantina Sociale Casarsa, Casarsa della Delizia (Pordenone)
Conti G. G. di Porcia, Pordenone (Pordenone)

THE FRIULI SEABOARD

Isonzo (65: 8.3.75; 287: 20.10.79)

ISONZO CABERNET

A dry red wine with a minimum alcoholic content of 11%.

Producers
Marco Felluga, Gradisca d'Isonzo (Gorizia)
Formentini, San Floriano del Collio (Gorizia)
Prandi d'Ulmhort, Romans d'Isonzo (Gorizia)
Giovanni Scolaris, San Lorenzo Isontino (Gorizia)

ISONZO MALVASIA ISTRIANO

A dry white wine with an alcoholic content of 10·5%.

Producers
Marco Felluga, Gradisca d'Isonzo (Gorizia)
Prandi d'Ulmhort, Romans d'Isonzo (Gorizia)

ISONZO MERLOT

A dry red wine with an alcoholic content of more than 10·5%.

Producers
Barone Codelli, Cormons (Gorizia)
Marco Felluga, Gradisca d'Isonzo (Gorizia)
Giovanni Scolaris, San Lorenzo Isontino (Gorizia)

ISONZO PINOT BIANCO

A dry white wine with a minimum alcoholic content of 11%.

Producers
Marco Felluga, Gradisca d'Isonzo (Gorizia)
Prandi d'Ulmhort, Romans d'Isonzo (Gorizia)
Giovanni Scolaris, San Lorenzo Isontino (Gorizia)

ISONZO PINOT GRIGIO

A dry white wine with a minimum alcoholic content of 11%.

Producers
Marco Felluga, Gradisca d'Isonzo (Gorizia)
Formentini, San Floriano (Gorizia)
Giovanni Scolaris, San Lorenzo Isontino (Gorizia)

ISONZO RIESLING RENANO

A dry white wine with a minimum alcoholic content of 11%.

Producer
Marcello Brotto, Ronchi (Gorizia)

ISONZO SAUVIGNON

A dry white wine with a minimum alcoholic content of 11%.

Producers
Marcello Brotto, Ronchi (Gorizia)
Prandi d'Ulmhort, Romans d'Isonzo (Gorizia)

ISONZO TOCAI

A dry white wine with a minimum alcoholic content of 10.5%.

Producers
Barone Codelli, Cormons (Gorizia)
Marco Felluga, Gradisca d'Isonzo (Gorizia)
Formentini, San Floriano (Gorizia)
Giovanni Scolaris, San Lorenzo Isontino (Gorizia)

ISONZO TRAMINER AROMATICO

A dry white wine with a minimum alcoholic content of 11%.

Producer
Francesco Pecorari, San Lorenzo Isontino (Gorizia)

ISONZO VERDUZZO

A dry white wine with a minimum alcoholic content of 10·5%.

Producers
Marcello Brotto, Ronchi (Gorizia)
Marco Felluga, Gradisca d'Isonzo (Gorizia)
Franco Visintin, Gradisca d'Isonzo (Gorizia)

Latisana (292: 5.11.75)

LATISANA CABERNET

A dry red Cabernet which may be blended with Cabernet Franc
with a minimum alcoholic content of 11·5%.

LATISANA MERLOT

A dry red wine with a minimum alcoholic content of 11%.

LATISANA PINOT BIANCO

A dry white wine with a minimum alcoholic content of 11·5%.

LATISANA PINOT GRIGIO

A dry white wine with a minimum alcoholic content of 11%.

LATISANA REFOSCO

A dry red wine with a minimum alcoholic content of 11%.

LATISANA TOCAI FRIULANO

A dry white wine with a minimum alcoholic content of 11%.

LATISANA VERDUZZO FRIULANO

A dry white wine with a minimum alcoholic content of 11%.

Producer
Cantina Sociale di Latisana, Latisana (Udine)

Aquileia (290: 31.10.75)

AQUILEIA CABERNET

A dry red wine with an alcoholic content of 11·5%.

AQUILEIA MERLOT

A dry red wine with an alcoholic content of 11%.

AQUILEIA PINOT BIANCO

A dry white wine with an alcoholic content of 11·5%.

AQUILEIA PINOT GRIGIO

A dry white wine with an alcoholic content of 11%.

AQUILEIA REFOSCO

A dry red wine with an alcoholic content of 11%.

AQUILEIA RIESLING RENANO

A dry white wine with an alcoholic content of 11%.

AQUILEIA TOCAI FRIULANO

A dry white wine with a minimum alcoholic content of 11·5%.

Producers
Cantina Sociale Cooperativa del Friuli Orientale, Cervignano
  (Udine)
Isola Augusta, Palazzolo dello Stella (Udine)

Recommended non-DOC Friuli 'claret'

VIGNE DAL LEON

A dry, *barrique*-aged red wine (Cabernet Sauvignon, Cabernet
Franc, Merlot).

Producer
Vigne dal Leon (Udine)

15
Emilia Romagna

Most people think of Milan and Turin as the driving forces of Italy – the factories, the efficiency and the money. But I cannot help feeling that the real economic wisdom and wealth and, for that matter, the real efficiency, is in the valley of the Po.

When the rest of Italy, a few decades ago, willy-nilly dumped agriculture as a shameful occupation for modern man in favour of an industrialization policy, the Emilia-Romagnians ignored the propaganda and invested their last lira in their land, in orchards, in cows, pigs and vineyards, to make one of the most fruitful and profitable areas in all Europe. The spin-off from agriculture has been great food-processing industries, including Parmesan cheeses, Parma hams, salamis from Bologna and, above all, wine, with an output that has long ago passed the billion-litres-a-year mark.

For all that, the wine connoisseurs look a trifle askance at Emilia Romagna: it is not that good, honest and pure wine is not produced there, it is mostly that other places produce better wine. And this, of course, is true, though at times the criticism is gratuitous and offensive.

Winewise, in fact, Emilia Romagna has some unusual offerings. First, astride the Lombardy-Emilia boundary, there is the Gutturnio

– a hearty Barbera-Bonarda blend – an excellent everyday wine, very much to Italian taste; then a certain amount of respectable Trebbiano DOC which has not hit the headlines, not even of the parish magazines. This area, however, is becoming better known due to the creative wine-making of the Fugazza sisters who are using the traditional Barbera and Bonarda as blends and single varietals, along with some experimental Pinot Noir.

Moving to the flatlands of the River Po, one meets with an inundation of wine, starting with Reggio Emilia. This is the Lambrusco that is so often under fire. But the major producers of it, the RIUNITE co-operative, with its 12 million cases exported to the USA every year in 12,000 container loads and with a $12-million advertising budget, cry all the way to the bank. In collaboration with Villa Banfi, as mentioned earlier (p. 15), they are now producing a white Lambrusco which is nearly as successful as the red and I believe that the Bianco di Scandiano (a nearby wine zone) is responsible for the most part, though there is no impediment to their importing good white wine from Puglia or Umbria to make a non-DOC Lambrusco. In all events, the Villa Banfi-inspired RIUNITE (with 50 per cent of the USA's total wine-import market) is extending its list to more 'serious' wines and charmats. Technologically, one can only take off one's hat to them. I have not, however, succeeded in getting samples of these latter novelties and, since they are not for sale in Italy, I cannot therefore give further detail.

There are large Lambrusco companies – Cavicchioli, Chiarli and Giacobazzi – who make DOC and more traditional Lambruscos. There is a small production of Lambrusco Terra Calda Scorza Nera which is a sort of Riserva, darker, stronger, drier and better! This is made by Remigio Medici and Ina Maria Pallerano.

Further down the river, one arrives at one of the world's major gastronomy centres, Bologna. Their wines, until recently, were not comparable to their cuisine. The old argument was that a light, low-alcohol wine like Lambrusco was ideal with their multi-course meals, as not only could one drink a bottle or two without getting drunk, but Lambrusco was ideal for cutting down one's cholesterol count.

However, they also drank large quantities of Sangiovese della Romagna which, in recent years, has improved notably. The Superiore is a strong red with an equally strong vinous aroma and good body: a wine to go with grills and barbecues. If vinified as a young wine, it is much lighter and goes with cooked and spiced seafood magnificently. These wines should have the advantage of not being expensive. This Sangiovese (not Sangioveto) is a traditionalist wine with a lot of vigour.

The two whites, Albana and Trebbiano, are as good as who makes them: Conte Pasolini dall'Onda and Fattoria Paradiso are recommended sources.

There is an island of wine that has surfaced – at least in reputation if not materially. I am sure somebody can prove that Pliny the Elder or Martial planted vines there way back in history. It has a DOC title that nobody can be expected to remember. It is, optionally, Colli Bolognesi di San Pietro, Colli Bolognesi-Monte San Pietro, Colli Bolognesi dei Castelli Medioevali or just Monte di San Pietro. In all events, it has six DOC disciplines also (for Barbera, Albana, Merlot, Pinot Bianco, Riesling and Sauvignon) of which one has gone into orbit, the Pinot Bianco. Though a non-DOC – just as though six disciplines were not sufficient to choose from – the Vallania winery has perfected a Cabernet Sauvignon, presented as a lowly table wine and called Terre Rosse. In view of the wealth in those parts, the enormous appetites and their eternal thirsts, not much of this fine wine will even be required to travel far. However, it should at least be saluted *en passant*.

THE PIACENZA HILLS

Gutturnio dei Colli Piacentini (203: 14.8.67)

A dry red wine made with Barbera (60%) and Bonarda (40%) offers an alcoholic content of 12%.

Producers
Fratelli Bonelli, Rivergaro (Piacenza)
La Solitaria, Zaino (Piacenza)
Giuseppe Molinelli, Ziano Piacentino (Piacenza)
Pusterla, Vigolo Marchese (Piacenza)
Valtidone Cantina Cooperativa, Borgonovo Val Tidone
    (Piacenza)
Fugazza Castello di Luzzano (Piacenza)
Cantine Romagnoli (Piacenza)

Monterosso Val d'Arda (321: 9.12.74)

A dry white wine made from Malvasia di Candia (50%) and a blend of Moscato Bianco, Trebbiano Romagnolo and Sauvignon, with a minimum alcoholic content of 11%. It is also made amabile.

Producers
Enoteca Castellarquato, Castel'Arquato (Piacenza)
Pusterla, Vigolo Marchese (Piacenza)

Trebbianino di Val Trebbia (100: 15.4.75)

This dry white wine, based on Ortrugo grapes (35–50%), Malvasia di Candia (10–30%), Trebbiano Romagnolo or Moscato (15–30%) and Sauvignon (15%), is an 11% alcohol content wine that may be processed either as a completely dry or as an abbocca-to-frizzante wine.

Producer
Fratelli Bonelli, Rivergaro (Piacenza)

REGGIO–MODENA–BOLOGNA

Bianco di Scandiano (37: 9.2.77)

This wine is made from Sauvignon (locally called Spergola or Spergolina (85%)) with a balance from Malvasia di Candia or Trebbiano Romagnolo. It is made as sweet, semi-sweet and dry; in all cases, the alcoholic content is 10·5%. It is mostly made as a sparkling wine, in which case it must have an alcoholic content of 11%.

Producers
Cooperativa Colli di Scandiano, Scandiano (Reggio-Emilia)
Consorzio Vini Scandiano, Reggio-Emilia (Reggio-Emilia)

Colli Bolognesi di San Pietro or Colli Bolognesi–Monte San Pietro; Colli Bolognesi dei Castelli Medioevali (318: 2.12.75)

COLLI BOLOGNESI BARBERA

A dry red wine produced solely from Barbera grapes to provide an alcoholic content of 11·5%. With 12·5% and three years' ageing in the wood, the wine may be called Riserva.

Producers
Cantina Consorziale Comprensorio di Monte San Pietro
  Cooperativa, Zola Predosa (Bologna)
Bruno Negroni (Bologna)
Sassoli, San Martino in Casola (Bologna)
Torre Ca'Bianca, Zola Predosa (Bologna)
Vallania, Zola Predosa (Bologna)

COLLI BOLOGNESI BIANCO

A dry white wine made from Albana (60%) and Trebbiano (40%), with an alcoholic content of at least 11%.

Producers
Cantina Consorziale Comprensorio di Monte San Pietro
  Cooperativa, Zola Predosa (Bologna)
Sassoli, San Martino in Casola (Bologna)
Vallania, Zola Predosa (Bologna)

COLLI BOLOGNESI MERLOT

A dry red wine with an alcoholic content of 11·5%.

Producers
Cantina Consorziale Comprensorio di Monte San Pietro
  Cooperativa, Zola Predosa (Bologna)
Sassoli, San Martino in Casola (Bologna)
Vallania, Zola Predosa (Bologna)

COLLI BOLOGNESI PINOT BIANCO

A dry white wine produced entirely from Pinot grapes to provide an alcoholic content of at least 12%.

Producers
Cantina Consorziale Comprensorio di Monte San Pietro
  Cooperativa, Zola Predosa (Bologna)
Vallania, Zola Predosa (Bologna)

COLLI BOLOGNESI RIESLING ITALICO

A dry white wine with an alcoholic content of at least 12%.

Producers
Cantina Consorziale Comprensorio di Monte San Pietro
  Cooperativa, Zola Predosa (Bologna)
Sassoli, San Martino in Casola (Bologna)
Vallania, Zola Predosa (Bologna)

COLLI BOLOGNESI SAUVIGNON

A dry white wine with a minimum alcoholic content of 12%.

Producers
Cantina Consorziale Comprensorio di Monte San Pietro
  Cooperativa, Zola Predosa (Bologna)
Sassoli, San Martino in Casola (Bologna)

Recommended non-DOC St Peter's Mount wines

CABERNET SAUVIGNON

Producer
Vallania (Bologna)

Lambrusco Grasparossa di Castelvetro (203: 12.8.70)

A red sparkling wine, produced both dry and amabile with a minimum alcoholic content of 10·5%.

Producers
Cavalli, Scandiano (Reggio-Emilia)
Chiarli e Figli, Modena (Modena)
Angelo Giacobazzi, Nonantola (Modena)
Contessa Matilde–Selezione Premiovini, Brescia (Brescia)
Cantina Sociale di Castelvetro, Castelvetro (Modena)
Cantina Sociale di Settecani, Settecani (Modena)

Lambrusco Reggiano (223: 4.9.71; 32: 1.2.79)

A sparkling red wine produced both dry and amabile with a minimum alcoholic content of 10·5%.

Producers
Cantine Cooperative Riunite di Reggio-Emilia, Reggio-Emilia
(Reggio-Emilia)
Cavalli, Scandiano (Reggio-Emilia)
Ermete Medici, Villa Gaida (Reggio-Emilia)

Lambrusco Salamino di Santa Croce (204: 13.8.70)

A red sparkling wine produced both dry and amabile with a minimum alcoholic content of 11%.

Producers
Cantarelli, Gualtieri (Modena)
Cantine Cooperative Riunite di Reggio-Emilia, Reggio-Emilia
(Reggio-Emilia)
Chiarli e Figli, Modena (Modena)
Severi Vini, Baggiovara (Modena)
Nedo Massetti, Cibemo Carpi (Modena)
Cantina Sociale di Carpi, Carpi (Modena)

Lambrusco di Sorbara (206: 17.8.70)

A sparkling red wine produced both dry and amabile with a minimum alcoholic content of 11%.

Producers
Chiarli e Figli, Modena (Modena)
Angelo Giacobazzi, Nonantola (Modena)
Contessa Matilde–Selezione Premiovini, Brescia (Brescia)
Severi Vini, Baggiovara (Modena)
Cantina Teleforo Fini, Bomporto (Modena)
Cantina Sociale di Sorbara, Bomporto (Modena)

Major producers of Lambrusco

RIUNITE (Reggio-Emilia)
Cavicchioli (Modena)
Chiarli (Modena)
Giacobazzi (Modena)
Remigio Medici (Reggio-Emilia)
Ina Maria Pellerano (Reggio-Emilia)

THE ROMAGNA HILLS

Albana di Romagna (209: 21.8.67; 253: 6.10.69; 63: 6.3.75)

The Albana is a white wine that is made both dry at 12% alcoholic content and amabile at 12·5%. The legislation also permits its being processed into a sparkling wine by natural methods.

Producers
Cooperative Riolo Terme Baldrati, Lugo (Ravenna)
Colombina, Bertinoro (Forli)
Guarini Matteucci, San Tome (Forli)
Pantani Torino e Edo Casa, Mercato Saraceno (Forli)
Fattoria Paradiso, Capocolle di Bertinoro (Forli)
Pasolini dall'Onda, Montericcio (Bologna)
Tenuta Amalia, Villa Verucchio (Forli)

Sangiovese di Romagna (203: 14.8.67; 253: 6.10.69; 343: 27.12.76)

A dry red wine from the Sangiovese vine with a minimum alcoholic content of 11·5%; if with 12%, the wine qualifies as Superiore, and, if aged for two years, may be labelled as Riserva.

Producers
Luigi Baldrati, Lugo (Ravenna)
Cantina Braschi, Mercato Saraceno (Forli)
Coop. Agricola, Riolo Terme (Ravenna)
Ferrucci, Castelbolognese (Ravenna)
Fattoria Paradiso, Capocolle di Bertinoro (Forli)
Pasolini dall'Onda, Montericcio (Bologna)
Tenuta Amalia, Villa Verucchio (Forli)

Trebbiano di Romagna (327: 20.12.73; 15: 16.1.78)

A dry white wine produced from Trebbiano grapes (100%) with an alcoholic content of 11·5%. This may also be made as a spumante wine by natural methods.

Producers
Luigi Baldrati, Lugo (Ravenna)
Fattoria Paradiso (Forli)
Pasolini dall'Onda, Forli (Forli)
Tenuta Amalia, Villa Verucchio (Forli)

16
Tuscany

CARMIGNANO

Carmignano is amongst the oldest wine-producing areas of Italy: documentation is said to go back to the 1300s. Today, which is what matters, it has a reputation for high-quality, well-made wines. What is more, some ten or so years ago they managed to change their DOC status, leaving the Chianti zone and its four-wine blend in favour of an independence which permitted the use of 10 per cent Cabernet Sauvignon which is what all of Tuscan Chianti country is dreaming of.

Keeping a low profile, they obtained what they wanted and are the envy of all. The major producer, Contini Bonacossi, has a low yield and only 100 acres of vineyards. He does not need fifteen-second commercials on TV to sell his wares.

Carmignano (222: 21.8.75)

Carmignano was a Chianti that withdrew from the Chianti discipline to formulate one of its own. Its style is individual due to its unusual blend: Sangiovese (45–60%), Canaiolo Nero (10–15%), Cabernet (6–10%), Trebbiano Toscano, Canaiolo Bianco, Malvasia del Chianti (10–20%), Mammolo, Colorino and Occhio di Pernice (up to 5%). It has a minimum alcoholic content of 12·5% and a minimum ageing in the wood of two years; with three years' ageing, two in the wood, the wine may be termed Riserva.

Producers
Artimino, Artimino (Carmignano, Firenze)
Bacchereto, Carmignano (Carmignano, Firenze)
Contini-Bonacossi, Capezzana (Carmignano, Firenze)
Il Poggiolo, Carmignano (Carmignano, Firenze)
Sghedoni, L'Albanella, Verghereto (Carmignano, Firenze)

THE CHIANTI HILLS – BRUNELLO – VIN NOBILE DI MONTEPULCIANO – VIN SANTO AND TUSCAN WHITES

This is the land of ancient traditions, nineteenth-century traditions and a whole lot of brand-new ones.

In Chapter 6, the Age of Graceful Ageing, Chianti, Chianti Classico and their respective Riservas show up as well aged wines, along with Vin Nobile di Montepulciano, Brunello and Carmignano, all of which are cousins and DOC-regulated wines. Only Brunello is a single vine varietal: the others are blends. The quintals-per-hectare figures, however, do not show the internal changes that have occurred with most of these fine wines (some have been reduced appreciably). First, they have undergone, at least in part, the New Enology – slow fermentation, malolactic fermentation and some other processes. They probably contain much less white wine than in the past and some have made up for this loss by adding some Cabernet Sauvignon, beginning with Carmignano. The results, in all events, are greater complexity and higher quality. Some wineries have shown respect for the old Sangioveto grape and, as with Brunello, made wine 100 per cent Sangioveto, though often giving it a little *barrique* time.

Brunello is basically a Sangioveto Grosso vine that was selected a hundred years ago or so by grandfather Ferruccio Biondi Santi who liked it and who cloned it to plant out at Montalcino; since then many have jumped on the bandwagon. Though Brunello is a cousin of the other Sangioveto vines of Tuscany, it has its own distinctive characteristics; Vin Nobile di Montepulciano, another cousin, still has to include white wines in its blend and, though an excellent wine, it will be even better when and if the DOC regulations change.

The world-class wineries such as Villa Banfi, Antinori, Frescobaldi, Paglierese, Castello Volpaia and Avignonesi, lead the way; but one should also raise one's hat to enologists and enologist–owners such as Ezio Rivella (Villa Banfi), Giacomo Tachis (Antinori), Raffaele Rossetti (Capannelle), Carlo Mascherone and Giovanella Stianti (Volpaia), Maurizio Castelli (Castellare), Sergio Manetti (Monte Vertine), Piero Stucchi Prinetti (Coltibuoni) and Ferruccio Biondi Santi (Il Greppo) who would seem to be head and shoulders above the crowd as creators of wine.

Ezio Rivella stands alone at the top for the astonishing panorama of wines he has made, invented or resuscitated in Tuscany and in Piedmont. Giacomo Tachis is also around the top of the class but for a more limited Cabernet expertise, used as a single varietal and blended with Sangioveto, which has had, however, earth-shaking effects. His new wines – Sassicaia, Tignanello, Solaia and others – are dealt with in Chapter 4, pp. 30–31.

There are a few unusual wines that the reader might like to note: Palazzo Altesi, a *barrique*-matured Brunello-style table wine: Castellare's I Sodi di San Niccolò, a 90 per cent Sangioveto and *barrique*-aged for a year; Coltassala and Castello di Volpaia, both 85 per cent Sangioveto and duly aged; Capannelle and Pergole Torte, both 100 per cent Sangioveto and *barrique*-aged. These wines demonstrate that the autarky-born Sangiovese (Sangioveto) is not a failure, as some wine-writers would have it, but that it stands better alone (or nearly) than in a Chianti mix. The last is the Ca' del Pazzo, made by a Brunello producer, which is a 50 per cent Brunello and 50 per cent Cabernet table wine, *barrique*-aged for ten months and refined (as are all these fine wines) for a year in the cellar in bottles. This last looks very similar in blend to Rivella's forthcoming Castello Banfi.

As things stand, it seems as though Chianti Classico will, at some future date, be either a Sangioveto-Cabernet Sauvignon or a 90–100 per cent *barrique*-aged Sangiovese. Baron Ricasoli's four-wine blend will be forgotten or kept alive as a curiosity. Tuscany, then, is in a state of flux ... but a good one which promises very well.

Among the outstanding whites are a number of Vin Santos, some sparkling spumantes, chiefly Moscadellos from Villa Banfi and a Brut from Antinori, followed by some Chardonnay from each, plus some Galestro/Bianco della Lega, a light summery wine from the major producers, and, finally, a few great wines such as Antinori's Pomino Chardonnay-Sauvignon, Villa Banfi's Fontanelle Chardonnay and Centine. Some names also to remember are La Selva (Siena), Montecarlo Winery (Lucca) for white wines, Giovanni Bianchi's Chardonnay-based Villa Cilnia and Vernaccia di San Gimignano from the Fattoria Ponte.

The only widely-known non-DOC, short-aged Brunello – called Vigneti di Brunello ('from the Brunello Vineyards') – goes under the brand name of Centine and is produced by Villa Banfi. It is also a brand-new world-class wine worthy of attention. Other Brunello wineries are following in Rivella's footsteps.

Chianti Classico (217: 30.8.67; 253: 6.10.69)

A composite wine, based on Sangiovese, (see CHIANTI, p. 29), made in the historically delimited zone of Central Tuscany. It has a minimum alcoholic content of 12% and, if aged for two years, may be called Vecchio. If with 12·5% alcohol and aged for three years, it may be labelled Riserva. Almost all producers make an aged, completely dry Vin Santo dessert wine. More than 90% of the producers belong to the guild called the Consorzio del Chianti Classico but only 50% of the wine reaches the quality to get the Black Rooster seal on the bottle.

Producers
Agricentro, Castellina in Chianti (Siena)   FATTORIA ROCCA
  DELLE MACIE AND VILLA BANFI
Marchesi L. and P. Antinori, Palazzo Antinori, Florence
  (Firenze)   VILLA ANTINORI, FATTORIA SANTA CRISTINA
Ruspoli Berlingueri, Castellina in Chianti (Siena)   FATTORIA DI
  CAMPALLI

Fabrizio Bianchi, Barberino d'Elsa (Firenze) FATTORIA
MONSANTO

Contessa Bonucci, Querciagrossa (Firenze) FATTORIA
FORTILIZIO, IL COLOMBAIO

Giovanni Cappelli, Greve in Chianti (Firenze) FATTORIA
MONTAGLIARI, FATTORIA LA QUERCIA

Capellini, Greve in Chianti (Firenze) CASTELLO DI
VERRAZZANO

Conte Neri Capponi, Greve in Chianti (Firenze) FATTORIA
CALCINAIA

Castelbarco Albani, Greve in Chianti (Firenze) CASTELLO DI
UZZANO

Kunz Asburgo, Castello di Poppiano, Barberino d'Elsa (Firenze)

Cesare Canessa, Gaiole in Chianti (Siena) CASTELLO DI SAN
POLO IN ROSSO

Luigi Cecchi, Castellina in Chianti (Siena)

Marchese Corsini, San Casciano Val di Pesa
(Firenze) FATTORIA DI MONTEPALDI

Principe Corsini, San Casciano Val di Pesa (Firenze) CASTELLO
DI PROMIANO VILLA LE CORTI

Pian d'Albola, Radda in Chianti (Siena) FATTORIA PIAN
D'ALBOLA

Alberto de Marchi, Valiano (Siena) FATTORIA DI VALIANO

Palmina and John Dunkley, Gaiole in Chianti (Siena) AZIENDA
AGRICOLA RIECINE

Fideli e Rivella, Castellina in Chianti (Siena) FATTORIA IL
CAGGIO

Giovanni Ginanneschi, Gaiole in Chianti (Siena) FATTORIA DI
AMA

R. Grierson, Castellina in Chianti (Siena) and London
(UK) PODERE LA PUZZOLA

ICARO Spa, Mercatale Val di Pesa (Firenze) FATTORIA
CASTELLO DI GABBIANO

La Pagliaia, Pianella (Siena) FATTORIA LA PAGLIAIA

John Matta, Greve in Chianti (Firenze) and London
(UK) CASTELLO DI VICCHIOMAGGIO

Lapo Mazzei, Castellina in Chianti (Siena) CASTELLO DI
FONTERUTOLI

Melini, Pontassieve (Firenze) FATTORIA DI GAGGIANO

Renzo Olivieri, San Casciano Val di Pesa (Firenze)   FATTORIA
   DI PALAZZO AL BOSCO
Conte Filippo Pandolfini, San Polo, Greve in Chianti
   (Firenze)   FATTORIA DI TIZZANO
Roberto Pandolfini, Via San Gallo 74, Florence
   (Firenze)   SELECRU CHIANTI CLASSICO SELECTIONS
Pecchioli, Greve in Chianti (Firenze)   CASTELLO DI
   MONTEFIORALLE
Produttori Chianti Geografico, Gaiole in Chianti
   (Siena)   COOPERATIVE
Marchese Emilio Pucci, Pianella (Siena)   FATTORIA CASTELLO
   DI CERRETO
Contessa Radicati, Vagliagli (Siena)   FATTORIA LODOLINE
Barone Bettino Ricasoli, Piazza V. Veneto, Florence
   (Firenze)   CASTELLO DI BROLIO
Ricasoli Figli, Firadolfi, Gaiole in Chianti (Siena)   FATTORIA DI
   CACCHIANO
Ruffino, Pontassieve (Firenze)   FATTORIA DI NOZZOLE
San Felice, Castelnuovo Berardenga (Siena)   FATTORIA DI SAN
   FELICE
Ranieri Sanminiatelli, Greve in Chianti (Siena)   FATTORIA DI
   VIGNAMAGGIO
Biasotto Sanguineti, Borgo San Gusmè (Siena)   FATTORIA
   PAGLIARESI
Conte Serristori, San Casciano Val di Pesa
   (Firenze)   MACHIAVELLI
Stucchi Prinetti, Gaiole in Chianti (Siena)   BADIA A
   COLTIBUONO
Lorotelli Taddei, Montefioralle di Greve (Firenze)   FATTORIA IL
   GUERRINO
Vitagricola, Castellina in Chianti (Firenze)   FATTORIA LA
   CAPRAIA
Viticola Toscana Immobiliare, Gaiole in Chianti
   (Siena)   FATTORIA CASTELLO DI MELETO
Castello Querceto (Florence)
Fattoria dell'Ugo (Florence)
Fattoria dei Pagliarsi (Florence)
Le Capannelle (Siena)
Castellare di Castellino (Siena)
Monte Vertine (Siena)

Altesino (Siena)
Avignonesi (Arezzo)
Tenuta Caparzo (Siena)
Vinattieri, Castello Volpaia (Siena)

CHIANTI

Like the Chianti Classico, Chianti is a composite wine made from
the same four varietals: Sangiovese, Canaiolo, Trebbiano and Malvasia del Chianti. However, if aged for two years and with an
alcoholic content of 12%, instead of its regular 11·5%, it may be
labelled Vecchio; and Riserva if aged for three years and more.
Almost all producers make an aged, completely dry Vin Santo
dessert wine.

Producers
Biondi Santi, Montalcino (Siena)　FATTORIA I PIERI
Conte Guicciardini, Montespertoli (Firenze)　CASTELLO DI
　POPPIANO
Contini Bonacossi, Carmignano (Firenze)　VILLA CAPEZZANA
Marchesi De'Frescobaldi, Palazzo Frescobaldi
　(Firenze)　FATTORIA NIPOZZANO, FATTORIA POMINO
A. Malenchini, Antella (Firenze)　VILLA LILLIANO
Melini, Pontassieve (Firenze)　STRAVECCHIO MONNALISA
　Pasolini dall'Onda Borghese, Barberino Val d'Elsa (Firenze)
　VILLA PASOLINI
Conte Spaletti, Rufina (Firenze)　FATTORIA POGGIO REALE
Gotti Lega, Capannoli (Pisa)　VILLA CAPANNOLI
Guicciardini Strozzi, San Gimignano (Siena)　VILLA CUSONA
Borghini Baldovinetti, San Fabiano (Arezzo)　FATTORIA SAN
　FABIANO
Cantina Vini Tipici Aretini, Ponte a Chiani
　(Arezzo)　COOPERATIVE
Conte Mancini Griffoli, Foiano della Chiana
　(Arezzo)　FATTORIA SANTA VITTORIA
Amedeo di Savoia Aosta, San Giustino Valdarno
　(Arezzo)　FATTORIA IL BORRO
Vecchia Cantina di Montepulciano, Montepulciano
　(Arezzo)　COOPERATIVE

Majnori Guicci Ardim, Vico d'Elsa (Firenze)
Serristori, Macchiavelli, San Casciano (Firenze)

Recommended non-DOC red wines

SASSICAIA

70% Cabernet Sauvignon, 30% Cabernet Franc.

Producer
Marchese Inchisa della Rocca. Distributor Antinori (Florence)

SOLAIA

75% Cabernet Sauvignon, 25% Cabernet Franc.

Producer
Marchesi Antinori (Florence)

TIGNANELLO

80% Sangioveto, 20% Savignon Franc.

Producer
Marchesi Antinori (Florence)

A shortlist of some distinguished Tuscan whites and their makers

Giovanni Bianchi, Villa Cilnia (Arezzo)
Marchesi Antinori (Chardonnay) (Florence)
La Parrina (Grosseto)
Fattoria Buonamico (Carmignano)
Colombini, Fattoria Barbi (Siena)
Abbazia di Coltibuoni (Siena)

A shortlist of noted producers of Tuscan light wine

This is called Galestro in the Classic zone and Bianco della Lega in the other Tuscan areas.

Marchesi Antinori (Florence)
Ruffino (Florence)
Cecchi (Siena)
Frescobaldi (Florence)
Ricasoli (Siena)
Agricoltori Geografico (Siena)

A shortlist of distinguished producers of Vin Santo

Avignonesi (Siena)
Marchesi Antinori (Florence)
Ricasoli Brolio (Siena)
Contini Bonacossi (Carmignano)
Colombini (Siena)
Frescobaldi (Florence)
Ginori Conti (Siena)
Biondi Santi (Siena)
Giovanni Cappelli (Florence)
Vicchiomaggio (Florence and London)

BRUNELLO AND THE MONTEPULCIANO HILLS

Brunello di Montalcino (132: 30.5.66)

This famous wine is made from the Sangiovese Grosso grape alone and has a minimum alcoholic content of 12·5%. It must be aged for four years in the wood; if it is aged more than five, it may be labelled Riserva. This is a DOC-G.

Producers
Barbi, Colombini, Montalcino (Siena)
Biondi Santi, Il Greppo, Montalcino (Siena)
Col d'Orcia, Montalcino (Siena)
Il Colle al Matrichiese, Montalcino (Siena)
Poggio alle Mure, Montalcino (Siena)
Tenuta Il Poggione, Montalcino (Siena)
Tenuta Caparzo, Montalcino (Siena)
Villa Banfi, Sant'Angelo Scalo, Montalcino (Siena)
Fattoria Val di Siga, Bonconvento (Siena)
Argiano (Siena)

Vin Nobile di Montepulciano (233: 19.9.66)

Produced from the Sangiovese Grosso (Prugnolo) grape (50–70%), with some Canaiolo Nero (10–20%), Malvasia del Chianti and Tuscan Trebbiano (10–20%) and not more than 8% of Grechetto Bianco and Mamolo, this wine provides an alcoholic content of 12%. The legislation requires two years' ageing in the wood; should ageing be for more than three years, the wine may qualify as Riserva and, if for over four years, it may be labelled Riserva Speciale.

Producers
Fassati, Montepulciano (Siena)
Sant'Agnese Fanetti, Montepulciano (Siena)
Vecchia Fattoria, Montepulciano (Siena)
Avignonesi (Siena)
Poliziano (Siena)

Bianco Vergine Val di Chiana (310: 29.11.72)

This wine, a dry white, contains Trebbiano (75%) with a contribution of Malvasia del Chianti. It must have a minimum alcoholic content of 11%.

Producers
Mancini Griffoli, Foiano (Arezzo)
Il Poggetto, Rigutino (Arezzo)
Eugenio Razzarti, Bucine (Arezzo)
Aldo Casacini, Rigutino (Arezzo)

A listing of Villa Banfi non-DOC Tuscan wines

MOSCADELLO DI MONTALCINO

An Asti Spumante-style wine, light in alcohol, sweet in flavour.

CHARDONNAY FONTANELLE

A premium white wine, well *barrique*-aged in Californian style.

CENTINE CHARDONNAY

A traditional young Chardonnay, fruity and characteristic.

CENTINE BRUNELLO

A rich young red made with Brunello grapes and with a year of *barrique*-ageing.

SAN ANGELO PINOT GRIGIO

A wine with a lively bouquet, soft on the palate and with a memorable aftertaste.

A listing of Frescobaldi non-DOC Tuscan wines.

POMINO BENEFIZIO

A premium white wine subtly blended, but, being non-DOC, it has only its in-house discipline.

Producer
Frescobaldi (Florence)

THE TUSCAN SEABOARD

There are only three major wines in this area and they have already been dealt with earlier in this text. They are Marchese Incisa della Rocca's Sassicaia from Leghorn which once won the *Decanter* Cabernet-Sauvignon Prize and was the turning-point in the philosophy of Tuscan enologists.

There is the La Parrina DOC zone with its traditional, but also prize-winning, reds and whites and, finally, the new Morellino di Scansano, that has one producer, head and shoulders above the others: Le Pupille produced by the Fattoria (farm) of the same name and sold through the agency of the Institute of Italian Enology in Verona. This is 85% Sangioveto, *barrique*-aged first and then aged in the bottle. Experts think they have a great wine in the making; already, it is showing the stuff needed for long ageing.

It is all in the future, which is, to a great extent, what wine is all about. This Tuscan Seaboard, never heard of twenty years ago, is becoming very interesting.

Bianco Pisano di San Torpe (300: 31.10.80); Vin Santo Pisano di San Torpe

A dry white wine made with Tuscan Trebbiano and with 11% alcoholic content.

The Vin Santo is a golden dessert wine with at least 16% alcoholic content.

Producers
Niccolini, Ponsacco (Pisa)
Cantina delle Colline Pisane, Cenaia (Pisa)
Fattoria Castellare dal Canto, San Pietro Belvedere, Capannoli (Pisa)
Tenuta Torre a Cenaia, Cenaia (Pisa)

Bianco di Pitigliano (132: 30.5.66)

This dry white wine is produced in the volcanic soil of the province of Grosseto; it is made with Trebbiano Toscano (65–70%), Greco (30–35%), and Malvasia Bianca Toscana and Verdello (15%) grapes to a minimum alcoholic content of 11·5%.

Producers
Cantina Sociale di Pitigliano, Pitigliano (Grosseto)
Vinicola Toscana Agricola Immobiliare, Pitigliano (Grosseto)

Candia dei Colli Apuani (243: 4.9.81)

A very small production dry white wine from the Massa Carrara area.

Elba Bianco and Elba Rosso (200: 10.8.67)

The red is a Sangiovese with an alcoholic content of 12%, and the white is a Trebbiano with 11%; both are dry.

Producers
La Pianella, Proccio Elba (Livorno)
Tenuta Acquabona, Portoferraio Elba (Livorno)
La Chiusa di Magazzini, Elba (Livorno)

La Parrina (246: 29.9.71)

The Parrina DOC legislation allows for both a red and a white. The red is Sangiovese and the white, Trebbiano: the former has an alcoholic content of 12% and the latter of 11·5%.

Producer
La Parrina, Albinia di Orbetello (Grosseto)

Montecarlo Bianco (283: 8.11.69)

This dry white wine is made from a blend of grapes including Tuscan Trebbiano, Semillon, Pinot Gris, Pinot Bianco, Vermentino, Sauvignon and Roussanne. The minimum alcoholic content is 11·5%.

Producers
Carrara Vasco, Chiesina Uzzanese (Pistoia)
Fattoria Buonamico, Montecarlo (Lucca)
Mazzini Franceschi, Montecarlo (Lucca)

Montescudaio (37: 9.2.77)

The Montescudaio DOC permits both a red and a white dry wine. The red is Sangiovese (65–85%) with a balance of either or both Tuscan Trebbiano and Malvasia del Chianti. The white is Trebbiano Toscano (70–85%) with the rest made up of Malvasia del Chianti and Vermentino. Both have a minimum alcoholic content of 11·5%. A Vin Santo at 14% may also be made within this discipline.

Producer
R. Moschen, Montescudaio (Pisa)

Morellino di Scansano (92: 4.4.78)

A Sangiovese red wine (85%) with 15% of other approved red grapes grown in the same vineyards to reach a minimum alcoholic content of 11%. If, however, the wine is aged for two years, one of which is in the wood, and the alcohol content is 12%, the wine may be labelled Riserva.

Producers
Cantina Sociale del Morellino, Scansano (Grosseto)
Fattoria Le Pupille, Scansano (Grosseto)

Rosso delle Colline Lucchesi (186: 23.7.68)

The red is made from Sangiovese (40–60%) with a contribution of Canaiolo (5–15%), Ciliegiolo and Colorino (10–15%), Trebbiano Toscano (10–15%) and 5–10% Vermentino and Malvasia Toscano. It offers a minimum alcoholic content of 11·5%.

Producers
Scola Camerini, Pieve, San Stefano (Lucca)
Leoni, San Genaro (Lucca)

Vernaccia di San Gimignano (110: 6.5.66)

Produced from the Vernaccia vine, this dry white wine offers a minimum alcohol content of 12%. A Riserva is permitted if the wine is aged for one year in the bottle. Vernaccia may also be fortified.

Producers
Fattoria Pietrafitta, San Gimignano (Siena)
Strozzi e Guicciardini, Fattoria Clusona, San Gimignano (Siena)
Fattoria di Monte Oliveto, San Gimignano (Siena)
Fattoria Ponte a Rondolino (Siena)

Valdinievole or Bianco della Val-di-Nievole (140: 28.5.76)

This dry white wine is produced more inland towards Pistoia from the Trebbiano grape and with 25% of Malvasia di Chianti and

Vermentino. It has a minimum alcoholic content of 11%. Vin Santo is also included in this DOC legislation and three versions may be made; dry, semi-dry and sweet.

17

The Marches

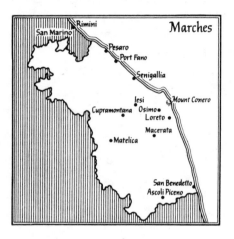

The Marches, though hilly and even mountainous, is a neat and tidy place with every little parcel of land well manicured and productive. Though it has never been a big wine-producer, each smallholder made their own wine for home consumption. Few had enough land from which to make a complete living, so they got into cottage industries and piece-work rather than exiling themselves to the Bronx. The industriousness of the Marchigiani is proverbial in Italy.

Twenty years ago, the Marches were gratuitously denominated by the Common Market as having a vocation for wine production and were given soft loans that they put to good use; they have become even notable exporters – particularly of Verdicchio whites and sparklers, charmat- and champenois-system. They have now nine DOC disciplines, half reds and half whites.

The best of the reds is the Cònero Rosso, a 100 per cent Montepulciano varietal which is more than just good table wine; it has temperament, vigour and a liveliness that make a change from the harmonious wines of the more cultivated north. This same temperament is found in the Sangioveses of the Romagna and in the Abruzzi reds to the south. Throughout history, the Marches did a lot to supply Rome and the Papacy with agricultural products, including wine, as well as the courts of the various milords temporal responsible for the defence of the frontier. Today, it supplies the millions of tourists who cook themselves on the sandy beaches of the Adriatic.

Bianchello del Metauro (143: 10.6.69)

Made from the Bianchello grape with an addition of Malvasia Toscano (5%), this dry white wine has an alcoholic content of 11·5%.

Producers
Anzilotti-Solazzi, Fano (Pesaro)
Consorzio Agrario di Pesaro, Pesaro (Pesaro)

Bianco dei Colli Maceratesi (177: 5.7.75)

This dry white wine must be made with Trebbiano Toscano (more than 50%) and a balance of Maceratino, Malvasia Toscano and Verdicchio; it has a minimum alcoholic content of 11%.

Producers
Villamagna, Macerata (Macerata)
Attilio Fabrini, Serrapetrona (Macerata)

Falerio dei Colli Ascolani (226: 26.8.75)

A dry white wine made with Trebbiano Toscano (not more than 80%) grapes; the balance may be Passerina, Verdicchio, Malvasia Toscano or Pinot Bianco, either singly or blended, with the option of using Malvasia Toscano (up to 7%). The minimum alcoholic content is 11·5%.

Producers
Consorzio Agrario Provinciale, Ascoli Piceno (Ascoli Piceno)
Pennesi, Sant'Elpidio a Mare (Ascoli Piceno)
Constantino e Rozzi, Folignano (Ascoli Piceno)
Tatta di Ciarrocchi, Porto San Giorgio (Ascoli Piceno)
Giovanni Vinci, Cupramarittima (Ascoli Piceno)
Emidio Costantini Brancadoro, San Benedetto del Tronto (Ascoli Piceno)
Villa Pigna, Offida (Ascoli Piceno)

Rosso Cònero (210: 22.8.67; 128: 12.5.77)

Produced from the Montepulciano vine, to which may be added Sangiovese (15%), this dry red wine provides an alcoholic content of 11·5%.

Producers
Fazi-Battaglia, Castelplanio (Ancona)
Gioacchino Garofali, Loreto (Ancona)
Umani Ronchi, Osimo Scale (Ancona)
Giuseppe Pennesi, Sant'Elpidio (Ascoli Piceno)
Emidio Costantini Brancadoro, San Benedetto del Tronto (Ascoli Piceno)

Rosso Piceno (245: 26.9.68)

This dry red wine is made from a blend of Sangiovese (50%) and Montepulciano (40%) with a balance of Trebbiano or Passerina. It has a minimum alcoholic content of 11·5%; with a minimum of 12% and one year's ageing, the wine may qualify as Superiore.

Producers
Aurora, Cupramontana (Ancona)
Consorzio Agrario Provinciale, Ascoli Piceno (Ascoli Piceno)
Consorzio Agrario Provinciale, Macerata (Macerata)
Costantini, Passo Sant'Angelo (Macerata)
Umani Ronchi, Osimo Scalo (Ancona)
Cantina Sociale Val di Nevole, Corinaldo (Ancona)

Sangiovese dei Colli Pesaresi (20: 9.8.72)

This dry red wine is produced from Sangiovese grapes (85%), with the addition of Montepulciano and Ciliegiolo (15%), and has a minimum alcoholic content of 11·5%.

Producers
Cantina Colli-Vigneti Mancini, Pesaro (Pesaro)
Fattoria San Cristoforo, San Lorenzo in Campo (Pesaro)

Verdicchio dei Castelli di Jesi (245: 26.9.68; 79: 21.9.79)

This dry white wine is produced from Verdicchio (80%), Trebbiano Toscano (up to 20%) and Malvasia Toscano. It has a minimum alcoholic content of 12%. Made from grapes produced in vineyards in the historically limited zone the wine may be labelled Classico.

Producers
Aurora, Cupramontana (Ancona)
Consorzio Agrario Provinciale Ancona, Enopolio di Majolati, Ancona (Ancona)
Fazi-Battaglia Titulus, Castelplanio Stazione (Ancona)
Gioacchino Garofali, Loreto (Ancona)
Umani Ronchi, Osimo Scalo (Ancona)
Val di Nevola Cantina Sociale, Corinaldo (Ancona)
Cantina Sociale di Cupramontana, Cupramontana (Ancona)
Villa Bucci (Ancona)

Verdicchio di Matelica (211: 30.8.67; 157: 9.6.79)

This wine closely resembles the Verdicchio di Jesi in composition and characteristics. The DOC legislation permits the making of sparkling wines from the base with natural methods.

Producers
Consorzio Agricolo di Macerata, Enopolio di Matelica, Matelica (Macerata)
La Monacesca, Matelica (Macerata)
Aurora, Cupramontana (Ancona)

Vernaccia di Serrapetrona (222: 4.9.71; 142: 25.5.79)

A sweet or amabile wine made from Montepulciano grapes and Sangiovese and Ciliegiolo (up to 20%). This is customarily made as a full spumante wine with a minimum alcoholic content of 11·5%.

Producer
Attilio Fabrini, Serrapetrona (Macerata)

18
Umbria

The wine scene in Umbria has changed a great deal in the last decade and promises to change more, always for the better. Umbria has a natural vocation for producing fine grapes for wine-making. It is, to all intents and purposes, an extension of Tuscany, culturally, agriculturally, gastronomically and scenically – though always in a minor key. It has usually been dominated by Florentines. Today the dominator is Antinori which has, in the last two decades, updated and upgraded its winery at Castello della Sala. As always with Antinori, one has complete confidence that what must be done has been done; cutting corners is not in their style.

Orvieto wines used to be the only named wines of Umbria, but even they were mostly owned by Florentines. The big production of Umbrian reds and whites found its way in bulk to the *négociants* of Tuscany to be bottled and labelled as Tuscan specialities. Today, there is a Lake Trasimeno co-operative that sells its Umbrian wines under the name of Trasimeno Hills DOC zone (even to Canada). Within this DOC zone, something of importance has occurred that will have a publicity value of its own. The designer and maker of space-age sports cars, Ferruccio Lamborghini, has set his mind to making the traditional wines of Umbria on his estate by Lake Trasimeno, using the most modern techniques. Though his are the best of the zone, they have not yet reached pinnacles of fame. The high technology he has introduced will surely have an ameliorating effect on wine generally as it is learned and adopted by the local smallholders and their co-operative. He has now sold his racing-car interests to the Chrysler Corporation and returned to the basis of his fame and wealth – agriculture and the manufacture of tractors.

The subtle and delicate Orvieto wines are a delight that one tends to forget; like Umbria itself, they are too shy to make a fuss and clamour about their charms. The slightly sweet Orvieto is the real and traditional one; it reflects the gentleness of Umbria. There is now, however, a fully dry version that has become the standard Orvieto today; it is a valuable all-purpose wine that has been re-styled to modern taste. Orvieto red – a traditional Sangiovese, though non-DOC – is a wine that can face the world on its own qualities and characteristics that are well up to Tuscan standards.

The relatively new, and very important, arrival on the Umbrian scene is the production of the Torgiano winery, a few miles outside Perugia. Over the last thirty years, due to the far-sightedness of its owner, Dr Giorgio Lungarotti, the winery has gained a solid, world-wide reputation for its impressive Rubesco red and for its white Trebbiano blend, called Torre di Giano. Both wines are composites: the red is a Chianti-like blend, while the white Trebbiano has softer touches of aromatic Grechetto and Malvasia di Candia. Incidentally, Dr Lungarotti has set up a fascinating museum of wine-making implements.

Much more fascinating today are his three new non-DOC wines which are now well established as world-class products: San Giorgio, Chardonnay di Miraduolo and Cabernet Sauvignon di Miraduolo. The first has 25 per cent of Cabernet Sauvignon and 75 per cent of Sangioveto and Canaiolo; it is briefly *barrique*-aged and then given four years of bottle-ageing in the Lungarotti cellars. The two Miraduolos are equally estate-grown and -bottled, but are 100 per cent single varietals.

The latest arrivals on the scene are not in the same class, though perhaps they will develop: wines seem to require a long running-in period till they hit the right rhythm and style to show off their talents. One of these is the Upper Tiber Hills (Altotiberini) zone. It has always been of good quality but there is quite a leap between having good basic grapes and having good, blended and bottled wine. There is also the Montefalco DOC which, though small, is offering some good strong country wine called Sagrantino. It is a red seduction wine that has aroused admiration from all quarters, which does demonstrate that a good product does not need a 'bush', or TV commercials to make known its existence and merits. However, as things stand, you are unlikely to find any unless you tour Umbria; and there are many worse things to do in this vale of tears. The ancient cities of Orvieto, Assisi, Perugia and Spoleto, not to forget Gubbio and Todi, are lovely to look at and the food is simple yet imaginative and always well prepared.

As a tailpiece, one should remember a wine that needs no technology but only a magic touch, and which is made in fair quantities in Umbria, as it is in Tuscany: Vin Santo. It is either a sweet or, more often, a bone-dry wine (as with Sagrantino), rich, luxurious and velvety in taste and body and with a sherry-like (but not fortified) alcoholic content of around 17 per cent. It is made from semi-dried grapes and matures in the wood over many years. Lungarotti makes a nice one.

Colli Altotiberini (175: 27.6.80)

ALTOTIBERINI BIANCO

A dry white made with Trebbiano (90%) and Malvasia (10%) at 10·5% alcoholic content.

ALTOTIBERINI ROSSO/ROSÉ

The red is Sangiovese (55–70%) blended with Merlot (10–20%) and Tuscan Trebbiano and Malvasia del Chianti (up to 10%). The rosé has the same make-up as the red and the same alcoholic content of 11·5%.

Producers
COVIP, Ponte Pattioli (Perugia)
Colle del Sole, Umbertide (Perugia)
Arnaldo Caprai (Perugia)

Colli del Trasimeno (84: 29.3.72)

TRASIMENO BIANCO

The dry white Trebbiano (60–80%) may be blended with Malvasia del Chianti, Verdicchio, Verdello and/or Grechetto (up to 40%). It has a minimum alcoholic content of 11%.

TRASIMENO ROSSO

The red Sangiovese (60–80%) may be blended with Ciliegiolo, Gamay, Malvasia del Chianti and/or Trebbiano (up to 40%). It has a minimum alcoholic content of 11·5%.

Producers
Cantina Sociale Trasimeno, Castiglione del Lago (Perugia)
COVIP, Ponte Pattioli (Perugia)
Ferruccio Lamborghini, La Fiorita, Panicarola, Castiglione del Lago (Perugia)
SMOM (Sovereign Military Order of Malta), Magione (Perugia)

Montefalco Rosso or Rosso di Montefalco (108: 19.4.80); Montefalco Sagrantino or Sagrantino di Montefalco

MONTEFALCO ROSSO

A dry red wine made with Sangiovese (65–75%), Tuscan Trebbiano (15–20%) and Sagrantino (5–10%).

MONTEFALCO SAGRANTINO

This wine is made with passito (semi-dried) grapes to produce a 14%, slightly sweet and slightly sparkling wine. One year's ageing is required.

Producer
Fratelli Adanti (Perugia)
COVIP, Ponte Pattioli (Perugia)

Orvieto (219: 31.8.71)

The Trebbiano Toscano (50–60%), with the addition of some Verdello and Grechetto (20–30%), Drupeggio and Malvasia Toscana (up to 20%), produces a dry and an abboccato white wine with a minimum alcoholic content of 11·5%. If the grapes are harvested inside the original historic growing area, the wine may be labelled Classico.

Producers
L. e P. Antinori, Castello La Sala, Orvieto (Terni)
Luigi Bigi, Orvieto (Terni)
Cantina di Torriti, Civitella d'Agliano (Viterbo)
Cooperativa di Orvieto, Orvieto Stazione (Terni)
Achille Lemmi, Montegabbione (Terni)
Le Velette, Orvieto Canale (Terni)
Petrurbani, Orvieto (Terni)
COVIP, Ponte Pattioli (Perugia)
Bigi Winefood, Orvieto (Terni)

Torgiano (132: 25.5.68; 75: 16.3.73)

TORGIANO BIANCO (Tore di Giano)

This dry white wine is a Trebbiano Toscano (50–70%) blended with some Grechetto (15–35%) and Malvasia and Verdello (up to 15%), to reach a minimum alcoholic content of 11·5%.

TORGIANO ROSSO (Rubesco)

This dry red wine is a Sangiovese (50–70%) blended with some Canaiolo (15–30%) and Trebbiano Toscano (10%) and up to 10% of Ciliegiolo and Montepulciano, with an alcoholic content of 12%. If the wine is aged for three years, it may be labelled Riserva.

Producers
COVIP, Ponte Pattioli (Perugia)
Dott. Giorgio Lungarotti, Torgiano (Perugia)

Recommended non-DOC speciality wines from the Lungarotti–Torgiano Winery

San Giorgio
Chardonnay di Miraduolo
Cabernet Sauvignon di Miraduolo
Vin Santo
Falò, Vino Novello

19
Lazio (Latium)

THE ETRUSCAN HILLS

Lazio is one of the major wine-producing regions of Italy, though this is hard to believe. The only valid explanation is that a city of two million wine-drinkers can polish off a great deal of wine. There are exports of Fontana Candida, Marino and some Colli Albani, but I doubt that many others, except Enotria and Colli dei Cavalieri on the ex-Pontine Marshes, send anything appreciable across the regional boundaries. In fact, there are imports of wine from the south, from Sardinia and from the ex-Pontine Marshes that are blended to make non-DOC products. Though the wines, mostly whites, are not the most distinguished of Italy, they are unassuming, easy to drink with any type of cooking and nowadays are well made and will travel.

Starting from the north, we have two wines which seem to have an uncertain fate ahead of them. The Aleatico di Gradoli is a sweet red dessert wine made with *passito* grapes and comes also in a fortified version at 18 per cent. Dessert wines are having a hard time, nowadays, particularly those of the south: the habit of sipping velvety wines and nibbling a biscuit at mid-morning seems to have died – a civilized habit but it certainly requires a less rushed world than ours. The Est! Est! Est! is currently in the phase of adapting itself to the New Enology but not getting a very good press despite the fact that Antinori and Bigi have entered the lists.

Aleatico di Gradoli (217: 22.8.72)

A red dessert wine produced from the Aleatico grape with a minimum alcoholic content of 12%. A fortified version with a total alcoholic content of 17% is permitted.

Producers
Cantina Sociale di Gradoli, Gradoli (Viterbo)
Bigi, Orvieto (Terni)

Cerveteri (64: 7.3.75)

CERVETERI ROSSO

This dry red wine is made from a blend of Sangiovese and Montepulciano (exceeding 60%): Cesanese may contribute (to the extent of 25%) and other grapes such as Canaiolo Nero, Carignano and Barbera make up the balance. The alcohol content may not be less than 12%.

CERVETERI BIANCO

This dry white wine is made up of Trebbiano (at least 50%), to which may be added Malvasia di Candia or Lazio (35%); the balance is of Verdicchio, Tocai, Bellone and Bombino. The minimum alcoholic content is 11·5%.

Producer
Cantina Sociale di Cerveteri, Cerveteri (Roma)

Est! Est! Est! di Montefiascone (111: 7.5.66)

A dry white wine produced from the Trebbiano Toscano (65%) and the Malvasia Toscano (20%) and Rossetto (15%), with a minimum alcoholic content of 11%.

Producers
Bigi, Orvieto (Terni)
Cantina Cooperativa di Montefiascone (Viterbo)
Italo Mazziotti, Bolsena (Viterbo)
Marchesi Antinori (Florence)

ROME AND CASTELLI

Few realize that in the seventeenth century, when Rome was a small town, outside its walls, in what is now a part of the town itself, were vineyards. The Via Veneto, of *La Dolce Vita* fame, and the Parioli residential quarter were vineyards until 100 years ago. The last vine in central Rome is now in the service-entrance courtyard of the Grand Hotel. It is very old and very big and of a strain that is no longer even known. The hotel management and staff proudly make a few dozen bottles of wine from it every year. I suspect that one cannot stop Italians making wine by any means short of Islamic democracy.

The finest wines of Rome come from less than ten miles from the centre of town, just past Ciampino Airport. It is over ten years since I have tasted them but I am assured that they are still magnificent. Sadly, and probably inevitably, they are almost unobtainable. For the record, then, Prince Boncompagni Ludovisi makes two whites and a red: one white is straight Malvasia (malmsey) of Candia and the other a Sémillon, while the red is a Merlot-Cabernet. All are called Fiorano, just in case you come across a bottle. The whites are still treated with old-world courtesy and a little barrel-age, a compliment they return generously. The red, of course, is aged for over two years.

Another non-DOC wine that is little known, though its cheaper versions may be found in the supermarkets of the city, is that of Maccarese, a large agricultural estate that, like so many of Italy's enterprises, was taken over by the IRI (a state corporation for rescuing industries from bankruptcy by taking over ownership and management – a Fascist invention). It lies on the plains next to Rome's Fiumicino Airport, by the beach resort of Fregene. Particularly fine is the aged red San Giorgio made from Montepulciano and Merlot. It is aged in the wood for at least two years (though there is no rule) and can take more in the bottle. It is a state-subsidized wine, which gives it an added charm.

Fontana Candida, of course, has made an international reputation but the Marino Superiore is preferred by the Romans as it is more vinous: it is exported by Villa Banfi under the non-DOC label 'Roman Wine'.

As always, when there is a levelling spirit abroad, choosing the best becomes difficult: time is the best helper. Frascati wins out but Monteporzio-Catone, a few miles down the road, has also got itself head and shoulders above the others, which means that a lot of people have been voting with their cheque books. In 1974, I could only trace, with difficulty, a couple of wineries in those parts and they only sold wine in demi-johns. Among the producers, today, is the owner of one of Rome's best Enotecas, Piero Costantini.

The Castelli Romani have eight DOC zones, when one would be enough, given a little flexibility in the blending of the wines and the wording of the legislation. The difference between them, today, is not so much between one zone and another as between one winery and another; when one, for example, is still back in the 1960s with its processing methods and the other is up to date. The difference starts at around a million pounds sterling to fix up a winery with modern equipment and not everybody has that sort of money for investment.

Low-tech Castelli wine was great to drink sitting under a tree on a sunny day in Frascati, Grottaferrata or Castelgandolfo. Way back, they used to make it amabile which travelled and lasted a bit better, but when dry became the rule, the barrel wine could be relied on to play tricks, particularly in summer, when it needed sulphur tablets to stop it fermenting again, while the drinkers needed Alka-Seltzers. Nowadays, even the jug wine sold in demi-johns is stabilized and hot-bottled. You could load it on the space-shuttle and it would orbit the earth in perfect condition, I am sure. Some of Italy's best enologists (including Ezio Rivella) have given Castelli wines their full attention for many years and beaten its caprices, including 'noble rot' which, unlike in France and Germany, is considered a curse.

These whites go under the zonal names of Frascati, Colli Albani, Colli Lanuvini, Marino, Montecompatri-Colonna, Velletri, Zagarolo and Cori. They are all made up of Malvasias and Trebbianos and a few local varietals such as Bonvino, Greco and Bellone that are not permitted for more than a modest proportion. All these wines come from the hills up to twenty miles south-east of Rome. Among the more southerly is Velletri which brings the first red wine – a good one because one of its components is the Cesanese grape which, though little known, is most attractive and only needs the dedication and affection that have been given to other vines to cut a handsome figure. There is also, however, a little red wine produced on Frascati's little mountain, Rocca di Papa, which is not to be scorned.

Bianco Capena (292: 5.11.75)

A dry white wine made from a maximum of 55% of the three Malvasias (Candia, Lazio and Toscana) with Trebbiano (up to 25%) and 20% of local wines such as Bellone and Bombino (called 'Spanish grapes'). An alcoholic content of 11·5% is required; if 12%. the wine may be labelled Superiore.

Producer
Cantina Sociale di Feronia Capena, Capena (Roma)

Colli Albani (280: 5.11.70)

A Castelli Romani dry white wine made from the red or white Malvasia (60%), various Trebbiano strains (25–50%), Malvasia del Lazio (15–40%) and smaller quantities of Bonvino and Cacchione (15–40%). The minimum alcoholic content is 11·5%; an amabile version is also made.

Producer
Cantina Sociale Colli Albani, Cecchina (Roma)

Colli Lanuvini (182: 20.7.71)

A dry white Castelli Romani wine made from Malvasia di Candia (70%) and Trebbiano (30%) with an addition of Bellone and Bonvino (up to 10%). It has a minimum alcoholic content of 11·5%.

Producers
Cantina Sociale La Selva Viticoltori, Genzano (Roma)
Conte Raimondo Moncada, Genzano (Roma)

Cori (243: 25.9.71)

CORI BIANCO

This dry white wine is made from a blend of Malvasia di Candia (40–60%), Bellone (30%), Trebbiano Toscano (15–25%) and Trebbiano Giallo (5–10%). The wine is made in three versions – dry, amabile and sweet – but always with the same alcoholic content of 11%.

CORI ROSSO

The red wine is made of a blend of Montepulciano (40–60%), Nero Buono di Cori (20–40%) and Cesanese (10–30%) with an alcoholic content of 11·5%.

Producer
Giuseppe Palleschi, Cori (Roma)

Frascati (119: 16.5.66)

A dry, Castelli Romani white wine made from Malvasia Bianco. Malvasia del Lazio, Greco and Trebbiano Toscano blended as wines or fermented together. The minimum alcoholic content is 11·5%; if over 12%, the wine may be qualified as Superiore.

Producers
Cantina Produttori Frascati, Frascati (Roma)
Cantina Sociale di Marino, Frattochie (Roma)

De Sanctis, Frascati (Roma)
Fontana Candida, Frascati (Roma)
Valle Vermiglia, Frascati (Roma)
Santerelli, Frascati (Roma)
Anna Zambotti, Frascati (Roma)
Cantina Colli Catone, Monteporzio (Roma)
Villa Simone (Roma)
San Matteo (Roma)

Marino (279: 3.11.70)

A dry white Castelli Romani wine made from red or white Candia
Malvasias (60%), Tuscan Trebbiano (25–55%) and Malvasia del
Lazio (15–45%) and up to 10% Bonvino. It has minimum
alcoholic content of 11·5%.

Producers
Cantina Sociale di Marino, Frattocchie (Roma)
De Paolis, Lepanto, Frattocchie Marino (Roma)
Cantina Giancarlo Mastrofini, Finocchio (Roma)
Paola di Mauro, Marino (Roma)

Montecompatri Colonna (212: 17.8.73) or Montecompatri or Colonna

A dry white Castelli Romani wine made from Malvasia di Candia
(up to 70%) with the balance from Trebbiano (30%). Bellone and
Bonvino are permitted in small quantities. The minimum alcoholic
content is 11·5%; if above 12·5%, the wine may be labelled as
Superiore.

Producers
Silvano Lulli, Colonna (Roma)
Giuseppe Costanti, Colonna (Roma)

Velletri (190: 22.7.73)

VELLETRI BIANCO

This dry white Castelli wine is made from Malvasia di Candia
(70%) and Tuscan Trebbiano (30%) with small additions of

Bellone and Bonvino. It has a minimum alcoholic content of
11·5%.

VELLETRI ROSSO

The red wine is dry and a blend of Sangiovese (20–35%), Montepulciano (20–35%) and Cesanese (30%). It has a minimum alcohol
content of 11·5%.

Producers
Consorzio Produttori Vini, Via Oberdan, Velletri (Roma)
Cantina Sociale Colli Albani, Cecchina (Roma)

Zagarolo (215: 21.8.73)

This dry white wine is made from grapes of the Malvasia di Candia
(70%) and Trebbiano (30%) vines with small additions permitted
of Bellone and Bonvino. The minimum alcohol content is 11·5%
but with 12·5% the wine may be labelled Superiore.

Producers
Gregorio Lunati, Zagarolo (Roma)
Cantina Gabinia, Colle Pallavicino, Zagarolo (Roma)

SOUTH OF ROME

The Cesanese area comes further south towards Frosinone, from
the hills around the three mountain villages of Piglio, Affile and
Olevano Romano. Though there are three DOC disciplines, there
seems little basic difference except for their geographical position
and the fact that Olevano Romano is usually made as a velvety,
slightly sweet, full-bodied red, much loved in the proletarian wine
shops (which incidentally are getting rarer) of Rome in winter.

The most likely source of good, dry Cesanese, both young and
aged, is La Selva winery at Paliano (not to be confused with two
other La Selvas in central and north Italy). It has 100 or so hectares
of well-cared-for vineyards, a good processing plant and a good
eno-technician: he makes a DOC red and a La Selva non-DOC
blend. The latter is always the better.

In this text, I have tried to avoid writing about wines that are impossible to find on the market or are produced in quantities so small that you have to knock on the producer's door to beg a glassful. However, I have been asked to mention Torre Ercolana which comes from Anagni, that fabulous medieval papal city which nobody visits. The wine is made with Cesanese, some Cabernet and some Merlot. Connoisseurs insist that not only is it proof of the virtues of the Cesanese grape but a wine of international stature – but less than 3,000 bottles are made annually and I have not knocked on the door.

The last Lazio zone is that of Aprilia, a small town on the former Pontine Marshes. These were drained in Mussolini's day and homesteads were given to his veteran troops, chiefly from the Veneto. They built a flourishing agricultural economy there and, after the Second World War, the present republican government encouraged light industry.

However, the twist of fate that has brought the most wealth to this zone was the return of Italian wine-producers from North Africa. They, with their own methods, have made the one-time Pontine Marshes flourish as never before and produce immense quantities of wine. They are highly competent but not idealists like so many Italian wine-producers.

The area produces, according to the pruning methods and processing systems, both regular table wines and strong cutting wines. Nobody can deny that the former are of good quality though they do not reach the standards that they might – neither, on the other hand, do their prices. They suit the Roman supermarket clientèle to perfection and that is not to be discarded lightly; in fact, it is the essential part of the wine industry that Italy has never ignored and does not ignore now. As for the cutting wines, they vanish into northern mists, as do so many of those of the south, in tanker TIRS and tanker freighters, and nobody ever asks their destination.

There is one exception to this commercial ambience: a major amelioration project for the growing of vines and wine-processing is underway, supported chiefly by the Casale del Giglio (the use of their land *et al.*) and the Lazio Regional Government (the cash). Top agrarian experts and eno-technicians have been engaged to carry out practical experiments while the results are being published for all to read and copy. Casale del Giglio, particularly with its unusual pale pink Sangiovese, has got a long way ahead of the others in the quality field and young Tony Santarelli, who is taking over from his father, Dino, should have some interesting crops and vintages soon – perhaps he has them already – ageing in his cellars.

Cesanese di Affile, Cesanese di Piglio, Cesanese di Olevano Romano (225: 22.8.73; 216: 22.8.73; 221: 28.8.73)

This dry red wine is made, with slightly different results, in three different areas of southern Lazio. It is often made amabile and sometimes sparkling. It has a minimum alcoholic content of 12% in all cases.

Producers
Cantina Sociale di Piglio, Piglio (Frosinone)
Cantina Sociale Cesanese, Olevano (Roma)
Azienda La Selva, Paliano (Frosinone)
Tenuta Manfredi Berucci, Piglio (Frosinone)

Merlot di Aprilia, Trebbiano di Aprilia, Sangiovese di Aprilia (174: 16.7.66)

These wines are all single-grape varietals made with a minimum alcoholic content of 12%.

Producers
Cantina Sociale Tres Tabernae, Cisterna di Latina (Latina)
Cooperativa Enotria, Aprilia (Latina)
Colli dei Cavalieri, Campoverde (Latina)
Casale del Giglio, Le Ferriere (Latina)

A recommended non-DOC Cesanese-Cabernet-Merlot

TORRE ERCOLANA

Producer
Luigi Colacicchi (Frosinone)

20

The Abruzzi and Molise

THE ADRIATIC VALLEYS

As is the case in most of Italy, they have been making wine in the Abruzzi mountains since the Iron Age: not very good wine. The monks from Spanish Naples in the seventeenth century are said to have tidied up their vine-dressing (they used to drape their vines from one tree to another) and, by the nineteenth century they were selling strong cutting wine to the north. In the first half of this century, with improved processing and bottling, something of a reputation, which was not only local, was made. It has been the last twenty-five years – as in so many other cases – that have, with steel vats and New Enology, changed the picture. A great deal of modernizing and experimentation is now going on and this can only be to the good.

Of the Molise region, somebody said that it was 'an enological silence' where two new and obscure DOC zones have come into existence: Pentro and Biferno. I can, however, break that silence since I spent a couple of hours with two charming young producers in the Molise wine trade at the Verona Wine Fair.

We drank and talked about their wines, which were a sort of meeting place between north and south, as is the Molise region itself. They were both reds, rich, full-bodied, generous wines of the south with more than a touch of the elegance of a Chianti: their names were Serramacaglia of Pietracatella and Masseria Di Majo Novante of Campomarino. It is probably because they are partly made with the Sangiovese grape that they have that touch of Tuscan elegance.

Just as French vines have infiltrated into north and central Italy, the stalwart Sangioveses, Montepulcianos and even Trebbianos are extending their terrain to the south and to the islands as blenders; they produce well-structured wines in lands where the local grapes tend to be fragile as table wines and for ageing, despite their apparent robust nature.

Montepulciano d'Abruzzo (178: 15.7.68)

This dry red wine is produced from Montepulciano (85%) grapes with a balance of Sangiovese and a minimum alcoholic content of 12%. A Cerasuolo version of this wine is slightly rosé.

Producers
Consorzio Aprutino, Roseto degli Abruzzi (Teramo)
Consorzio Vini d'Abruzzo, Ortona (Chieti)
Azienda Pepe, Torano Nuovo (Teramo)
Cooperativa San Vitale, San Salvo (Chieti)
Casal Thaulero, Roseto degli Abruzzi (Teramo)
Camillo Valentini, Loreto Aprutino (Pescara)
De Prospero, Pratola Peligna (L'Aquila)
Vittorio Janni, L'Aquila (L'Aquila)
Dino Illuminati (L'Aquila)

Trebbiano d'Abruzzo (221: 25.8.72)

This dry white wine, made of Trebbiano (85%) and a balance of suitable local wines, has an alcoholic content of 11·5%.

Producers

Consorzio Aprutino, Roseto degli Abruzzi (Teramo)
Consorzio Vini d'Abruzzo, Ortona (Chieti)
Azienda Pepe, Torano Nuovo (Teramo)
Camillo Valentini, Loreto Aprutino (Pescara)
Casal Thaulero, Roseto degli Abruzzi (Chieti)
Edoardo Valentini, Loreto Aprutino (Pescara)
Vittorio Janni, L'Aquila (L'Aquila)

21

Campania

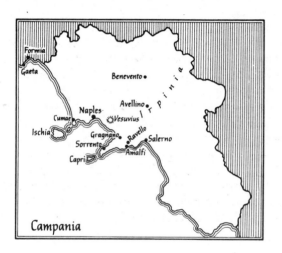

Campania

THE BAY OF NAPLES AND HINTERLAND

It would seem from the lack of English importers that there is a profound lack of confidence in Neapolitan wines; and, with the exception of a handful, this is fairly well justified. If one is to make a shortlist of Italian wines, here is a good place to start pruning back, although it could result in a certain injustice.

A shortlist, however, should include Antonio Mastroberardino of Atripalda whose formidable and unexpected Taurasi has earned itself a 'world-class' medal as a 'big' red wine. It comes from a lonely mountainous area behind Naples that is not at all southern – it has good agricultural land and forests; and it even rains, which is a rarity in the south. Yet the population has been draining away for a century. Better to be a shivering night watchman on a building site in Rome than work in the fields at home which have the discouraging and discomforting defect of being prone to earthquakes.

The Atripalda Taurasi wine is from the Aglianico vine. Another southern world-class wine, equally curious, is also an Aglianico (which means Greek) – Aglianico del Vulture ('Vulture' being an extinct volcano in Lucania, upon which it grows). Both of them are relics of an arcane past world that has continued to our day but risks extinction for extraneous economic reasons and, perhaps, earthquakes.

The other great wines of the Naples region are also from the same Mastroberardino – the Fiano di Avellino and the Greco di Tufo. Unlike the three years of ageing in the wood of the Taurasi, these whites are given a year to good effect, a rounding-out rather than an oxidation of dessert-wine dimensions.

The only other major wine from the Campania region is the Lacryma Christi which, though made from Vesuvius's grapes, is processed best by the same Mastroberardino. This frizzante wine comes rosé and white; in the long past, the pink version was considered the real thing. If only because it is part-and-parcel of the myth of Naples, one hopes that its good name will no longer be degraded by unprincipled *négociants* and that it will only improve, both in image and substance.

Capri (339: 14.12.77)

CAPRI BIANCO

This dry white wine is made with approximately half-and-half of Falanghina and Greco and has a minimum alcoholic content of 11·5%.

CAPRI ROSSO

A red wine made from Piedirosso (more than 80%) and the balance of other locally authorized wines. It has minimum alcoholic content of 11·5%.

Producer
Marchese Ettore Patrizi, Capri (Napoli)

Ischia (112: 9.5.66)

ISCHIA BIANCO

The white is made from the Forestera (65%) and Biancolella (20%) vines with a minimum alcoholic content of 11%. With selected grapes and a 12% content, the wine may be labelled Superiore.

ISCHIA ROSSO

A red made from Guarnaccia grapes (50%), Piedirosso (40%) and Barbera (10%). It has an alcoholic content of 11·5%.

Producers
D'Ambra, Panza di Ischia (Napoli)
Perazzo, Naples (Napoli)

Fiano di Avellino (241: 29.8.78)

A dry white wine produced from Fiano (85%) and from a blend of Greco, Coda di Volpe and Trebbiano Toscano for the remainder. It has a minimum alcoholic content of 11·5%. One year's ageing is customary but not obligatory.

Producer
Michele Mastroberardino, Atripaldi (Avellino)

Greco di Tufo (130: 25.5.70; 157: 9.6.79)

A dry white wine is produced from Greco (80–100%) grapes with Coda di Volpe (20%). It has a minimum alcoholic content of 11·5%. One year's ageing is customary but not obligatory.

Producer
Michele Mastroberardino, Atripalda (Avellino)

Solopaca (28: 30.1.74)

SOLOPACA BIANCO

A dry white wine made from Trebbiano Toscano (up to 70%), Malvasia di Candia (20–40%) and some Malvasia Toscano and Coda di Volpe. It has a minimum alcoholic content of 12%.

Producers
La Guardiense Cantina Sociale, Guardia Sanframondi
  (Benevento)
La Vinicola Ocone Ponte (Benevento)

Taurasi (129: 25.5.70)

A dry red wine chiefly made from the Aglianico vine (70%) with a maximum (30%) blend of Piedirosso, Sangiovese and Barbera, and a minimum alcoholic content of 12%. All Taurasi wines must be aged for three years, of which at least one must be in the wood; if aged for four years, the wine may be labelled Riserva.

Producers
Michele Mastroberardino, Atripalda (Avellino)
Scuola Enologico di Avellino, Avellino (Avellino)

Recommended non-DOC Lacryma Christi

Producer
Antonio Mastroberardino (Avellino)

22

Basilicata (Lucania)

Here we find the other 'Greek' wine, the Aglianico del Vulture, mentioned in the Campania section (Chapter 21, p. 209). The Basilicata (or Lucania, as it is often called), where the wine is produced, is among the most forgotten and abandoned stretches of Italy; even the volcano on the slopes of which the vines grow is extinct.

Throughout history, the region has been a colony of Puglia. During the period of the late Roman Empire, it was overrun by Greek Basilian monks whose astonishing convents, cut out, in trogloditic spirit, of the living rock and painted and frescoed, are still being discovered in the most improbable places in the abandoned countryside. Perhaps they brought the Aglianico Greek vines with them.

This Aglianico presents a wine, especially when aged for five years to become a Riserva, subtly yet profoundly different from the claret–Barolo–Chianti world. It speaks Italian with a foreign accent after 1,500 years of residence and therein lies a lot of its charm. Rather like the Greek philosophers who came to this land, called Magna Graecia, they would never have flourished and reached their paramount wisdom had they not been transferred to Italy.

The Lucanians are slowly awakening: they are discovering that the vine grows well also down by the sea at Metaponto. We must remember to check this out occasionally to see how they are getting on; perhaps we shall not have to wait a millennium. The last word from those lonely parts was that they had struck a huge crude-oil deposit.

Aglianico del Vulture (129: 22.5.71)

The dry red wine is made from grapes of the Aglianico vines. Normally, it must provide an alcoholic content of 11·5%; if with 12·5% and aged for three years, two of which are in the wood, it may be labelled Vecchio. If it has five years' ageing, it may be called Riserva.

Producers
Azienda Agricola Vini del Vulture (Winefood), Venosa (Potenza)
Centrale Cooperativa Riforma Fondiaria Puglia, Lucania, Molise;
    Centrale di Rionero, Rionero (Potenza)
D'Angelo di Donato, Rionero (Potenza)
Ente Sviluppo, Enopoli di Rionero, Maschito e Acerenza
    (Potenza)
Paternoster, Barile (Potenza)
Premiovini, Brescia (Brescia)
Miali, Martina Franca (Taranto)
Torre Sveva, Barletta (Bari)

23
Puglia

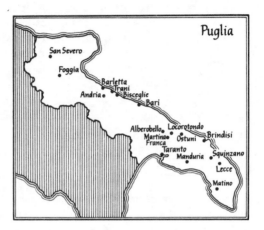

The flood of wine – about a billion litres – that Puglia can and usually does produce annually is formidable. It is, for the most part, wine of good quality. There are many wineries, both private and co-operatives, with long-standing reputations for their bottled table wines. Most of the wine used for the making of vermouth and other wine-based apéritifs is from Puglia. Quantities of inexpensive wine are bottled in flagons and demi-johns and still there is a surplus, after even vaster quantities of cutting wines have been despatched by ship and tanker-TIR to the north – some 100 million litres that is destined to end its days at cost price as industrial alcohol; which, incidentally, nobody knows what to do with.

The new situation in Puglia is complex and evolving. Puglia is no longer struggling to make a living and like the rest of Italy has little difficulty in raising investment capital. Puglia, therefore, has got its New Enology high-tech equipment.

The region divides, roughly, into two different sectors: the Heel of Italy, part of the body of Italy, which is hilly; and the Salento Peninsula, which is not. The table wines of the former have been moved out of the plains to the hills to gain a lighter touch, while those of the Salento stay and broil on the plains where the great high-sugar cutting and dessert wines come from. Their mitigation from the heat of the long summer is in slow, cold fermentation and refrigerated storage vats. This has made these former cutting wines into giants that have shaved off their beards, had a haircut, and put on a business suit. I have drunk a Primitivo of Manduria of 20 per cent alcoholic content, which is theoretically impossible for an unfortified wine – a thought-provoking experience. Such wines may be too strong as table wines but, by God, they would be good if you were snowed in for the winter. For the record, these emasculated cutting wines go under the names of Pampanuto, Primativo (or Primitivo), Bombino, Troia, Negroamaro (or Negramaro), Verdeco; whilst Barbera, Montepulciano and Sangiovese, when grown in the deep south, become cutting wines.

Already, names such as San Severo (from D'Alfonso del Sordo), Castel del Monte (from Rivera De Corato) and Torre Quarto (from Farrusi of Cerignola) are a part of Italian eno-gastronomy and, as such, nobody who knows his way around Italian wines would spurn any of them: they are wines redolent of the south even if their defects have been removed by advanced technology.

An aged Torre Quarto in particular is a fine dinner wine, that I would feel confident of serving to the most critical of guests, sure they would not fault me. The Rivera rosés are something on their own: they are apéritifs that blend with all sorts of light food, from lobsters to strawberries and cream. They are dry, velvety, round and a fabulous pink: good wines for a buffet supper.

In all, there is much pleasure to be had from the quality table wines of Puglia and their sales and reputations are spreading considerably. The Torre Quarto, I should have mentioned, is unusual in that its only component is the French vine, the Malbec, which plays a small part in the make-up of claret.

The Torre Quarto is not a band-wagon novelty, but has existed as long as I can recall. However, Gancia's entry on the scene as an experimenter in French vines in Puglia is new. Basing themselves on the theory that the Puglia climate is 'Californian', they are planting out Sauvignon, Pinot Bianco, Riesling and Chenin Blanc to see what happens.

The Salento wines are big, full-bodied and something to remember. The dessert wines are a symbol of the deep Italian south. Just as the ladies of the south do not go out when it rains, they do not drink vodka martinis in singles bars, but stay at home and sip dessert wines – or, at least, they used to. The Moscatos of Trani (by Gennaro Marasciulo and Picardi of Trani) are well known in this discreet tippling field, as are the masterpieces of Leone de Castris.

Of the new DOC wines that are made from cutting wines, it is still too early to see which one is going to get head and shoulders over the others. Copertino is a good wine and might well win, especially as it is made in the little town where their patron saint, St Joseph, used to fly around the ceiling of the parish church;* perhaps after drinking a bottle we might all do so.

Recently, draught frizzante wine has been observed in a few bars in Italy: it is stowed under pressure, like beer, in what would appear to be five-gallon metal kegs. That tasted by this writer was not memorable, though the idea of bringing wine in an economic dress to new customers is not one to discard lightly.

THE HEEL OF ITALY

Aleatico di Puglia (214: 20.8.73)

This sweet dessert wine is produced in two versions, natural sweet and fortified. It is made from Aleatico (85%) grapes with the balance made from Negro Amaro, Malvasia Nera and Primitivo. As a sweet red wine, it has a minimum total alcoholic content of 15% and, as a fortified wine, 18·5%. If aged for three years, the wines may be called Riserva.

Producer
Centrale Cantina Riforma, Cantina di Corato (Bari)

* See *Old Calabria* by Norman Douglas.

Cacc'e Mmitte di Lucera (82: 29.3.76)

This dry red wine is a composite, including Troia (35–60%), Montepulciano, Sangiovese and Malvasia Nera di Brindisi (up to 35%) and a balance of Trebbiano Toscano, Bombino Bianco and Malvasia del Chianti. It has a minimum alcoholic content of 11·5%.

Producer
Cantina Cooperativa Riforma Fondiaria, Lucera (Foggia)

Brindisi (111: 23.4.80)

Both a dry red and a dry rosé are made under this discipline with Negro Amaro grapes (70%) and with Montepulciano and Sangiovese for the remaining 30%.

Producer
Cantina Messapia di Zanarelli, Brindisi (Brindisi)

Castel del Monte (188: 26.7.71)

CASTEL DEL MONTE BIANCO

A dry white wine made with Pampanuto grapes with additions of Trebbiano Giallo and Toscano, Bombino Bianco and Palumbo (up to 35%). It has a minimum alcoholic content of 11·5%.

CASTEL DEL MONTE ROSSO/ROSÉ

The red and rosé are made with Uva di Troia and an addition (up to 35%) of Bombino Nero, Montepulciano and Sangiovese is permitted if needed. The red has a minimum alcoholic content of 12% and the rosé of 11·5%. If the red has three years' ageing in the wood, it may be labelled Riserva.

Producers
Rivera de Corato, Andria (Bari)
Fattoria Torricciola, Andria (Bari)
Riforma Fondiaria, Andria (Bari)
Vini Chiddo, Bitonto (Bari)

Locorotondo (211: 19.8.69)

The Locorotondo dry white wine is made with the Verdeca (50–60%) and d'Alessano (35–50%) grapes with a minimum alcoholic content of 11%.

Producers
Cantina Sociale di Locorotondo, Locorotondo (Bari)
Leone de Castris, Salice Salentino (Lecce)
Rivera, Andria (Bari)
Riforma Fondiaria, Andria (Bari)

Martina or Martina Franca (211: 19.8.69)

The dry white wine is produced from the Verdeca (50–65%) and Bianco d'Alessano (35–50%) grapes, with a minimum alcoholic content of 11%.

Producers
Centrale Cantina Cooperativa di Puglia, Lucania, Molise, Bari (Bari)
Vinicola Miali, Martina Franca (Taranto)
Riforma Fondiaria, Andria (Bari)

Moscato di Trani (63: 6.3.73)

A sweet white dessert wine produced from the Moscato di Trani (or Moscato Reale) vine with a total alcohol content of 15%, of which 2% is a sugar residue. A fortified version is permitted at 18%, with the same 2% sugar residue.

Producers
Gennaro Marasciulo, Trani (Bari)
Nuovo Vinicola Picardi, Barletta (Bari)

Ostuni (83: 28.1.72)

OSTUNI BIANCO

The dry white Ostuni is made from the Impigno (50–85%) and Francavilla (15–50%) grapes and Bianco d'Alessano and Verdeca if required (to 10%). It has a minimum alcoholic content of 11%.

OSTUNI OTTAVIANELLO ROSSO

This dry red Ostuni is made from grapes of the same name with some Negro Amaro (15%); it has an alcoholic content of 11·5%.

Producer
Cantina Sociale di Ostuni, Ostuni (Brindisi)

Rosso Barletta (278: 12.10.77)

A dry red wine made from the Troia vine. The minimum alcoholic content is 12%; if aged for two years, the wine may be labelled Invecchiato (aged).

Producers
Fattoria Torricciola, Barletta (Bari)
Cantina Sociale di Barletta, Barletta (Bari)

Rosso Canosa (198: 20.7.79)

A dry red wine made from Canosa-Troia (65%) and Montepulciano (35%) grapes. The minimum alcohol content is 12%. With three years' ageing, of which two are in the wood, the wine may be labelled Riserva.

Producer
Cantina Sociale Nicola Rossi, Canosa di Puglia, Bari (Bari)

Rosso di Cerignola (285: 31.10.74)

This dry red wine comes from grapes of the Troia vine (55%) and the Negro Amaro (15–30%), with optional contributions of Sangiovese, Barbera, Montepulciano, Malbec and Trebbiano Toscano (up to 15%). The minimum alcoholic content is 12%. If the wine is aged for two years in the wood and has a 13% alcohol content, it may be qualified as Riserva.

Producers
Cirillo Farrusi, Cerignola (Bari)
Avello, Cerignola (Bari)
Italvini, Cerignola (Bari)

San Severo (138: 1.6.68)

SAN SEVERO BIANCO

A dry white made from the Bombino Bianco and Trebbiano Toscano; it has a minimum alcoholic content of 11%.

SAN SEVERO ROSSO/ROSÉ

The dry red and rosé are both made from Montepulciano d'Abruzzo and Sangiovese with an alcoholic content of 11·5%.

Producers
D'Alfonso del Sordo, San Severo (Foggia)
Cirillo Farrusi, Cerignola (Foggia)
Riforma Fondiaria, Andria (Bari)

THE SALENTO DEEP SOUTH

Copertino (27: 29.1.77)

This wine comes in two versions: red and rosé. Both are made from Negro Amaro grapes alone with a minimum alcoholic content of 12%. If the red wine is aged for two years and has 12·5% alcohol, it may be labelled Riserva.

Producers
Barone Fabio Bacile di Castiglione, Copertino (Lecce)
Cantina Sociale di Copertino, Copertino (Lecce)

Leverano (41: 12.2.80)

LEVERANO BIANCO

A dry white wine made with white Bombino and Trebbiano Toscano; it has a minimum alcoholic content of 11%.

LEVERANO ROSSO/ROSÉ

Both the red and the rosé are made with Negro Amaro (90%) and Malvasia Bianco (10%): the red, however, has a minimum alcoholic content of 12% and the rosé 11·5%.

Producer
Cantina Sociale di Leverano, Leverano (Lecce)

Matino (187: 24.7.71)

MATINO ROSSO/ROSÉ

Both these wines are from the Negro Amaro vine but may be blended with some Malvasia Nero and Sangiovese if required. Both versions have an alcoholic content of 11·5%.

Producers
Leone de Castris, Salento (Lecce)
Cooperativa A.M., Matino (Lecce)

Primitivo di Manduria (60: 4.3.75)

This is a red dessert wine produced in three versions: natural sweet, fortified sweet and fortified dry at 16, 17·5 and 18% total alcoholic content, of which, respectively, 3%, 2·5% and 1·5% of sugar residue is left.

Producers
Cantina Sociale di Lizzano, Lizzano (Taranto)
Giovanni Soloperto, Manduria (Taranto)

Salice Salentino (224: 25.8.76)

SALICE SALENTINO ROSSO/ROSÉ

Both of these wines are made from Negro Amaro grapes; permitted additions to this wine are Malvasia Nera di Brindisi and Malvasia Nera di Lecce (to the extent of 20%). The minimum alcoholic content is 12·5%. Both the red and the rosé may be aged: in the case of red, it may be called Riserva after two years' ageing, of which one must be in the wood. The rosé, after one year, may be called Prodotto Invecchiato (aged product).

Producers
Leone de Castris, Salice Salentino (Lecce)
Gennaro Marasciulo di Trani (Lecce)
Picardi di Trani (Lecce)

Squinzano (230: 31.8.76)

SQUINZANO ROSSO/ROSÉ

Both of these wines are made with the Negro Amaro grape (up to 85%) and with the Malvasia Nera (up to 15%). Both have the same alcoholic content of 12·5%; but the red, if aged for two years, of which six months is in the wood, and with more than 13% of alcohol, may be qualified as Riserva.

Producer
Renna, Squinzano (Lecce)

Non-DOC draught frizzante wine

Producer
Lupini (Palagiano, Taranto)

Recommended non-DOC Salento Rosé

ROSATO DEL SALENTO

Producer
Giuseppe Calò (Lecce)

24
Calabria

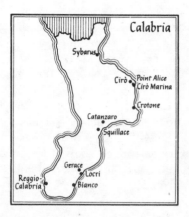

Like the Aglianico and the Taurasi, the Cirò is a wine of Greek origin from ancient times. The production is fairly large and reaches its apex in the classic zone and with its three-year-old Riservas. The town of Cirò is on the instep of Italy at the widening of the Gulf of Taranto into the Ionian Sea. This is, of course, the land of Greek and Bacchic myth where one finds the excavated ruins of Sybarus, the Greek city which lived it up so well that it earned itself a place as an adjective in the English language (sybaritic) for its luxury.

A little further down the coast – under Italy's big toe, so to speak – there is the town of Bianco which would probably have passed unnoticed by most travellers to those parts, were it not for its two remarkable wines, the Greco di Gerace (or Greco di Bianco, as it is called as a DOC wine) and the Mantonico, both whites. The former is a dessert wine, sweet when young, that quickly becomes dry with ageing, with an alcohol content of 16–18 per cent. It is very well made by Umberto Ceratti. It is expensive because each vine only yields one bottle of golden wine from the sun-baked soil – but what a bottle! The other, the Mantonico, equally amber-coloured and with an intense bouquet, requires a little ageing but not too much, for oxidation reasons. They are not party or gossip-group wines but rather something special to be shared with one other person in moments of supreme tranquillity, – seduction wines, perhaps, now one comes to think about it.

Wine production in the hills of Calabria was tidied up and extended by the Ente Sila, a para-governmental corporation capitalized for the purpose of developing the agriculture and animal husbandry in all the mountainous hinterland. The wines, due in part to the fact that they are grown at 2,000 feet above sea-level, are not cheap and, since they are not widely known, do not find an easy market.

Most impressive to me is the bright rosé Pellaro – a wine with a hint of abboccato, considerable body and a big bouquet. The Enotria white (non-DOC) seems redolent of sea-breezes and mountain pines and is very pleasing. Also to be given some, but perhaps not too much, attention are the Savuto and Pollino reds, the Donnici, the Melissa Cirò and the Sant'Anna, all dry table wines from the highlands.

This little Switzerland in the heart of the Mediterranean has only in the last three decades been opened up with roads and a few hotels. It will probably be some years before any of the new DOC disciplines produces a world-class wine, but Cirò Classico, if well worked on, might. I think Mr Ceratti does not fuss about such things and, in any event, he does not make enough wine to worry the Gallo Brothers of California.

Cirò (139: 4.6.69)

CIRÒ BIANCO

This dry white wine is made from Greco Bianco with Trebbiano Toscano (up to 10%) for a minimum alcoholic content of 12%.

CIRÒ ROSSO/ROSÉ

These are both produced by grapes from the Gaglioppo (95%) vine, with Trebbiano Toscano and Greco Bianco (up to 5%). They have a minimum alcoholic content of 13·5%. If with a minimum of 13·5%, and aged for three years, the wines may be labelled Riserva. There is a long-established limited zone around the town of Cirò from which wines produced in it may be designated Classico.

Producers
Caparra e Siciliani, Cirò Marina (Catanzaro)
Cirovin, Cirò Marina (Catanzaro)
Vincenzo Ippolito, Cirò Marina (Catanzaro)
Cantina Sociale Torre Melissa, Torre Melissa (Catanzaro)
Librandi (Catanzaro)
Fratelli Caruso (Catanzaro)

Donnici (225: 25.8.75)

DONNICI ROSSO/ROSÉ

These wines must both be made up of 50% Gaglioppo (locally called Mantonico Nero), Greco Nero (10–20%) and not less than 20% of Malvasia Bianco, Mantonico Bianco and Pecorello, either singly or together. The minimum alcoholic content is 12%.

Producers
Cantina Sociale Donnici, Piane Crati (Catanzaro)
Azienda Pasquale Bozzo, Donnici Inferiore (Catanzaro)

Greco di Bianco (252: 12.12.80)

Processed as a table wine, the Greco is required to have a minimum alcoholic content of 13%. However, it is customarily made with semi-dried grapes to make a sweet Passito dessert wine with a total alcohol content of 17%, of which 14% is converted. Also called Greco di Gerace.

Producers
CACIB Cooperative, Bianco (Reggio Calabria)
Umberto Ceratti, Caraffa del Bianco (Reggio Calabria)

Lamezia (96: 5.4.79)

This dry red wine comes from the Nerello grape (30–50%), the Gaglioppo (25–30%) and the Greco Nero (25–35%); it has a minimum alcoholic content of 12%.

Producer
Cantina Sociale Torre Melissa, Torre Melissa (Catanzaro)

Melissa (326: 28.11.79)

MELISSA BIANCO

This dry wine comes from the Trebbiano Toscano and Malvasia Bianco with a minimum alcoholic content of 11·5%.

MELISSA ROSSO

The dry red is made from Gaglioppo grapes with a small contribution of Greco Nero, Trebbiano Toscano *et al*, with a minimum alcoholic content of 11·5%; if 12·5%, the wine may be labelled Superiore.

Producers
Cantina Sociale di Melissa, Torre Melissa (Catanzaro)
Cantina Sociale di Neto, Scandale (Catanzaro)

Pollino (291: 3.11.75)

A dry red wine produced from not less than 60% of Gaglioppo (locally called Arvino or Lacrima) and at least 20% of Greco Nero, Malvasia Bianco (locally called Verdana and Iuvarella); Mantonico Bianco and Guarnaccia Bianca either singly or together should not exceed 20%. Normally, the wine should have a 12% alcoholic content; if 12·5%, and with two years' ageing, it may be labelled Superiore.

Producer
Cantina Sociale Vini del Pollino, Castrovillari (Cosenza)

Sant'Anna di Isola Capo Rizzuto (158: 11.6.79)

A dry red wine made chiefly from the Gaglioppo vine, but with some Nerello and Nocera. It has a minimum alcoholic content of 12%.

Producer
Cantina Sociale di Sant'Anna, Isola Capo Rizzuto (Catanzaro)

Savuto (291: 3.11.75)

SAVUTO ROSSO/ROSÉ

Both the dry red and the dry rosé of this DOC category are made with the same composition: 35–40% Gaglioppo (locally called Magliocco and Arvino) plus 35–45% of Greco Nero, Nerello, Cappuccio, Magliocco Canino and Sangiovese; however, there must not be more than 10% of Sangiovese. Malvasia Bianca may be added with Pecorino, either singly or together, up to a maximum of 25%. The minimum alcoholic content is 12%, but if 12·5% and with two years' ageing, the wine may be labelled Superiore.

Producer
G. B. Longo Azienda Vitivinicola, Marina di Cleto (Cosenza)

Recommended non-DOC whites wines

Producers
Umberto Ceratti (Reggio Calabria)
Mantonico

25
Sicily

The history of Sicily begins when the Greeks and the Phoenicians finally went to war for the ownership of this highly delectable island, but neither won. The Romans, by then, having conquered all of south Italy, decided that they could make good use of Sicily's corn and wine. Many centuries later, when the Roman Empire fell, Sicily was occupied by just about every possible band of adventurers and self-anointed kings – Byzantines, Moslems, Normans, Hohenstaufens, Swabians, Angevins, Spaniards, Bourbons, the French again (this time under Napoleon), the Bourbons for a second round, Garibaldi and then the Piedmontese. The Sicilians found themselves briefly, towards the end of the Second World War, with nobody telling them what to do. They nearly succeeded in seceding from Italy to make themselves an independent State, but finally opted for autonomy within the Italian Republic. Such a catalytic outburst of new energy, however, had its effect in arousing this land of antique civilization to come to terms with the present.

Sicily is pejoratively called 'the inexhaustible Cellar of Europe'. It has 180 co-operatives, most of which are in the province of

Trapani, on the west coast, which is the part of Sicily that was occupied by the Phoenicians. There is also, today, an astonishing grand total of 650 different wines of all types bottled and labelled in Sicily. The best known are the various Marsalas, the Corvo di Salaparuta wines, the Regalealis and the Etna wines of Barone Villagrande. Less known are those of the d'Angelo winery of Alcamo, the Di Giuseppe of Partinico, the Diego Rallo of Marsala (also a producer of good table wines), Faustus of Casteldaccia and Florio, producer of Marsala and brandy: there is a list of some thirty producers at the end of this chapter whose wines are worthy of investigation.

On the subject of Marsala, it can be said that it represents, along with madeira, port and sherry, nineteenth-century imperial Britain's sally into the wine-producing field. The sun may never have set on the Empire, but England itself remained a very chilly place where a glass of rich, warm and strong wine, elegantly fortified with wine-alcohol and processed with concentrated must and cooked wine, then aged in a complex but basically economical way – the solera system – was most welcome at any hour of the day or night. All four wines are full-bodied, hot-climate wines and made from grapes that have completely matured in a broiling sun. The addition of wine-alcohol guaranteed the stability of the wine, ensuring that it would arrive in the London docks or in any part of the far-flung Empire in prime condition. This was very important in a period of history when enology had not overcome stability problems, particularly those which involved taking casks of wine in sailing ships across the Equator and around the Cape of Good Hope.

In the more recent past, Marsala was labelled not only as Superiore Riserva (four years in the wood), Vergine (five years in the wood) and Soleras Stravecchio (ten years in the wood) but these top categories were (and are still) amber coloured and dry without the concentrated and cooked cutting wines permitted for the lower-quality types which include Fine and Superiore. To confuse the Marsala parade of wines even further, there used to be – one hopes they no longer exist – a variety of fancy labels such as 'Italia' and 'Inghilterra' and letters such as SOM, OP, PG, COM, and GD, which respectively meant: Superior Old Marsala, Old Pale, Particularly Genuine, Choice Old Marsala and Garibaldi Dolce. The less said about strawberry- and banana-flavoured Marsala the better;

though it must be admitted that, with today's fruit-flavoured wines, they were on to something before everybody else. However, it was this tomfoolery that got Marsala its bad name and only today is it recovering some of its lost honour.

Over the years, the ownership of Marsala left British hands and the tradition was continued by Sicilian growers and shippers. Today, one might say that Giovanni Agnelli, the chairman of the FIAT motor company, has taken the place of Messrs Woodhouse, Whitaker and Ingham through the Florio Marsala company, a subsidiary of the Cinzano Vermouth company which, in turn, is a subsidiary of FIAT.

Marsala is again becoming more popular as an apéritif and as a post-prandial drink, and it is certainly much better made today than when Lord Nelson used to buy it for his fleet in the nineteenth century. It comes dry, sweet, long-aged and less-aged. Superiore can be used in the kitchen for flavouring a whole range of dishes from veal cutlets to the famous zabaglione, the egg-yolk-based pick-me-up which can be taken straight or used in pastry-making as a *recherché* filling. The same ingredients – Marsala, sugar and raw egg yolks, plus a little wine-alcohol for fortification – are used to make Marsala *all'uovo*: this wine is the staff-of-life of Italy's street-walkers on cold nights.

The Zibibbo grape, no matter who vinifies or bottles it, makes, in my very personal opinion, a most cheerful and delicious drink: it is the basis of the Tanit dessert wine of Pantelleria Island which is gaining some ground and distinction. It is most suitable for breaking the ice at the more stuffy of receptions, the only risk being that the guests might break into a Tarantella. If a Corvo Brut Spumante, a sparkler of great qualities, were also served, the risk might turn into certainty.

Sicily has opened up a Bacchic dream of abundance based on modern technology that has no limits. But it has not succeeded on a world-class level. The closest is, perhaps, Conte Tasca's Rosso del Conte Riserva, which comes from the Regaleali estate that lies 1,500 feet up in the central hills. This was one of the first wineries that Rivella, as a young enologist, re-designed.

The Corvo Salaparuta wines are excellent and the white was created by the Duchess Topazia Alliata Salaparuta, another lady to add to the roll-call of female wine-makers. The Rapitalà white has made a lively reputation for itself in a remarkably short time: perhaps this will become a banner for Sicilian wines.

For the rest, we have the reds that come from nearly 3,000 feet up Mount Etna. I recommend the reader to go to Baron Villagrande's winery and look at the cellars. The enormous black barrels (never have I seen such big ones) surely were never transported there; they must have been assembled in the cellars. The villa and the garden of the winery have a vast and fabulous panoramic view over a hundred miles of coastline and blue Mediterranean Sea.

This leaves us with Carlo Hauner's excellent Lipari malmsey and Conte de Bartoli's Vecchio Samperi Marsala: this latter is a straight, ten-year-aged, non-DOC, very strong wine without the traditional additives. Conte de Bartoli has a unique and noble calling; may he succeed in persuading the world that Vecchio Samperi is the tops. It is certainly a great wine, lovingly made.

However, all this new wine that has been created should not be spurned simply because most of it has never been *barrique*-aged, or gained a world-class label. The reds especially are great drinking wines (I hate the word 'quaffing' – I, categorically, do not quaff wine), rather than sipping wines. There is a shortlist of recommended producers (mostly co-operatives) and their best product at the end of this chapter.

Etna (244: 25.9.68)

ETNA BIANCO

The Etna dry white wine comes from the Carricante and Catarratto vines with a contribution of locally approved grapes (15%): it has a minimum alcoholic content of 12%.

ETNA ROSSO/ROSÉ

The red and the rosé are both from the Nerello Mascalese vine with an addition of some Mantellato and approved, neutral white grapes (up to 10%). Both are required to have a minimum alcoholic content of 12·5%.

Producers
Cantina Sociale Le Vigne dell'Etna, Linguaglossa (Cantina)
Etnea Vini, Catania (Catania)
Barone Nicolosi di Villagrande, Milo (Catania)
SALVINA, Sant'Agata Li Battiati (Catania)

Faro (61: 4.3.77)

A dry red wine produced from the following vines: Nerello Mascalese (45–60%), Nocera (5–10%), Nerello Cappuccio (15–30%) and, permitted also, Calabrese (locally called Nero d'Avola), Gaglioppo (Mantonico Nero) and Sangiovese (up to 15%). It has a minimum alcoholic content of 12%.

Producer
Spinasanta, Messina (Messina)

Malvasia delle Lipari (28: 30.1.74)

A sweet dessert wine produced from the grapes of the Malvasia delle Lipari vine with Corinto Nero (5–8%).

LIPARI MALVASIA SWEET

An alcoholic content of 11·5%, of which 8% is converted.

LIPARI MALVASIA PASSITO

An alcoholic content of 18%, of which 12% is converted into alcohol, 6% remaining as sugar.

LIPARI MALVASIA LIQUOROSO

An alcoholic content of 20%, of which 4% is sugar residue.

Producers
Cantina Sperimentale di Milazzo, Milazzo (Messina)
Salaparuta-Corvo, Casteldaccia, Palermo (Palermo)
Sciascia, Marsala (Trapani)
Carlo Hauner, Lipari (Messina)

Marsala (143: 10.6.69)

This dessert wine is produced from the Catarratto, Grillo and Inzolia vines, yielding white grapes at not more than 100 quintals per hectare. This is a fortified wine with a complex process of vinification and ageing. Its colour varies from amber to tawny, and its alcoholic content is never less than 17%. The Marsala tends to greater dryness with greater ageing.

Producers
Di Giuseppe, Partinico (Trapani)
Florio, Marsala (Trapani)
Diego Ralli e Figli, Marsala (Trapani)
Carlo Pellegrino, Marsala (Trapani)
Scia-Scia, Marsala (Trapani)
Vito Curatolo Arini, Marsala (Trapani)

Moscato di Noto (199: 30.7.74)

A sweet amber-coloured dessert wine produced from the Moscato Bianco grape; it has an alcoholic content of 8% and 3·5% of sugar residue. The fortified version has 16% alcohol and 6% sugar residue. A spumante version is also permitted that is also very sweet, with 5% sugar and 8% alcohol.

Producer
Cantina Sperimentale, Noto (Ragusa)

Moscato di Pantelleria and Passito di Pantelleria (239: 22.9.71)

Pantelleria comes in five versions. All are based on an amber-coloured sweet wine made from the Zibibbo grape.

PANTELLERIA MOSCATO

A dessert wine with a total alcoholic content of 12·5% of which 4·5% remains in sugar form and is not converted into alcohol, i.e., the alcoholic content is 8%.

PANTELLERIA PASSITO

A dessert wine, made with semi-dried grapes, it has an alcoholic content of 14% and 3·5% sugar residue.

PANTELLERIA LIQUOROSO

The fortified version has a total alcoholic content of 21·5%, of which at least 15% is converted into alcohol (leaving 6·5% as sugar residue).

PANTELLERIA LIQUOROSO EXTRA

A fortified wine with a total alcoholic content of at least 23·9%, of which at least 15·5% is converted into alcohol, the balance remaining as sugar residue.

PANTELLERIA SPUMANTE

A sweet sparkling wine is also permitted under this DOC discipline.

Producers
Cossyra Maccotta, Marsala (Trapani)
Carlo Pellegrino, Marsala (Trapani)
Diego Rallo, Marsala (Trapani)
Agricoltori Associati di Pantelleria (Trapani)

Moscato di Siracusa (315: 6.12.73)

A sweet amber-coloured dessert wine from the Moscato grape with a minimum alcoholic content of 16·5%, of which 14% must be converted into alcohol, leaving a 2·5 sugar residue.

Producer
Giovanni Bonvicino Aretusa, Syracuse (Siracusa)

Alcamo (249: 22.9.72)

This dry white wine is produced from the Catarratto Bianco with a permissible addition of Damaschino, Grecanico and Trebbiano Toscano (20%); it has a minimum alcoholic content of 11·5%.

Producers
Aurora Cooperativa, Salemi (Trapani)
Corsorzio Produttori, Alcamo (Trapani)
Conte de la Gatinais, Alcamo (Trapani) – 'Rapitalà'

Cerasuola di Vittoria (221: 28.8.73)

This amber-coloured dessert wine, produced from the Frappato (40%) and Calabrese (60%) grapes, with the addition of Grosso Nero and Nerello Mascalese if required, offers a minimum alcoholic content of 16%. The wine is noted for its long ageing, sometimes being bottled after thirty years in the wood.

Producers
Giuseppe Coria, Villa Fontane, Vittoria (Ragusa)
Buccellato, Vittoria (Ragusa)

Some recommended non-DOC wines from Salaparuta Corvo (Palermo)

Colomba Platino white
Spumante Brut
Stravecchia di Sicilia
Bianco Vino Fiore

Some recommended non-DOC wines from Conte Tasca d'Almerita (Palermo) Regaleali

Rosso del Conte Riserva
Bianco Sauvignon

Some recommended Sicilian wines

Aurora Cooperative, Salemi CASTELVECCHIO
Cantina Sperimentale di Milazzo, Milazzo MAMERTINO
Consorzio Produttori Bianco Alcamo, Alcamo MEDORO
Cantina Sociale Enocarboj, Sciacca CARBOJ
Cantina Sociale Europa, Marzara del Vallo CRECANICO
Cantina Sociale La Vite, Partanna DONZELLE
Cantina Sociale Le Vigne, Linguaglossa ETNA NIBBIO,
  GABBIANO
Cantina Sociale Saturnia, Partanna DRACENO
Settesoli Cantina Sociale, Menfi BIANCO DI MENFI
Cantina Sociale Valdelia, Marsala GRECANICO
Az. Agr. Fontanarossa, Palermo CERDESE
Solunto, Palermo SOLUNTO
Cantina Sociale Birgi, Marsala BIRGI ROSSO
Cantina Sociale Mozia, Mozia FENICIO
Az. Vinicola Siciliana di Noto, Noto ELORO
Diego Rallo, Marsala NORMANNO
D'Angelo, Alcamo GEBBIA
C/S Saturnia, Partanna SATURNO
Agricoltori Associati Pantelleria, Pantelleria ZIBIBBO, TANIT,
  SOLIMANO SPUMANTE
Rocche di Rao, Corleone ROCCHE DI RAO
Torre di Salsa, Palermo NOE, VOSSIE
Cooperativa Vitese, Marsala MAKANI
SIV, Marsala TORRE MARINA
SALVINA, Catania CORBERA, NIBBIO
Etnea Vini, Catania CICLOPI
Az. Coria, Vittoria CERASUOLO
De Bartoli, Marsala VECCHIO SAMPERI
Ericino, Marsala ERICINO
Adelkam, Palermo RAPITALA

26
Sardinia

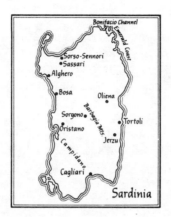

Sardinia should always be considered separately from mainland Italy, as its history, from its rising out of primordial waters to its millennia of solitude and geo-politics, is different. There are many animal species on the island, such as hares, rabbits, ponies and donkeys, that are far smaller than those of Europe; the birds are different, there are no frogs or poisonous snakes, and the honey is often bitter instead of being sweet.

Sardinia was, in fact, the only part of Europe where the Phoenicians of Tyre and Carthage set up home with no fear of attack, so good were their relations with the Sardinians; they traded in corn, wine and salt and exported silver, lead and other metals that they mined together. Much the same economic pattern exists today, with the addition of crude-oil refining and some petro-chemicals.

There is a lot of discussion about the origin of Sardinian vines, but scarcely any consensus of opinion. Some say they came from Spain in the fourteenth century, others that they are much older, perhaps native, or perhaps brought by the Phoenicians from the

Lebanon as much as 4,000 years ago. Mediterranean man, in the misty past, when making a long journey with no date of return always carried with him his favourite seeds and cuttings (just as he does today). Even the origin of Carignano (Sardus Pater, in Sardinian) vines is thrown into doubt. Yes, perhaps they came from France, but not in living memory; more likely they came via Spain. The Malvasias (the malmseys) are believed to have come from Greece – not via Venice at the time of the Crusades but with the Byzantines in the fifth century.

In all, the wines of Sardinia have a character of their own and, like the Sardinians, a language (in fact, several languages) of their own. Since they have so little to do with the wines of the mainland and the rest of Europe, it is unfortunate that the visitors and holiday-makers to Sardinia come in summer and thus do not indulge themselves in the strong mountain wines that are more winter wines to accompany grills and game on the spit.

Also, unlike mainland Italy, most of Sardinia's grapes come from the 70,000 smallholders who furnish the thirty-nine co-operatives which process the wine and sell it in bottles or in bulk. The only estate of any size is that of Sella & Mosca (1,600 acres); the other dozen or so labels are of *négociants* and small producers who specialize in Cagliari dessert wines and Oristano Vernaccias.

If you ask anybody where the surplus wine goes, you will get the quick answer: 'France', but this is not as true as it used to be. Long ago, the Sardinian wines certainly went to France, where they played a large role in saving the French industry during the *phylloxera* plagues. Today, West Germany has become the major importer of Sardinian wines – in bulk and, recently, also of bottled wines.

Co-operatives have set up efficient production and bottling plants and a fairly wide variety of local wines is now available in the grocery stores; there is quite a lively export to mainland Italy and some to the rest of Europe and even the USA, but not much. Sella & Mosca is the first company to set itself up as an international supplier, which has aligned itself with the most modern methods and delivery deadlines. My only criticism of Sella & Mosca is that they tend to make very light wines and only their port-like Anghelu Ruju is a heavyweight.

The firm is of Piedmontese origin, of the Sella family of statesmen, economists and bankers, and its present capital and executives come from Piedmont, too. Piedmont was, until 1870, part of the Kingdom of Sardinia, which explains the connection. The Piedmontese like the wild-boar hunting in Sardinia, for which the island was, and is now to a lesser extent, famous. At all events, Sella & Mosca is moving to place Sardinian wines on the shelves of the wine shops of the world.

In the past, three great wines were the main protagonists of the bulk-wine trade: the Cannonau and the Monica, both subtle yet forceful reds from all over the island, and the Nuragus white from the broiling plains of the south. Today, much bottled Cannonau is available under various labels but always with a natural 13·5 per cent of alcoholic content. If aged in the wood, it may be called Riserva; if it has 15 per cent of alcohol (without sugaring, of course), it may be called Superiore. There is also the previously mentioned sub-category called Oliena and Capo Ferrato that is produced best by Mario Mereu of Tortolì, the Deina Winery at Oliena, the Cantina Sociale there and that of Jerzu. The Capo Ferrato comes entirely from the Castiadas co-operative and is made by 'Tunisians': that is to say by Sicilian families who were constrained to abandon their vineyards in Tunis over twenty years ago for political reasons. These expert 'Tunisini' are to be found also on the south-west coast, making Carignano. The bottled version of the Nuragus, nowadays, is made from vines grown in the hills on trellises and vinified with slow fermentation to produce a more delicate wine: it is a neutral wine, like the mainland Trebbiano, and is blended with up to 15 per cent of aromatic wines.

Sardinia has several particularly strong, yet delicate white wines: the S'Eleme, the Abbaia, the Giogantino and the Aghiloia; all Vermentinos from the Gallura in the north-east, near the Aga Khan's Emerald Coast. They make most welcome apéritifs and partners for fish and other light dishes, though the Superiore (Aghiloia), at a minimum of 14 per cent of alcohol, is by no means as 'light' as it might seem, as it may well turn out to be a 15 per cent wine and that requires a good head.

Two other whites that have suave and enticing personalities are the Torbato and the Dorato di Sorso. The former is a Sella & Mosca product safely at 11·5 per cent, whereas the latter is made also *passito* at over 16 per cent.

The Sella & Mosca company has its own dessert wine called the Red Angel (Anghelu Ruju) which is sweet (7 per cent residual sugar), *passito* and fortified so that it has 18 per cent of alcoholic content, after which it is aged for three to four years in the wood. It is well suited for cocktails and for being passed around the table at the end of a convivial dinner. It is made from the ubiquitous Cannonau grape.

The Monica of Sardegna has made great strides in the last five or ten years as a light, dry red such as is fashionable nowadays: an undemanding wine with a low total acidity requiring little attention. The Monica Superiore, at 14 per cent and with a little ageing, is to be taken more seriously. The Sardinians have also a non-DOC Sibiola based on Monica, from the Dolianova co-operative, which they like very much and which, I learn to my surprise, is sold on the US market. Relatively new as DOC-zone wines are the Terralba and Carignano: both are 'blacks' with big bodies and strong bouquets. They do not seem to have much potential for long ageing.

The wines that have been recognized in Sardinia and by no means ignored on the mainland are the dessert wines. Curiously, they were noted in Milan in the seventeenth century when Lombardy was, like Sardinia, a Spanish colony. In the listings, the reader will find further details of Malvasia di Bosa, Malvasia di Cagliari, Moscato di Cagliari and Nasco di Cagliari, which are all liquid golds, while the Girò di Cagliari and the Monica di Cagliari are deep, luxuriant, velvety reds. They come in a range of sweet to dry, natural *passito* to fortified.

When *Italian Wines* (1983 edition) was being written, the Sardinians were experimenting with sparkling wines. They were sending their various Vermentinos, Torbatos and Moscatos to the professional spumante-makers of the Veneto and Piedmont to see what would happen and they also slipped them on to the local market to see who would stand up and salute them. Coming back to Sardinia some years later, I found that Sardinian charmat, made on the island, was the standard and had pushed most of the Italian and French bubbly to the back of the shelves: surprisingly so, as Sardinia, on the whole, is the opposite of autarky-minded and loves things foreign.

In the forefront of these are chiefly the Brut Vermentinos from the three major co-operatives (Berchidda, Monti and Tempio), Solais Brut from Santadi (also a Vermentino), the sweet moscato from Mogoro and Sella & Mosca's Brut Torbato.

In the same time-lapse, we have a few Novellos: two from Sella & Mosca (Rubicante rosé and a ruby red Tanca Farrà); also to be found are the San Giacomo Novello of the Santadi Coop and the Santa Caterina of Dorgali's.

Sardinia would seem to be reducing the quantity of its production and to have improved quality through more effective vine-dressing and processing methods. Except for Sella & Mosca's range, however (created by Dr Mario Consorte who has spent his whole long working-life there since he was a teenager and has constructed an ideal, idealized and idealistic world of manicured vineyards, shady gardens and a spotless winery), unless a latter-day Villa Banfi comes to the rescue, little of Sardinia's offerings will reach foreign shores ... though, perversely, they do reach foreign stomachs which is much the same. The one or two million (in any case, much more than the total population of the island) Italian and foreign tourists who invade Sardinia from May to October mostly consume Sardinian wines which they find more than satisfactory, thus saving the Sardinians the problem of exporting them. For the record, all Sella & Mosca's wines, all the spumantes and Novellos, are non-DOC – which, by now, will surprise nobody. An exception is the new cru Cala Viola Vermentino.

Cannonau di Sardegna (248: 21.9.72)

The Cannonau is the major red wine of Sardinia and is processed in various ways to produce different wines.

CANNONAU TABLE WINE

This red is made both dry and amabile with a minimum 13·5% alcohol content; it may also be made as a rosé. In all cases, the wine must be aged for one year. When it is aged for three years it may be called Riserva.

CANNONAU DI OLIENA AND CAPO FERRATO

This is an exceptionally sturdy wine with an alcoholic content that can rise to more than 15–17%. Ageing as for above.

CANNONAU DI ALGHERO

A dry red wine with a minimum 12% alcoholic content, aged three years, of which two are in the wood.

CANNONAU DESSERT WINE

This sweet red wine is processed as Naturale, Secco, Naturale Amabile and Naturale Dolce; in the case of the latter two sweeter varieties, the ageing required is two years against one for the former two. The total alcoholic content is 15%.

CANNONAU LIQUOROSO

This fortified sweet red wine is processed either as Secco or Dolce Naturale. Both have at least 16% alcoholic content and the Dolce Naturale has at least 2% sugar residue.

Producers
Cantina Sociale di Castiadas, Capo Ferrato (Cagliari)
Cantina Sociale di Dorgali (Cagliari)
Cantina Sociale di Jerzu (Nuoro)
Cantina Sociale di Marmilla, Sanluri (Cagliari)
Cantina Sociale di Oliena (Nuoro)
Deiana, Oliena (Nuoro)
Mereu, Tortoli (Nuoro)
Sella e Mosca, Alghero (Sassari)

Campidano di Terralba or Terralba (61: 6.3.76)

This is a dry red wine produced from Bovale (both Sardinian and Spanish varieties) grapes with the addition of up to 20% of Pascale di Cagliari, Greco Nero (locally called Gregu Nieddu) and Monica from the same vineyards; the wine must have an alcoholic content of not less than 11·5%.

Producers
Cantina Sociale di Campidano, Terralba (Cagliari)
Cantina Sociale di Arborea, Arborea (Cagliari)
Cantina Sociale Marrubiu, Marrubiu (Oristano)

Carignano del Sulcis (281: 14.10.77)

CARIGNANO ROSSO/ROSÉ

Both the red and the rosé are produced from the Carignano vine along with grapes from the Monica, the Pascale and the Alicate Bouschet, singly or together but from the same vineyards. The minimum alcoholic content for both red and rosé wines is 11·5%, though the red may be labelled Invecchiato (aged) if matured for one year.

Producers
Cantina Sociale di Calasetta, Calasetta (Cagliari)
Cantina Sociale di Santadi, Santadi (Cagliari)
Cantina Sociale di Sant'Antioco (Cagliari)
Cantina Sociale di Pula (Cagliari)

Girò di Cagliari (249: 22.9.72; 274: 6.10.79)

This red dessert wine is produced in sweet, dry, fortified and Riserva versions from the Girò vine.

GIRÒ DOLCE

An alcoholic content of 15·5% of which 2·5% is left unconverted as sugar residue.

GIRÒ SECCO

An alcoholic content of 15·5% of which 1% is left unconverted as sugar residue.

GIRÒ LIQUOROSO

Both the Liquoroso Naturale and Liquoroso Secco fortified wines have a total alcoholic content of 17·5%.

GIRÒ RISERVA

Girò that has been aged for at least two years.

Producers
Cantina Sociale di Monserrato, Monserrato (Cagliari)
Zedda-Piras, Cagliari (Cagliari)

Malvasia di Bosa (255: 28.9.72)

This is a white dessert wine produced from the Malvasia di Sardegna vine.

BOSA DOLCE NATURALE

A total alcoholic content of 15%, of which 13% is converted into alcohol; i.e., with 2% sugar residue.

BOSA SECCO

A total alcoholic content of 15%, of which 14·5% is converted.

BOSA LIQUOROSO DOLCE NATURALE

A total alcoholic content of 17·5%, of which 15% is converted.

BOSA LIQUOROSO SECCO

A total alcoholic content of 17·5%, of which 16·6%, is converted into alcohol.

Producers
Deriu Mocci, Bosa (Nuoro)
Emilio Arru, Magomadas, Bosa (Nuoro)

Malvasia di Cagliari (228: 1.9.72; 164: 16.6.79)

A white dessert wine produced from the Malvasia di Sardegna vine in the following versions:

MALVASIA DOLCE NATURALE

A total alcoholic content of 15%, of which 13% is converted.

MALVASIA SECCO

A total alcoholic content of 15%, of which 14·5% is converted.

MALVASIA LIQUOROSO

A total alcoholic content of 17·5%, of which 15% is converted for Dolce.

MALVASIA LIQUOROSO

A total alcoholic content of 17·5%, of which 16·5% is converted for Secco.

MALVASIA RISERVA

A Liquoroso aged for two years, one in the wood.

Producers
Cantina Sociale di Campidano, Serramanna (Cagliari)
Cantina Sociale di Campidano, Terralba (Cagliari)
Cantina Sociale di Dolianova, Dolianova (Cagliari)
Cantina Sociale di Villacidro, Villacidro (Cagliari)
Cantina Sociale Marmilla, Sanluri (Cagliari)
Zedda-Piras, Cagliari (Cagliari)

Monica di Cagliari (Dolce Naturale: Secco) (217: 22.8.72)

A red, aged dessert wine that comes in two versions, sweet and dry: made from the Monica grape.

MONICA DOLCE NATURALE

A minimum alcoholic content of 15·5%, of which 13% is converted.

MONICA SECCO

An alcoholic content of 15·5%, of which 14·5% is converted.

MONICA LIQUOROSO, DOLCE AND SECCO

A total alcoholic content of 17·5%.

MONICA LIQUOROSO RISERVA

The fortified version aged for two years, one at least in the wood.

Producers
Cantina Sociale di Campidano, Serramanna (Cagliari)
Cantina Sociale di Campidano, Terralba (Cagliari)
Cantina Sociale di Villacidro, Villacidro (Cagliari)
Zedda-Piras, Cagliari (Cagliari)
Sella e Mosca, Alghero (Sassari)

Monica di Sardegna (309: 28.11.72)

This red table wine is produced from grapes from the Monica (85%) vine and, for the remainder, a blend of Pascale di Cagliari, Carignano, Bovale Grande and Bovale Sardo. The minimum alcoholic content is 12%; but if the wine has one year's ageing and a minimum content of 13% it may be called Superiore.

Producers
Cantina Sociale della Riforma, Santa Margherita di Pula Cagliari
  (Cagliari)
Cantina Sociale del Campidano, Serramanna (Cagliari)
Cantina Sociale di Sant'Antioco, Sant'Antioco (Cagliari)
Cantina Sociale di Marmilla, Sanluri (Cagliari)
Cantina Sociale di Terralba, Terralba (Cagliari)

Moscato di Cagliari (222: 25.8.79; 164: 16.6.79)

An amber-coloured dessert wine made exclusively from the Moscato Bianco grape with a natural alcoholic content of 16%.

MOSCATO DI CAGLIARI

A sweet wine with 3% sugar residue.

MOSCATO LIQUOROSO DOLCE NATURALE

An alcoholic content of 15%; 3·5% sugar residue.

MOSCATO LIQUOROSO SECCO

A wine with 1–3·5% sugar residue.

MOSCATO LIQUOROSO RISERVA

The Dolce requires one year's ageing; the Secco two years.

Producers
Vini Classici di Sardegna, Pirri (Cagliari)
Zedda-Piras, Cagliari (Cagliari)
Efisio Meloni, Selargius (Cagliari)

Nasco di Cagliari (220: 24.8.72; 153: 6.6.79)

A white dessert wine produced exclusively from the Nasco vine.

NASCO DOLCE NATURALE

A total alcoholic content of 15·5%, of which 13% is converted into alcohol.

NASCO SECCO

A total alcoholic content of 15%, of which 14% is converted into alcohol.

NASCO LIQUOROSO

An alcoholic content of 17·5%.

NASCO LIQUOROSO DRY

An alcoholic content of 16·5%.

NASCO LIQUOROSO RISERVA

Qualification after two years' ageing in the wood.

Producers
Cantina Sociale di Marmilla, Sanluri (Cagliari)
Cantina Sociale di Dolianova, Dolianova (Cagliari)
Sella e Mosca, Alghero (Sassari)
Zedda-Piras, Cagliari (Cagliari)
Efisio Meloni, Selargius (Cagliari)

Moscato di Sardegna (143: 2.6.80)

An amabile white wine made from the Moscato grape with a total alcoholic content of 11·5%, of which only 8% is converted into alcohol, leaving a sugar residue of 3·5%. This wine is much used for making sparkling wines.

Producers
Efisio Meloni, Selargius (Cagliari)
Sella e Mosca, Alghero (Sassari)

Moscato di Sorso-Sennori (193: 26.7.72)

A sweet dessert wine produced exclusively from the Moscato Bianco grape to provide a total alcoholic content of 13%; however this is converted so as to leave a 2% sugar residue. This wine is also used for making sparkling wines.

Producer
Cantina Sociale di Sorso Sennori, Sorso (Sassari)

Nuragus di Cagliari (66: 10.3.75; 160: 19.6.79)

This dry white wine is obtained from the Nuragus di Cagliari vine, with 15% permitted from the Trebbiano Toscano, the Romagnolo

Trebbiano, Vermentino, Clairette and Semidano vines; it has a minimum alcoholic content of 11%.

Producers
Cantina Sociale di Dolianova, Dolianova (Cagliari)
Cantina Sociale di Marmilla, Sanluri (Cagliari)
Cantina Sociale di Mogoro, Mogoro (Cagliari)
Efisio Meloni, Selargius (Cagliari)
Zedda-Piras, Cagliari (Cagliari)
Cantina Sociale di Serramanna (Cagliari)

Vermentino di Gallura (173: 2.7.75)

This dry white wine is obtained from Vermentino (up to 95%) and not more than 5% of locally approved grapes. With a 14% alcoholic content, instead of the normal 12%, the wine may be labelled Superiore.

Producers
Cantina Sociale di Giogantino, Berchidda (Sassari)
Cantina Sociale del Vermentino, Monti (Sassari)

Vernaccia di Oristano (247: 30.9.71)

This dry white dessert wine is produced exclusively from the Vernaccia grape. It has an alcoholic content of 15%; if 15·5% or more, and the wine is aged for three years in the wood, it may be labelled Superiore.

Producers
Cantina Sociale della Vernaccia, Oristano Rimedio (Oristano)
Silvio Carta, Baratili San Pietro (Oristano)
Attilio Contini, Cabras (Oristano)
Produttori Riuniti, Baratili San Pietro (Oristano)
Josto Puddu, San Vero Milis (Oristano)

The range of recommended non-DOC wines produced by Sella & Mosca (Alghero, Sassari)

BRUT TORBATO   a dry, white charmat Torbato, 11.5%.
TERRE BIANCHE   a dry, white Torbato, 11·5%.

TORBATO DI ALGHERO   a dry, white Torbato, 10%.

VERMENTINO DI ALGHERO   a dry, white, 10%.

TANCA FARRÀ DI ALGHERO   a dry, red Cannonau and Cabernet blend, a Novello.

ANGHELU RUJU   an aged, port-like sweet fortified wine.

RUBICANTE   a dry, red Cannonau and Sangiovese blend, Novello.

I PIANI   a dry, red Sangiovese and Carignano blend, 12%.

NURAGHE MAJORE DI ALGHERO   a dry white, Trebbiano and Malvasia blend, 10%.

Wines from the Dolianova co-operative, the major producer of bottled Sardinian wines

NURAGUS OF CAGLIARI   a dry white, min. 11% alcoholic content. 15% of Trebbiano, Vermentino, Clairette and Semidano grapes permitted.

NASCO DI CAGLIARI   a white dessert wine exclusively from Nasco grapes. Circa 15% of alcoholic content.

MOSCATO DI CAGLIARI   a sweet, white dessert wine with 16% of alcoholic content: made in four versions.

MALVASIA DI CAGLIARI   a white desert wine with 15% of alcoholic content, made in five versions.

GIRÒ DI CAGLIARI   a red dessert wine with 15.5% of alcoholic content, made in four versions.

MONICA DI SARDEGNA   a dry, white table wine, 85% Monica at 12% alcoholic content.

PARTEOLLA   a dry (10%) white of Trebbiano and Nuragus.

Recommended 'Geographic Denomination' wines

REDS

ABBAIA   a strong dry wine from the Vermentino Cooperative at Monti; to drink young.

EMBARCADOR   a highly-fortified (20–21%) dry red with a trace of sweetness; for ageing. Made by Bulla-Mugoni of Alghero.

LE BOMBARDE   a sturdy red made by the Cantina Sociale Santa Maria La Palma from Cannonau and Sangiovese. Can age a few years.

MANDROLISAI a light red Cannonau of good quality. To be drunk young and fresh; from Mandrolisai Cooperative.

PERDA RUBIA a deep red wine of great distinction made by Mario Mereu at Gairo Cardedu. Customarily of well over 14% alcohol.

SIBIOLA a pleasing red wine to be drunk young: a good 12·5% alcoholic content.

SU 'IGANTE a good, rich fortified dessert wine made by Zedda-Piras of Cagliari. Not a wine for ageing. Over 17% alcohol.

ROSÉS

PERDA RUBIA ROSATO like the red of the same name, a formidable wine, strong in alcohol and character; will age. Serve with roast fish and spiced poultry dishes.

SANDALYON a gentle wine made by the Monteserrato Cooperative (11·5%).

THAORA ROSATO from the Vermentino Cooperative at Monti. A delicate yet strong (12·5%) wine, high coloured and suitable for a wide range of dishes including white meats. Also apéritif.

WHITES

ARAGOSTA a Vermentino-type wine, delicate, dry and harmonious with 12% of alcohol.

NINFEO a sweetish dessert wine produced from Tocai grapes by the Santa Maria La Palma winery of Alghero. Over 15·5% of natural alcoholic content.

SARDUS PATER a dry table wine made by the Sant'Antioco Cooperative with Trebbiano and Nuragus grapes (12%).

27

Some Lacunae in Availability

The selection of wines that Italy offers is too big and the problem is that it is getting bigger. It is scarcely reasonable to expect any wine-lover to cope with them all – especially in the abstract. And no flood of wine-tasting adjectives and colourful jargon is going to resolve the problem.

The ideal is to visit the major trade fairs and to taste the wines at all the stands, but this is not for everybody. Educated gossip, to my mind, along with friendly group tastings, is perhaps the best lead. One must, of course, write off exaggerated hype and PR-plugging but the producer who spends some money to get his wine known on a word-of-mouth basis is by no means necessarily phoney. Few producers use much straight media publicity, even in Italy. I can think only of three or four that take the occasional spot on TV, though there is a certain amount – not much – of TV and print-media publicity taken by the Ministry of Agriculture and the Regional Agricultural Boards that broadly encourage the drinking of wine, without naming names or styles of wine. There is, however, a sort of consensus as to who is making the best wine, traditional, high-tech, premium or world-class as they say nowadays. Here, the importers and stockists can give a good lead.

As mentioned earlier, the sparkling-wine sector of Italian wines has made a great leap in quality and an even greater one in quantity. It seems to be the least known abroad, which is odd because it offers champenois-system wines that are a serious rival to those of France and plenty of lesser charmat wines that can equally meet the requirements of the occasion – and at a much reduced price.

For dryness or sweetness, for bouquet, for perlage, for after-taste and for purity (low sulphur), Italian champenois-system and charmat sparklers can meet all the connoisseurs' demands. There are now approaching a hundred wineries that specialize in sparkling wines and, with RIUNITE's and Villa Banfi's entry on to the stage with their twelve million cases of charmat sold to the USA yearly, it can be considered an industrial breakthrough, though French champagne's total sales of 200 million bottles a year is still, I think, the world-beater. RIUNITE is by far Italy's greatest producer and shows every sign of growing fast with a whole new range of traditional and fruit wines.

What is odd about this Italo-American venture is that it might never have happened. Ezio Rivella might never have met John Mariani, might never have created an American Lambrusco nor had the astonishing opportunity to build the Montalcino winery. The old New York Banfi wine-importing company was amongst the major importers of French wines into the United States. The company executives visited the French growers several times a year, while John Jr, in particular, tried to interest French producers in a potential new US market, as he saw it – that is, for a slightly sweet and slightly sparkling, low-alcohol, three-dimensional, chillable wine with a dry after-taste. His theory failed to ring a bell anywhere in France, so he turned his search to Italy. How close we must have been to ten million cases a year of modified-Beaujolais, we shall never know! Therefore, the Marianis' choice of Italy was not, as most of us have probably thought, a 'returning to the old sod', because the French had the first option and rejected it.

The essence of the issue today is that immobility is not the answer to the problems or the way of the future. Never has the wine-lover been given such a wide choice which allows him to vote with his chequebook for what he fancies. Banfi has just acquired the world-distribution rights to five wines, none of which are from European countries. The cry over the last two decades has been for greater quality: there is also, however, a growing demand for novelty, originality and ever greater choice. Dozens upon dozens of Italian wineries are answering that demand from the public. I have mentioned the many wineries that have already won or are now gaining reputations for their new wines: one has only to think of the huge range of nearly seventy charmat sparklers and thirty champenois-system wines that have surfaced of recent years, which alone is sufficient to justify my listing them separately, along with a dozen Novellos which have also settled into the Italian landscape.

Here follows a listing of wineries that have, chiefly over the last ten years, started making sparkling wines and a second list of charmat-makers, including the major names in Pinot Brut, Asti Spumante, Prosecco and Verdicchio sparklers – as well as a dozen novellos.

Spumante Classico – Metodo Champenois

Marchesi Antinori (Florence) – Nature, Gran Spumante Brut, Cuvée Royale
Calissano (Alba) – Brut
Carpene Malvolti (Conegliano) – Brut
Contratto (Canelli) – Sabauda Riserva, Bacco d'Oro
EQUIPE 5 (Trento) – Brut
Giulio Ferrari (Trento) – Blanc de Blanc, Brut Rosé, Riserva del Fondatore
Carlo Gancia (Canelli) – Chardonnay Brut, Vallarino Gancia
Santa Maria della Versa (Pavia) – La Versa Brut
Riccadonna (Piedmont) – Conte Balduino

The above are members of the Spumante Classico Institute. Not less distinguished, however, are the following:

Arunda (Alto Adige) – Brut
Berlucchi (Lombardy) – Cuvée Imperiale Berlucchi
Ca' del Bosco (Lombardy) – Brut
Catturich-Ducco (Lombardy) – Brut
Clastidio Ballabio (Lombardy) – Brut
Conti Loredan Venegazzù (Veneto) – Brut
Girelli (Veneto) – Brut
La Scolca (Piedmont) – Brut
Villa Banfi Cellars – Brut
Lini (Emilia Romagna) – Brut
Maschio (Veneto) – Brut
Martini e Rossi (Piedmont) – Brut
Gioacchino Garofalò (Marches) – Brut
Pisoni (Veneto) – Brut
Villa Costa (Piedmont) – Brut

Valdo Vini (Veneto) – Brut
Zardetto (Veneto) – Brut
Anteo (Lombardy) – Brut
Bellavista (Lombardy) – Brut
Cesarini Sforza (Trento) – Riserva dei Conti Sforza
Danieli-Fisdan (Friuli) – Brut Mus
Fontanafredda (Piedmont) – Gattinera Brut, Rosa Pas Dosé

Spumante a Fermentazione Naturale
(Also called charmat, cuve-close or tank-method)

Cinzano (Turin) – Pinot-Chardonnay, Principe di Piemonte
Caneval (Treviso) – Cartizze
Angoris (Friuli) – Brut
Villa Banfi Cellars (Piedmont) – Pinot Brut
RIUNITE (Emilia) – Brut
Cora (Piemont) – Brut
Cantina Sociale di Vo' (Veneto) – Brut, Moscato
CAVIT (Trentino) – Brut, Chardonnay Brut
Bertani (Veneto) – Brut
Bolla (Veneto) – Brut
Cantina Sociale Valdobbiadene (Veneto) – Brut
La Selva (Lazio) – Brut
Salaparuta Corvo (Sicily) – Brut
Kettmeir (Alto Adige) – Brut
Franciacorta (Lombardy) – Brut
Naonis (Friuli) – Chardonnay Brut
Tenuta Amalia (Romagna) – Brut
Santa Margherita di Portogruaro (Veneto) – Brut
Fol (Veneto) – Brut
Adamo Cannel (Veneto) – Brut
Zonin (Veneto) – Brut, Durello, rosé
Cardinal (Solighetto, Veneto) – Brut
Cantina Sociale Lavis (Alto Adige) – Brut
Istituto Agrario San Michele (Alto Adige) – Brut
Sella & Mosca (Sardinia) – Brut Torbato
Diego Rallo (Sicily) – Brut
Carlo Pellegrino (Sicily) – Brut
Cossyra Maccotta (Trapani) – Brut
Agricoltori Assoc. Pantelleria (Sicily) – Brut

Villa Banfi Cellars (Piedmont) – Brut, dry
Cantina Sociale di Mogoro (Sardinia) – Nuraghe Moscato
Cantina Sociale di Berchidda (Sardinia) – Giogantino Brut
Cantina Sociale di Gallura-Tempio (Sardinia) – Ladas Vermentino
   Brut
Cantina Sociale di Santadi (Sardinia) – Solais Brut
Cantina Sociale di Gallura-Tempio (Sardinia) – Moscato
Villa Banfi (Montalcino, Tuscany) – Moscadello
RIUNITE (Emilia) – Dry, Brut etc.
Fazi Battaglia (Marches) – Brut
Federici & Gagliardini (Marches) – Brut
Collavini (Friuli) – Applause Nature, Brut, Il Grigio
Endrizzi (San Michele, Trentino) – Brut
Barone de Cles (Trentino) – Brut
Gancia (Piedmont) – Vallarino Non Dosato, Chardonnay Brut,
   Gancia dei Gancia
Romagnoli (Emilia) – Brut
Martini & Rossi (Turin) – Riesling Oltrepò Martini

Asti Spumante

Luigi Bosca (Asti)
Martini & Rossi (Turin)
Villa Banfi Cellars (Alessandria)
Luigi Calissano (Cuneo)
Cantina Sociale di Canelli (Asti)
Giorgio Carnevale (Asti)
Francesco Cinzano (Turin)
Cora (Turin)
Dogliotti (Asti)
Giuseppe Contratto (Canelli)
Fontanafredda (Cuneo)
I Vignaiuoli Sanstefanesi (Asti)
Dogliani Sette Cascine (Asti)

Prosecco di Conegliano – Valdobbiadene

Cantina Sociale di Valdobbiadene (Treviso)
Cantina Sociale di Soligo (Treviso)
Carpene Malvolti (Treviso)

De Bernard (Treviso)
Maschio (Treviso)
Pino Zardetto (Treviso)
Nino Franco (Valdobbiadene, Treviso)

The Superiore Proseccos are marketed as Cartizze and Classico and if vinified by the champenois-system, are made with 80 per cent or more of Pinot grapes.

Spumante Verdicchio (Marches)

Gioacchino Garofali (Loreto, Marches)

Vini Novelli (Vins nouveaux)

These wines, fermented by a variety of carbonic maceration methods and bottled for sale by October/November after the harvest, are a relative novelty in Italy. There are slightly less than 2,500,000 bottles made annually, almost all of which are made by the following wineries. These wines are also called *primeurs*.

Sella & Mosca – RUBICANTE and TANCA FARRA
Antinori – a Sangioveto called SAN GIOCONDO
Villa Banfi – a Brunello called SANTA COSTANZA
Gaja – a Nebbiolo called VINOT
Duca d'Aosta – a Grignolino called FIOR D'AUTUNNO
Rocca Delle Macie – a Sangioveto called DICEMBRINO
Col d'Orcia – a Brunello called NOVEMBRINI
Frescobaldi – a Sangioveto called NUOVO FIORE
Nino Negri – a Nebbiolo called CHIAVANNESCA
Carlo Gancia – a Pinot called SPUMANTE NOVELLO
Cantina Sociale di Santadi – a Carignano called SAN GIACOMO
Cantina Sociale di Dorgali – a Cannonau called SANTA CATERINA

These lively, but relatively short-lived wines, whose flavour has been enhanced by the new carbonic maceration process, should be drunk within six to eighteen months from vinification date, according to the vintners' recommendations.

28

Tailpiece

A few years ago, I met three South Africans, all important men in their wine-sphere, who were touring the world seeking the answer for their excess production of wine: most South Africans, white or black, drink beer. In Italy, their major interest was sparkling wines made by the charmat process; as for fruit-flavoured wines, Italy was way behind the South Africans who were already producing peach- and mango-tasting wines. It was Rivella who had to catch up quickly when Villa Banfi's position was threatened by Californian 'coolers'. His answer was an ingenious one in that it was a real 'wine-beverage', not a semi-soft drink like the coolers, which contained carbonated water, cane sugar and sorbates. Banfi's Sunny Apple, Royal Raspberry and Natural Peach are made with normal white wine to which fruit juice and grape juice are added to reduce the alcoholic content to 6 per cent and to give the fruit flavour. Banfi has already sold fifty million bottles. This is all a long way from the traditional concepts of cobwebby cellars and is a part of the future, like it or not.

These wines are reaching completely new markets, just as Lambrusco did years ago. Though I cannot speak with any authority on them, since they are not on sale in Italy, they – or at least one of them, Natural Peach – could be considered a traditional Italian drink. It is an Italian custom in summertime to marinate ripe peaches in wine – and strawberries, too, though perhaps not apples and raspberries. The sale of such beverages is illegal in Italy and they will be on sale in London before Rome. But, after all, they would seem to be little else than the fruit-cups which are not entirely foreign to summertime parties in England and they save a lot of time peeling fruit.

Though Villa Banfi growth is a centre of controversies today, it does, in fact, have less than 3,000 acres of vineyards and its estate-bottled wines are available only on allocation. Perhaps there will never be enough to go around. Their clout, however, lies elsewhere: with the RIUNITE, which has already extended its lines appreciably. I note that they have now yet a new range of quality wines, bottled for a company called VINIVIP which is presumably RIUNITE and possibly Villa Banfi, for sale only to restaurants. This includes a dry sparkling malmsey from Casa Torme (a RIUNITE property), a Pinot Grigio from the Oltrepò Pavese, a sparkling Lambrusco Reggiano DOC from Cantina Gallo of Reggio (a RIUNITE property) and a Franciacorta charmat.

Of even more recent note is the acquisition of a major New York importer by Villa Banfi which gives them exclusive rights on the production of five or more premium wine sources including non-European ones: Chile, Australia, Yugoslavia and others, not divulged. This surely is the age of choice.

Though this book seems to stress the New Enology and the use of *barriques* made with wood from France's Grand Massif, only the former is considered essential. *Barrique*-ageing is optional and, as far as Italy is concerned, by no means 100 per cent approved of. New *barriques* supply the wine with aromatic elements and tannin, but most of Italy's big wines have all the tannin they need – it is other wines that need it. California has led the way, however, and we must see where it leads us.

Come what may, quite counter to my expectations the panorama of Italian wines in the last five years has had a sea-change not only with Cabernets and Chardonnays but with sparkling wines and the beginnings of a new industry of fruit wines.

Another major change in the making is that the men – owners mostly, and some enologists – who have architected the Italian wine scene are getting on in years. A lot of them are already handing over the responsibility for their wineries to their sons and daughters: the average age of these youngsters would seem to be about twenty-nine, and, as often as not, the son is a fully qualified eno-technician. Plainly, the profession of wine-making is not phoney if it can gain such support from a wealthy younger generation that could just as easily have become stockbrokers, lawyers or playboys. As for the wine-writers, one of the most distinguished Italians, Buonassisi, celebrated his fifty years as a journalist recently: but there is a sprinkling of wine-writers with relatively new fifty-year-old Anglo-American blood. As for myself, I am ready to hand over the next edition of *Italian Wines* to a thirty year old.

Evolution is the cry of the day: nothing stands still any longer; even this book is in jeopardy. I, therefore, turn in fluid situations such as these to Francesco Guicciardini, my favourite amateur philosopher. He wrote in Florence, around 1525:

> The ability to do things or conduct one's affairs with absolute precision is most desirable ... it is equally a mistake to spend too much time making fine distinctions because even when you think you have got everything just right, you will find that you have succeeded in doing nothing at all.

Glossary

ABBOCCATO slightly, lightly sweet.

ACERBO tart.

ACIDITÀ FISSE fixed acids – tartaric, citric, malic and lactic – which cannot vaporize.

ACIDITÀ TOTALE total acidity – if too low, the wine is flat; if too high, bitter.

ACIDITÀ VOLATILE volatile acids – those than can vaporize.

ACIDO CARBONICO CO_2 – produced by alcoholic fermentation. The yeasts turn the sugar in the grapes into alcohol and CO_2.

ACIDO acid – a high degree of acids.

ACIDULO a wine with a high degree of acids but not necessarily displeasing.

AC Appellation Contrôlée – the French equivalent of the Italian DOC.

ACRE excessively acid.

ADULTERATO sophisticated – a wine made incorrectly and with prohibited materials.

AGGRESSIVO aggressive – a wine with exaggerated characteristics.

ALBERELLO vine pruned as a low bush and with low yield.

ALCOL COMPLESSIVO a total of the actual alcohol and the potential alcohol in the residual sugar.

ALCOL DA SVOLGERE the potential alcohol that could be produced from the residual sugar.

ALLAPPANTE astringent.

ALTERATO a wine that has been ill-treated or manipulated badly.

AMABILE sweeter than abboccato.

AMARO bitter.

AMARONE strong Valpolicella wine made with semi-dried grapes.

AMAROGNOLO a slightly bitter but pleasing characteristic.

AMBRATO a white wine that has darkened possibly through oxidation.

ANIDRIDE SOLFOROSO SO_2 – sulphur-dioxide, used in small quantities to regulate fermentation and as a disinfectant.

ANNATA   year of vintage.

ARDENTE   with a high alcohol content.

ARISTOCRATICO   with well-balanced organoleptic characteristics and high quality.

ARMONICO   harmonious.

AROMATIZZATO   used chiefly to describe, for example, vermouths with herbal aromatic additives.

ASCIUTTO   a wine that is bone-dry but short in its persistence of flavour.

ASPRETTO   meaning 'sharp' but pleasantly so.

ASPRIGNO   meaning 'sharp' but rather too acid to be pleasing.

ASPRO   a wine that has a high alcohol content, high tannin and acidity, giving a rough and harsh taste such as is to be found in 'big' wines in their early years.

ATM   Atmospheres, the meaurement of pressure. A champagne or Spumante wine is fixed at 6 Atms; a frizzante (like Lambrusco) at around 2 Atms.

AUSTERO   austere – rich in colour, full-bodied, a generous alcoholic content and a well-balanced acidity.

AUTOCLAVE   sealed vat that can be temperature-controlled.

AZIENDA AGRARIA   a farm.

AZIENDA VINICOLA   a wine-producing farm.

BARRIQUE   small barrel, usually of French oak, of 225 or 350 litres used for ageing fine wines.

BIANCO CARTA   paper-white, transparent, a white wine with the minimum of colouring.

BLANC DE BLANC   white wine from white grapes.

BOTTE   barrel (generic, of any size) for ageing wines.

BOUQUET   the perfume acquired during fermentation and ageing.

BRILLANTE   absolute clarity, bright.

BRUT   dry with less than 1·5% sugar residue per litre; refers to champagnes and spumantes.

CALDO   high-alcohol wine with a pleasing warmth to the palate.

CANTINA SOCIALE   a wine-producing plant run by a co-operative of growers.

CARATELLO   a 50-litre barrel used for making Vin Santo.

CARBONIC MACERATION   a fermentation method perfected by enologist Flanzy whereby he invented Beaujolais 'nouveau' wine, also called 'primeur' and, in Italy, 'novello'. See vino novello.

CATRAMOSO   a tarry taste due to the plentiful glycerine, alcohol and tannin, which with greater age becomes bitter.

CERASUOLO   dark pink.

CHAMPENOIS   the adjective of the place-name and sparkling wine of Champagne. Used in the form 'champenois-system' or 'champenois method' (or in French 'méthode-champenoise', in Italian 'metodo champenois'), it means, technically speaking, that the wine has had its second fermentation and ageing in the bottle and not as in the case of charmat, cuve close or spumante naturale made in bulk in vats (and often called 'mousseux' in French). Italian spumante classico, however, is made by the champenois-system in the bottle. Champagne is a copyright word, jealously defended by the French wherever possible in the world: the adjectival form 'champenois(e)' is not so protected.

CHAPTALIZATION the addition of sugar to wine during its fermentation to increase the alcoholic content: a system named after Count Chaptal in 1880.

CHARMAT a system of making sparkling mousseux and spumantes in bulk in autoclaves.

CHIARELLO a light-coloured red wine.

CHIARETTO pale red.

CLASSICO wine produced in a restricted area of a DOC zone, considered especially favoured.

COLLI hill.

COLLINE hills, but lower ones.

COMMERCIANTE *négociant*, trader, dealer.

CORPO body – rich in colour, acidity, alcohol and tannin but well balanced.

CORPOSO full-bodied – a wine with balanced and ample constituent components and consequently most pleasing to the taste.

CORTO short – a wine with limited organoleptic characteristics.

COTTO cooked – a heavy taste due to high temperature fermentation or hot-bottling.

COUPAGE *see* TAGLIO.

CRU a superior wine made from grapes produced on a limited area particularly suited to viticulture; also called 'growth'.

CUTTING WINE *see* TAGLIO.

CUVE-CLOSE *see* CHARMAT

DEBOLE thin.

DECREPITO decrepit – a wine that is disintegrating due to too long ageing.

DEGUSTAZIONE a wine-tasting.

DELICATO delicate.

DEPOSITO sediment.

DOC Denominazione d'Origine Controllata – the Italian equivalent of the French AC for regulating the various types of vines, their grapes, their processing, ageing and bottling.

DOC G DOC Garantita – a more demanding quality discipline.

DOLCE sweet.

DOLCIGNO   a pejorative name for sweet – not altogether pleasant.

DURO   hard – a wine that is rich in tannin, acidity and extracts.

ELEGANTE   elegant – fine but without strong characteristics, nevertheless pleasant.

ENOTECA   a place with a wide selection of fine wines – literally, a wine-library.

ENOTECNICO   an enologist, a qualified wine-maker.

EQUILIBRATO   balanced – a wine with the ideal proportions of its components and particularly a perfect balance between alcohol content and acidity.

ESTATE-BOTTLED   a wine that has not only been made on a specific estate but also processed and bottled there.

ETTOGRADO   see HECTOGRADE.

ETTOLITRO   100 litres.

FATTORIA   refers usually to a Tuscan farm where wine, usually Chianti, is made.

FEOGA   a Common Market fund raised by taxes on agricultural imports and spent on improving or subsidizing Common Market agriculture.

FERMENTAZIONE NATURALE   charmat, cuve-close, tank-method or autoclave fermentation system for spumante.

FIACCO   weak – a wine lacking body and acidity.

FINE   fine – a bouquet and taste that are harmonious, balanced.

FIORE   flower, the free-run (lightly pressed) must of a first pressing of grapes.

FLORAL ABORTION   a vine defect or disease whereby the flowering buds do not evolve healthily and many fall, producing a low (and scarcely economic) crop.

FONDO   dregs.

FRAGRANTE   fragrant – a bouquet and taste that are fresh, fruity and perfumed.

FRANCO   frank – a wine without defects but not necessarily a very fine one.

FRESCO   fresh – with a pleasant acidity.

FRUTTATO   fruity – a wine offering a sensation of fruit in its bouquet: often used nowadays to imply a trace sweetness.

FUGACE   fleeting – a wine whose taste and bouquet last briefly.

FUSTO   a barrel (generic, of any size) for ageing wines.

GENEROSO   of good body and ample flavour.

GENUINO   genuine – an honest wine, made according to the rules – but not necessarily a fine one.

GIOVANE   young – refers to an immature wine.

GOVERNO   a system used chiefly in Tuscany. After the fermentation of a Chianti, a small quantity of the same wine, made previously with slightly dried grapes, is added to the vat causing a second, but short, re-fermentation that gives the ultimate wine more character and stability.

GRADEVOLE   pleasing – harmonious and well made but not necessarily a great wine.

GROSSOLANO   coarse – heavy, hard and overly full-bodied.

HECTOGRADE   the metric system for measuring the alcoholic content in wine.

HECTOLITRE   100 litres.

INSIPIDO   insipid – a lack of character in organoleptic qualities and with low acidity; flat.

LEGGERO   light – of poor colour, low alcohol and light body but harmonious and therefore pleasant to drink.

LIEVITI   yeasts.

LIMPIDO   limpid, clear, with no particles in suspension, no sediment.

LIQUOROSO   fortified.

MADERIZZAZIONE   oxidation of the wine.

MAGRO   lean – lacking in quality, body and bouquet.

MALATO   spoiled.

MALMSEY   old English word for Malvasia.

MALOLACTIC FERMENTATION   a second fermentation, mostly provoked artificially in fine red wines, whereby the malic acid is turned into lactic acid, thus bringing the wine to its optimum; a process that has been perfected in the last decade or so.

MASSERIA   like a *fattoria*, a wine-producing farm.

MATURO   mature, ripe.

METALLICO   metallic – hard, dry cold taste reminiscent of iron – an impression that may be caused by the food eaten at the same time.

MÉTHODE CHAMPENOISE   the system of making champagne in bottles, called Metodo Champenois in Italian or Spumante Classico.

MEZZOGIORNO   the south of Italy, including Sicily, Sardinia and the smaller islands.

MOUSSEUX   French sparkling wines made by the charmat system: in Italian called Spumante or sometimes Metodo Italiano.

MUFFA   mould – a taste of or the actual presence of mould.

MUFFA NOBILE   *see* NOBLE ROT.

MUST   unfermented grape juice.

MUTO   mute – a wine that says nothing, often as a result of too much sulphur additive during processing.

NÉGOCIANT   one who bottles wine he has purchased in bulk; he may also do the blending and ageing of wines.

NERVOSO   highly strung – rich in acidity and full of verve.

NETTO   clean.

NEUTRO   neutral – without notable characteristics but of good body and satisfactory acidity.

NOBILE   noble – a wine that is far above the average.

NOBLE ROT   *muffa nobile* in Italian: *pourriture grise* in French and *Edelfäule* in German. The mould or mildew that attacks certain grapes to beneficial effect and others harmfully.

ODORE DI FUSTO   barrel smell – this can be positive and pleasant if moderate or unpleasant if excessive or the barrel is in poor condition.

OIDIUM   powdery mildew.

ORGANOLEPTIC   an all-purpose adjective used to cover the characteristics of a wine that can be noted by the human senses – colour and clarity, taste and tactility, smell and effect.

OSSIDATO   oxidized.

PASSITO   made with semi-dried grapes.

PASTOSO   rich in glycerines, of good body, structure and moderate acidity – generally speaking a good wine.

PERLAGE (PERLAGGIO)   refers to the bubbles in a glass of sparkling wine and how long they last.

PERSISTENTE   persistent – refers to the length of time that the bouquet and taste of the wine last.

PESANTE   heavy – refers to a full-bodied wine but a dull, low acidity one.

PÉTILLANT   frizzante – a 1–2 ATM, say, pressure of CO_2.

PHYLLOXERA   a vine pest, a genus of plant lice.

PIENO   full.

POURRITURE GRIS   *see* NOBLE ROT.

PRECOCE   a wine that reaches maturity quickly and, consequently, must be drunk early.

PROFUMO   the bouquet that comes through the fermentation and ageing.

PRONTO   clean – a wine without any extraneous odours or tastes.

PRONTO BEVA   ready to drink.

QUINTAL   100 kilos.

RETROGUSTO   aftertaste – the taste left after a wine has been drunk; it may be different, better or worse than the original organoleptic impression received by the palate.

RICCO   rich – a wine with plenty of colour and a good acidity.

RIPASSO PROCESS   (Veneto). This is similar in purpose and method to the Tuscan Governo in that the fermented wine is given a short second fermentation with its own lees which enhances the wine's body and richness of taste.

RISERVA   reserve – aged wine.

RISERVA SPECIALE   a wine aged a year more than a Riserva.

ROBUSTO   robust – a wine rich in alcohol and with a full body.

ROSOLIO   the prototype of liquors and liqueurs, first produced in Renaissance times from distilled wine, herbs and spices.

ROTONDO   round.

RUVIDO   rough – too much body, tannin, and therefore *aspro* but which may soften with barrel-ageing.

SALATO   salty.

SAPIDO   a wine full of all the right components and with a lively acidity and, therefore, with a satisfying taste.

SAPORE   flavour, taste.

SCARNO   thin or lacking in all the characteristics of a good wine.

SCHIETTO   a simple wine but one with marked characteristics of its category, thus wholly acceptable.

SCHIUMA   the froth that comes from the neck of a sparkling wine when poured.

SECCO   dry.

SFUGGENTE   fleeting – when the bouquet and taste are short-lasting.

SFUSO   wine sold in bulk.

SGRADEVOLE   not pleasant.

SNERVATO   a wine badly made or over-aged that has lost its characteristics.

SOLERA SYSTEM   an ingenious method of ageing strong wines, in particular sherry, by which the wine passes through and rests in a range of butts (which are never moved and are interconnected) and from which aged wine is drawn off and a similar quantity of new wine is added, thus maintaining steady quality and the organoleptic characteristics of the wine.

SOPHISTICATION   in the wine world, this word does not have its normal dictionary meaning of 'intricate, chic or elegantly refined', but only its secondary meaning of 'intentionally adulterated and debased': therefore, fraudulent or, at best, processed badly.

SOTTILE   lacking in alcoholic content and body but not without something of a harmonious nature.

SPOGLIO   a wine that has precipitated its major characteristics in sediment.

SPUMA   *see* SCHIUMA – though can also imply a chemical carbonization.

SPUMANTE   normally refers to a charmat-produced sparkling wine at 6 ATM, but may be used generically to include champenois-system and others.

STAGIONATO   correctly aged or matured.

STOFFA   stuff – good colour, body, alcoholic content and acidity duly harmonious and aged.

STUCCHEVOLE   too sweet or of a sweetness that is unattractive.

SUPERIORE   a wine with 1% more alcohol than 'normal' DOCs and some extra ageing.

SVANITO   a wine that has lost its intrinsic characteristics.

TAGLIO   Vino da Taglio means cutting wine; in French *coupage*. These wines are almost all from the Mezzogiorno and usually of ample alcoholic content, high colour and generous body. A noted exception is the Lancellotta Lambrusco, which is valued only for its high colour. These wines are added in small quantities to more northerly wines to correct deficiencies.

TANNICO   tannic – rich in tannin – referring chiefly to young red wines.

TAPPO   cork – taste of cork or mould from a defective or too old cork.

TEARS   also called 'legs': the drops of glycerine that can be observed on the inside of the glass when the wine is swirled.

TORBIDO   torbid – cloudy, with particles in suspension.

TRANQUILLO   still – a wine with no bubbles.

VECCHIO   often used pejoratively as 'old', and approaching decrepitude, but also favourably meaning 'aged'.

VDQS   Vin Délimité de Qualité Supérieur.

VELLUTATO   velvety – round, soft and smooth though not without a certain acidity and harmony of finish.

VERDOGNOLO   the greenish reflections that occur in some white wines.

VIN DU PAYS   local wines, usually not bottled and labelled but sold in demijohns. However, most of these nowadays in Italy are made by co-operatives with modern methods.

VIN SANTO   a white dessert wine made by traditional five- to six-year fermenting process in *caratelli*, mostly in Tuscany and Umbria.

VINO DA TAVOLA   a table wine, a wine not subject to DOC DOCG disciplines, which may be a modest wine or a very fine one which is outside the DOC system.

VINO NOVELLO   a wine, usually red, fermented by the carbonic maceration method, ready to drink in a few weeks and must be drunk within a year or so.

VINOSO   vinous.

VIOLACEO   purple colour that is found with many young wines.

VITE   vine.

VITIGNO   vine variety.

VIVACE   vivacious – a pleasing wine with a good acidity, generous CO_2 and piquant to the palate.

VIVO   alive – a harmonious wine that can take more ageing.

VOLPINO   foxy – an unpleasant taste characteristic of certain hybrid grapes.

VQPRD   Vin de Qualité Produit en Régions Déterminées: a Common

Market category meaning quality wines produced in specific areas – roughly equivalent to DOC and AC.

VUOTO   empty – lacking character in taste and bouquet.

ZOLFO   sulphur – a taste of SO_2.

ZUCCHERAGGIO   chaptalization.

Select Bibliography

Anderson, Burton, *Vino*, Little Brown & Co., Boston, 1980
Barr, Andrew, *Wine Snobbery*, Faber and Faber, London, 1988
Belfrage, Nicholas, *Life Beyond Lambrusco*, Sidgwick & Jackson, London, 1985
Guagnini, Enrico, *Lo Champagne*, Sansoni, Florence, 1979
Hazan, Victor, *Italian Wine*, Alfred A. Knopf, New York, 1982
Paronetto Lamberto, *Il Gusto del Vino*, A.E.B., Brescia, 1983
– *Enciclopedia dei Vini del Mondo*, Mondadori Editori, Milan, 1979
Piccinardi, Antonio, and Sassi, Gianni, *Berealto*, Mondadori Editori, Milan, 1986
Simon, André, *André Simon's Wines of the World*, Rainbird, London, 1981

Index